A
PSYCHOLOGICAL
THEORY OF
WORK ADJUSTMENT

A PSYCHOLOGICAL THEORY OF WORK ADJUSTMENT

An Individual-Differences Model
and Its Applications

René V. Dawis • Lloyd H. Lofquist
Department of Psychology
University of Minnesota

University of Minnesota Press
Minneapolis

Library of Congress Cataloging in Publication Data

Dawis, René V.
   A psychological theory of work adjustment.

   Bibliography: p.
   Includes index.
   1. Work—Psychological aspects. 2. Adjustment
(Psychology) 3. Difference (Psychology) I. Lofquist,
Lloyd H. II. Title.
BF481.D34 1984   158.7   83-23381
ISBN 0-8166-1316-8

The University of Minnesota is
an equal-opportunity educator and employer.

To Lydia and Lillian

Contents

Preface

The Theory of Work Adjustment was first published in 1964 with our colleague, George W. England, as a coauthor. It was revised in 1968, with the collaboration of David J. Weiss, and was given more extensive treatment in our book *Adjustment to Work* in 1969. The present book expands the theory and summarizes the research evidence in its support. The book also describes possible applications of the theory and its relationship to psychological theory in general.

Early work on the theory and on the development of measuring instruments for its variables was done in the Work Adjustment Project and was supported, in large part, by the Rehabilitation Services Administration, Social and Rehabilitation Service, U.S. Department of Health, Education, and Welfare. Research and development of the theory continues in the Work Adjustment Project, which includes a statewide Vocational Assessment Program conducted for the Minnesota Division of Vocational Rehabilitation, an adult Vocational Assessment Clinic, and a Vocational Psychology Research unit that develops, distributes, and scores instruments for application of the theory.

The influence of the late Professor Donald G. Paterson had much to do with shaping the direction of our research and with our commitment to the science of vocational psychology and its application to counseling psychology. It is hoped that the current statement of the theory in the broader context of the discussion in this book will stimulate research and provide at least a tentative frame of reference for the teaching and practice of vocational psychology and counseling psychology.

René V. Dawis
Lloyd H. Lofquist

A
PSYCHOLOGICAL
THEORY OF
WORK ADJUSTMENT

1

Introduction

We live in a work-oriented society. It is expected that an individual reaching physical maturity will engage in work, and full employment is a national goal. Many of our social institutions are associated with work. The importance of work in contemporary society is evidenced by the popularity of books such as *Working* (Terkel, 1972) and *Passages* (Sheehy, 1974) and by the continuous flow of articles about work and careers in the popular press. Governmental attention to work as it affects the quality of life, national productivity, full employment, and equal opportunity is illustrated by the work of a special task force (*Work in America*, U.S. Department of Health, Education, and Welfare, 1973). Recent landmark legislation established the importance of the opportunity to work as national policy. If work is as highly valued in our society as it appears to be, it is necessary and desirable to study the relationship of individuals to work and the problems faced in adjusting to work.

What does the word *work* mean to people? Typical definitions include activity engaged in for pay, to make a living or to earn money; activity that occupies much of the waking day (*occupation*); activity that uses abilities or skills in some social or economic enterprise (*employment*); activity that one is called upon to do (*vocation*); or activity that one contracts to do (*job*).

These definitions, however, do not bring out the full meaning of work to the individual. If work, as Roe (1956) pointed out, is truly the major focus of a person's activities and thoughts, then it assumes a larger meaning than these definitions imply. If work provides a focal point for the development of one's way of life and if it is an

3

important vehicle for one's total adjustment, then its meaning for the individual surpasses the activities listed above. Furthermore, the meaning of work cannot be understood properly unless it is viewed in the social context of the work values held by the individual's society. We may understand these values better if we briefly review the major thoughts people have had about work over the centuries (Tilgher, 1930).

Among the earliest recorded ideas (Hebrew, Greek) about work are references to it as a curse or punishment, an activity not included as part of the good life, or a necessary evil (needed only to sustain life). Many of these ideas were religious in origin, with work assuming meaning as a way to atone for sins. Work was viewed as the way in which the kingdom of God might be fashioned on this earth. To these meanings of work, the early Christians added the concept of work as a means by which charity (that is, love of God through neighbor) could be expressed.

With the passing of the centuries, a distinction developed between work that was intellectual, spiritual, and contemplative and work that was manual, physical, and exertive. The medieval universities, for instance, distinguished between the servile and the liberal arts (Pieper, 1952). The servile arts were undertaken to satisfy basic human needs; the liberal arts could not be put at the disposal of such utilitarian, albeit necessary, ends. Performance of a liberal art could not, rightly speaking, be paid for. The honorarium was nothing more than a contribution toward the living expenses of the liberal artist. On the other hand, a wage meant payment earned for a servile art— for a particular piece of work—with no necessary reference to the cost-of-living needs of the worker.

In the Middle Ages, work was seen as a natural right and duty; it was the basis of society, the foundation for property, and the source of prosperity (Pieper, 1952). The notion of investment and interest (of making money without work) was condemned. Work was still a necessity or obligation, but only insofar as it was necessary to maintain the individual and society. Beyond this lay the higher life, the better life, the life of the intellect or of contemplation.

With the advent of Protestantism, new meanings of work evolved (Tilgher, 1930). Martin Luther (1483-1546), the great German religious reformer, subscribed to the prevailing theory of work but added the idea that all who could work should work, including contemplatives and ascetics. Furthermore, work of whatever station, high or low, was a way of serving God. For Luther, there was one best way to serve God: by doing most perfectly the work of one's occupation or profession.

John Calvin (1509-64), another famous Protestant leader and

reformer, advanced radically new attitudes toward work. For Calvin, work alone sufficed to curb the evil bent of humans. Therefore, all persons—even the rich, the noble, and the ordained—needed to work. Work must be methodical, disciplined, rational, and continuous, not intermittent or occasional. To this command to work ceaselessly, the ascetic Calvin added a command to renounce the fruits of work. Max Weber (1930) asserted that the practice of investment gained religious sanction and impetus because of Calvin's teaching. It was the religious value of work and working, which was viewed as the highest means to asceticism and the strongest proof of religious faith, that Weber saw as the dominant influence in shaping the capitalistic attitude.

At about this time, a different view of work was emerging that expressed the spirit of the Renaissance. Leonardo da Vinci and his contemporaries saw work as the way by which nature was mastered. Through work (toil, art, and invention), humans drew farther from the animal and nearer to the divine, creating a second, higher nature of which they were the masters. As Tilgher (1930) pointed out, this was probably the first time in history that the idea of valuing work for its own sake, as both its own end and its own purpose, gained widespread acceptance.

Work, then, has had at least three basic meanings for preindustrial society: (1) a hard necessity, painful and burdensome; (2) instrumental, a means toward an end, especially a religious end; and (3) a creative act, therefore intrinsically good. All three meanings have probably been present in various proportions in all historical periods, one or another aspect receiving the greatest emphasis depending on the time, the place, and the person who was looking for the meaning of work.

With the Industrial Revolution and the advent of the machine, people became concerned with the relevance of work in the search for identity. Mechanization was seen as forcing individuals into a common mass or organizational mold, reducing them to marginal, isolated, normless, insecure parts of a person-machine system. In contemporary society, automation and computerization have accentuated these concerns and raised the specter of the individual being deprived of almost all work functions. With the "Second Industrial Revolution," the dehumanization of work is seen as reducing people to the humiliating status of tenders or watchers of machines. As machines perform an increasing number of work functions, society is faced again with questions about the meaning of work for the individual.

Another way to determine the meaning of work is to study the effect of removing work from people's lives. The unemployed and the retired are two groups that can be studied from this perspective.

Most studies on the unemployed are concerned with the economics of unemployment. A few deal with the psychological significance of unemployment to the unemployed. Bakke's studies (1934, 1940) on this problem are typical. From interviews with unemployed individuals both in the United States and in England, Bakke concluded that loss of work leads to a series of demoralizing influences that strike a terrible blow against the self-respect and self-confidence of the unemployed worker. The removal of furniture, lapse of insurance, cutting down on food, putting off the purchase of clothes, forgoing social events—these consequences of unemployment remove the individual from the world to which he or she so recently belonged. Bakke found that prolonged unemployment caused the unemployed person to move toward the attitudes of dependency and away from the desire to struggle back.

The unemployed expressed the meaning of work in various ways. Some talked of a sense of being lost without the work to which they were accustomed. Others found enforced idleness to be unbearable, worse than cutting down on food and clothing. Many felt a sense of hopelessness, a sullen and despondent mood that deepened as the weeks without work went by. Unemployment was described as especially hard on the heads of families, who were bitter about their incapacity to perform traditional roles and functions, all the more so when they felt it was not their fault that they were unemployed. A picture of the importance of work in the lives of these people emerges from Bakke's studies.

Another group for whom the meaning of work comes sharply into focus includes those workers who are coming to the end of their careers. Several studies of work and retirement have been undertaken, of which those by Friedmann, Havighurst, and their associates (1954) at the University of Chicago serve as examples. Among other conclusions, they found that work does not have the same meaning for all individuals; meanings vary as jobs and people vary. The significance of work, as interpreted by the worker, varies in two fundamental ways. First, it differs according to the particular recognition of the part that work has played in the person's life. Second, it differs according to the type of affective response the person has made to work.

Friedmann and his associates listed meanings of work that were common to the workers they studied. Work was the means of maintaining a certain standard of living, a certain level of existence, and also of achieving some higher standard or level. Work was something to do, a way to fill the day or pass the time. Work was a source of self-respect, a way to achieve recognition or respect from others. Work defined one's identity, one's role in society. Work provided the opportunity for association with others, for building friendships. Work allowed for self-expression, provided the opportunity for creativity, for new experiences. Finally, work permitted one to serve others.

One finding underscored by the Chicago group was the presence of negative as well as positive meanings of work. The other side of the coin, as expressed by some individuals, was the belief that work did not provide enough rewards. The pay was rarely satisfactory, and the work was dull, boring, exhausting, or dangerous. Work reduced one's self-respect and provided little prestige. Work forced people to associate with individuals that they did not like. Work was uninteresting and distasteful; one found little opportunity for service to others, for self-expression, for creativity.

Other studies that help us to understand the meaning of work to the worker include those about job satisfaction, vocational needs, and work values. In the many studies of job satisfaction, only a small proportion of workers (about 15 percent) expressed dissatisfaction with their work or, more precisely, with their jobs (U.S. Department of Labor, 1973). The reasons for job satisfaction included many of the meanings of work that have already been listed, such as security, opportunity for advancement, and good wages.

Roe (1956) stressed the importance that work has in the satisfaction of basic human needs. She wrote that, in our society, work is the single situation most capable of providing some satisfaction for all levels of needs. Other studies indicated that work is important in need satisfaction and that there are differences in the needs being satisfied by different kinds of work (for example, Weiss, Dawis, England, and Lofquist, 1964, 1965). Studies of work values (for example, Super, 1962), also yield information about the meaning of work.

This brief discussion of historical and research literature shows that work is central to human development and total life adjustment and that work provides a situation for satisfying needs. Even in the most advanced societies, two-thirds of the average individual's life and at least one-third of the average adult's day are spent in work activities. Work thus comprises the largest component of the total behavior of an individual and is, therefore, an appropriate area of study for the behavioral sciences, not only as an applied field but also as a vehicle for improving our understanding of human behavior. The present volume is a psychological study of work behavior, specifically of the way in which individuals adjust to work.

A psychological study of work obviously should draw upon the concepts and methods used by scientific psychology in the general study of behavior. Although we recognize that work behavior is complex and not easy to study in the laboratory, we also need to begin the study of work with the most reliable base of knowledge available to us, that provided by scientific psychology. The study of human behavior in contemporary psychology is typically based on a stimulus-response model. The responses of individuals are studied in relation to the stimuli that precede them (as in classical conditioning) or that follow them as reinforcers (as in instrumental conditioning). Studies are typically conducted under the highly controlled conditions of the laboratory, focusing on very specifically defined responses and stimuli that occur in relatively short periods of time. Much of our scientific knowledge of human behavior is based on such studies. They have provided concepts, principles, and theoretical approaches that can be used in the study of more complex, longer lasting, and larger units of behavior. The theory developed in this book makes use of such concepts as response and reinforcement derived from the laboratory, but it adapts them to larger units of individual behavior and environmental stimulation.

In work, an individual uses many related responses over an extended period of time in an environment that includes a variety of stimuli. To study how an individual adjusts to work, the researcher must attend to all the relevant responses and stimuli. We can make such a study manageable by focusing, as a first approximation, on more global groups of relevant responses and stimuli.

Our approach also recognizes the desirability of studying work behavior in its natural setting. Although it is recognized in science that laboratory studies offer the most dependable approach to the generation of knowledge, work behavior must first be studied in its natural setting to identify the significant variables for further scrutiny. Furthermore, there is no assurance that results from the laboratory study of more specific behavioral elements will generalize to the naturally occurring units of behavior when the laboratory elements are recombined into the larger units.

One useful approach to the study of work behavior in its natural setting is that of differential psychology, or the psychology of individual differences. This approach makes the following assumptions:

> People differ on any behavioral dimension.
>
> An individual's standing in a group may differ from one behavioral dimension to the next.
>
> For some behavioral dimensions, the individual's standing in a group will remain stable over time, whereas for others there may be change.

An individual's status on a behavioral dimension is the result of a unique genetic inheritance and a unique response-and-reinforcement history.

The phenomenon of individual differences lends itself to statistical methods of analysis, especially correlational techniques, which require reliable measurement of behavioral dimensions. Historically, progress in the study of individual differences has depended on rigorous measurement that, in turn, has produced a dependable technology for human assessment. This technology is available for use in the study of work behavior.

The approach taken in this book is an application of the individual-differences point of view. This approach to the study of work behavior requires the conceptualization of individuals and of work environments in terms of dimensions on which reliable differences can be measured, in recognition of the fact that people differ and environments differ. The most significant dimensions will be identified in subsequent chapters.

Our approach also uses a matching model in which people and work environments are described in the same terms (i.e., in measurements on the same or parallel dimensions). In addition, our approach conceptualizes people and work environments as being in continual interaction with each other. The theory of work adjustment that will be proposed, therefore, focuses on the work behavior of specific individuals who are in continuous interaction with specific work environments.

The theory of work adjustment advanced in this book can be summarized informally in the following statements:

• Work is conceptualized as an interaction between an individual and a work environment.

• The work environment requires that certain tasks be performed, and the individual brings skills to perform the tasks.

• In exchange, the individual requires compensation for work performance and certain preferred conditions, such as a safe and comfortable place to work.

• The environment and the individual must continue to meet each other's requirements for the interaction to be maintained. The degree to which the requirements of both are met may be called *correspondence*.

• Work adjustment is the process of achieving and maintaining correspondence. Work adjustment is indicated by the *satisfaction* of the individual with the work environment and by the satisfaction of the work environment with the individual, by the individual's *satisfactoriness*.

• Satisfaction and satisfactoriness result in *tenure*, the principal indicator of work adjustment. Tenure can be predicted from the correspondence of an individual's work personality with the work environment.

• Work personalities and work environments can be described in terms of structure and style variables that are measured on the same dimensions.

The structure and style of the work personality and the work environment should be described in the same terms and assessed on the same dimensions. This makes it possible to match work personality structure with work environment structure to determine degree of correspondence for the prediction of work adjustment; and to describe the continuous interactive process of work adjustment, thereby enhancing the prediction of work adjustment and the confidence that it will be maintained.

An understanding of the nature of the characteristics that individuals bring to work and those that the work environment presents to individuals helps to provide the context for a more formal treatment of adjustment to work.

REFERENCES

Bakke, E. W. *The unemployed man.* New York: Dutton, 1934.

Bakke, E. W. *The unemployed worker.* New Haven: Yale University Press, 1940.

Friedmann, E. A., & Havighurst, R. *The meaning of work and retirement.* Chicago: University of Chicago Press, 1954.

Pieper, J. *Leisure, the basis of culture.* New York: Pantheon Books, 1952.

Roe, A. *The psychology of occupations.* New York: Wiley, 1956.

Sheehy, G. *Passages.* New York: E. P. Dutton, 1974.

Special Task Force to the Secretary of Health, Education, and Welfare. *Work in America.* Cambridge, Massachusetts: The MIT Press, 1973.

Super, D. E. The structure of work values in relation to status, achievement, interests, and adjustment. *Journal of Applied Psychology,* 1962, *42,* 231-239.

Terkel, S. *Working.* New York: Pantheon Books, 1972.

Tilgher, A. *Work: What it has meant to men through the ages.* New York: Harcourt, 1930.

U.S. Department of Labor. *Survey of job satisfaction.* Washington, D.C.: U.S. Government Printing Office, 1973.

Weber, M. *The Protestant ethic and the spirit of capitalism.* New York: Scribner, 1930.

Weiss, D. J., Dawis, R. V., England, G. W., & Lofquist, L. H. Construct validation studies of the Minnesota Importance Questionnaire. *Minnesota Studies in Vocational Rehabilitation,* XVIII, 1964.

Weiss, D. J., Dawis, R. V., England, G. W., & Lofquist, L. H. An inferential approach to occupational reinforcement. *Minnesota Studies in Vocational Rehabilitation,* XIX, 1965.

PART I

The Individual and the Work Environment

2

The Individual

In seeking to understand human behavior, psychologists typically view the individual as a responding organism. The individual can be observed to respond in a variety of ways. Responses are made to different environmental conditions, that is, to sets of stimuli, or to stimulus conditions. Different responses are made at different times to what appear to be similar stimulus conditions. Some responses appear to be *reactions to* the environment. Other responses appear to be *actions on* the environment.

The individual has been observed to respond to different kinds of stimulation even before birth. At this stage, response is limited to such behavior as movement. In the earliest years of development, behavior consists mainly of reactions to the environment. As the individual develops, actions on the environment increase in number. The individual becomes increasingly capable of differential responses, and the response repertoire for use in coping with the environment expands. A variety of sensorimotor skills are developed, and ability to communicate with other individuals is soon manifested. Communication skills become more refined, more efficient, and more complex when the individual begins to talk.

As a responding and communicating organism, the individual is now able not only to respond but also to report on experiences with responses. The individual can report on experience with the stimulus conditions of the environment and on the nature of the response. Stimulus conditions and responses can be compared for different environments. Because the individual can report on past experiences, the presence of what is called memory may be inferred. Since each individual is unique at birth with respect to response potentials, and since no two environments will be exactly alike with respect to their stimulus conditions, the individual's memory provides a unique reference system for evaluating present experiences. Memory provides points of reference against which present experience can be compared. Present stimulus conditions and modes of response are reported as they are viewed in the context of past experience. Reports will, however, be uniquely those of the particular individual. They may not agree with reports by other observers of this individual's responses and of the stimulus conditions in which they occurred.

An individual's experiences with stimulus conditions in an environment, and with various modes of responding, can also be observed and described by another individual who, of course, would be using a different reference system (memory). The outside observer sees the response that accompanies specific stimulus conditions and the changes in response associated with changes in stimulus conditions. These observations permit the observer to make inferences about an individual's experiences. They also allow description, from an independent source, of the development of the individual's response repertoire.

An individual's report of his or her response experiences may differ, sometimes markedly, from the report of another individual acting as an observer. This suggests the desirability of considering both kinds of reports when describing an individual's behavior. Furthermore, reports made by different observers about an individual's behavior may differ in various degrees. Each other person observing an individual's behavior has a unique memory to provide reference points for observation and for the reporting of observed responses. The observers, then, may provide reports that are as much reflections of personal experience as they are assessments of the responses of the individual under observation. The use of several observers and of communicable standards for observation is helpful in increasing the reliability of these observations and minimizing the subjectivity of independent observers. Reports of this kind provide more objective reference points with which an individual's self-report of behavior can be compared. Even more objective reference points can be established by using mechanical observation devices, such as videotape recorders and mechanical behavior-recording devices.

In organized societies, an individual's behavior is viewed by others largely in terms of social norms or the social standards of behavior that have developed from the society's collective experience. In effect, society has written prescriptions for acceptable behavior for a variety of environments, such as the family, the church, the school, and the work setting. These prescriptions are modified with the passage of time. In a stable society, social norms remain relatively fixed. Patterns of acceptable behavior are well defined. Social institutions are set up to administer the social norms and to promote the development of individual behavior along the lines of the prescribed patterns. All of the responses of a developing individual are made in this context.

To summarize, an individual's self-reports of behavior are made in the contexts of both a unique memory and some level of knowledge of social standards. The independent observer's report of the individual's behavior, if made in the context of communicable standards for observation, may differ from the self-report. There are, then, at least two major, independent sources of data available for the description of an individual's behavior: the self-report of the individual and the reports of other persons. An understanding of an individual's behavior must be based on both sources of data. One source communicates from a private, or more subjective, frame of reference, the other from a public, or more objective, view of behavior. These two sources of data can be used to describe the individual as a responding organism. From such a description one might develop a concept of the individual that is called the individual's *personality.*

In observing an individual's behavior, one can identify recurring response sequences that tend to become modified and refined with repetition. They may be called *skills.* Over time, an individual develops a large repertoire of skills. Although each individual's repertoire is unique, it is feasible to identify similar response sequences in the repertoires of several individuals. This identification of a common skill for several individuals permits the definition of a *skill dimension* in terms of such characteristics as level of difficulty, economy of effort, and efficiency. Individual differences in a specific skill are reflected on a skill dimension; people can be ranked along such a dimension in terms of how skillful they are.

The number of skill dimensions is, however, extremely large. It is cumbersome to describe individual responses in terms of many skill dimensions. A more succinct system of description is provided by modern mathematical methods. Using factor analysis (Harman, 1970), we can identify a smaller number of more basic dimensions that underlie the several skill dimensions. These more basic dimensions, called *ability dimensions,* represent common elements in skill dimensions and can be used as reference dimensions to describe many skills. Obviously, it is more economical and more efficient to describe individual behavior in terms of ability dimensions.

Even when ability dimensions are used to describe individual response repertoires, the problem of measuring the full range of an individual's abilities remains formidable. Each dimension requires a specific measure, and there are many different ways to construct a measure for an ability dimension. Such measures are commonly known as ability tests, which can be constructed to measure ability dimensions that are derived by factor analysis. (See, for example, French, 1954.) Theoretically, any skill can be described by making reference to the measurements obtained by administering these tests.

Measurements of abilities taken at different points in the course of an individual's development will show change, typically in the direction of increased abilities. As the individual matures, less change is observed. An individual's abilities are characterized as mature when repeated measurements show stability.

Having ability is not the same as using it. Using ability requires the appropriate stimulus conditions for response, and an individual experiences a tremendous variety of stimulus conditions in a lifetime. As the individual develops, response is made in the context of many different stimulus conditions; as similar ones are encountered, the individual can report similarities not only in terms of describing the stimulus conditions and responses made but also of evaluating response under these conditions. In other words, the individual develops norms for evaluating stimulus conditions associated with responding. The evaluation is usually made in terms of how satisfying the stimulus conditions are. Such evaluations result in the establishment by the individual of stimulus-condition requirements for response that will be satisfying. Such requirements may be reported by the individual as preferences.

An outside observer can also describe the stimulus conditions under which a person responds and can compare responses under different stimulus conditions. However, to infer fully and accurately the individual's norms for evaluating stimulus conditions, an observer would have to observe and record an individual's total history from birth. Since this continuous observation is not feasible, the observer must infer the individual's preferences for stimulus conditions by observing samples of the individual's behavior under different stimulus conditions, comparing observations with those of others, and taking the individual's stated preferences into account.

When a set of stimulus conditions is observed to be consistently associated with an increased rate of response over the base rate, we refer to the stimulus conditions as *reinforcers* and to the increase and maintenance of response rate as the result of *reinforcement*. Different reinforcers maintain, or reinforce, responses at different frequency levels. In other words, different reinforcers have differential *reinforcement strengths* for an individual. In addition, the same reinforcer may differ in reinforcement strength for different individuals.

It is useful to speak of reinforcement strengths that are actual (experienced by the individual), stated (reported by the individual), and observed (reported by an observer). Stated reinforcement strengths may differ from observed strengths; actual strengths are inferred from stated or observed strengths.

An individual's experiences with different stimulus conditions result in the establishment of requirements or needs for reinforcement at particular levels of strength. Some reinforcers are required at higher levels of strength than others, and some at such low strengths as to be of little or no importance to an individual. A *need*, then, can be defined as an individual's requirement for a reinforcer at a given level of strength. The set of needs of an individual can be described as a required pattern of reinforcers at particular levels of strength.

It should be noted that the term *need* is used here in a way that differs from the common usage of the term as indicating a particular state of deprivation. Whereas deprivation may affect the strength of a reinforcer, the significant psychological point of interest lies in the requirement of a reinforcer at some particular strength, regardless of its derivation. For this reason, such needs can be thought of as *psychological needs.*

Psychological needs can be measured in at least two ways. Questionnaires (inventories, surveys) can be used to learn about an individual's reported preferences for stimulus conditions. Observers can judge the relative reinforcement strengths of particular stimulus conditions for an individual. Psychological needs, whether reported or observed, are said to be stable when successive measurements show little change. Measurements on a set of psychological need dimensions become, for most people, relatively stable as the individual reaches physical maturity. There are, of course, individual differences in the time when the set of needs becomes stable.

This concept of need stability is based on the observation that, for the most part, individuals live out their lives in relatively stable environments where similar stimulus conditions are experienced from day to day. With marked changes in environment, some change in an individual's psychological needs may result. Only in extremely rare instances will much change be expected if the marked environmental change occurs after psychological maturity, that is, after the set of needs has become relatively stable.

Need dimensions are potentially as numerous as the different stimulus conditions that may be required by different individuals. It is, therefore, more practical to describe these requirements for stimulus conditions in terms of the fewer, more basic dimensions that underlie the several needs. These more basic dimensions, which represent the common elements in need dimensions, are called *value dimensions.* They may be identified through factor analysis and used as reference dimensions for the description of the larger number of need dimensions.

Value dimensions are to needs what ability dimensions are to skills. Skills and needs are observable; abilities and values are inferred from the factor structures resulting from the organization of the common elements in skills and needs, respectively. It is more manageable to describe an individual's personality in terms of abilities and values than at the conceptual level of skills and needs. We would also expect measurements of abilities and values to be more stable than those of skills and needs because they represent common elements. For these reasons, most of our discussion will be at the conceptual level of abilities and values.

A set of complex interrelationships may be observed between abilities and values. For example, a high-level ability may be associated with one or several high-strength values. Similarly, a high-strength value may be associated with one or several high-level abilities. *Conflict* can occur when there is competition between contrasting values in relation to an ability or between contrasting abilities in relation to a value. For example, an altruistic value may conflict with an achievement value when the people who reinforce the individual do not permit full utilization of abilities; or the utilization of high verbal and high motor ability may produce conflict when an individual with a strong achievement value is offered a choice of tasks that use one ability but not both. However, most individuals exhibit few enduring conflicts and behave in relatively integrated fashion in most situations.

One common way in which individuals express ability-value relationships is by stating preferences (likes or dislikes) for various kinds of activities. These preferences appear to sample, in rough fashion, a number of classes of activity that the individual has experienced. For example, when asked about favorite activities, one may express preferences for bowling, playing golf, reading biographies, and tinkering with machines. These preferences may be termed *expressed* or *stated interests.* When we want an orderly and comprehensive sampling of activity preferences likely to have been experienced by most people (so that comparisons can be made among people), we create a structure (in the form of an interest inventory) within which each individual expresses preferences. Such activity preferences are scaled psychometrically to obtain the individual's *measured interests.* Because of the structure provided, these measured interests yield a better sampling of activities and a more comprehensive statement of an individual's total set of preferences than does an unstructured approach. The standard structure and conditions under which activity preferences are reported also allow us to assess consistency of measurement (reliability) and to compare measured activity preferences for different individuals and groups.

Preferences for activities may also be observed and continuously recorded in a systematic fashion. Records of participation in activities may be compiled by observers. The activities with which we are concerned are those for which an alternative to participation was available—in other words, ones in which the individual was not forced to participate. Observers may be the individual's teachers, employers, colleagues, friends, public officials, or behavioral scientists conducting a longitudinal study. These evidences of participation in activities may be termed *exhibited interests*. Where there is agreement between measured interests and exhibited interests, one might speak of *validated interests*.

Exhibited or validated interests, as opposed to vicarious interests, derive from experiences with specific combinations of values and abilities (or, more immediately, from experiences with specific combinations of needs and skills). The stability of interests is contingent upon the stabilization of an individual's set of values and abilities (that is, upon psychological maturity), which occurs in most people at physical maturity. Limitations of experience with specific combinations of values and abilities (or needs and skills) by the time of physical maturity may explain the later manifestations of what may be termed *latent interests*.

Another common way in which an individual expresses ability-value relationships is by stating the likelihood of behaving in particular ways, such as speaking out in public or talking to strangers. Such statements may be termed *expressed* or *stated personality descriptions*. When these descriptions are made within the framework of a psychometric instrument (usually an inventory) constructed to sample and scale a broad range of human behaviors in systematic fashion (for example, according to some theoretical orientation), one may speak of *measured personality descriptions* such as introversion and extroversion.

Personality descriptions can also be based on records compiled by observers; these evidences of ability-value relationships may be termed *descriptions of exhibited personality*. When the descriptions of exhibited personality agree with measured personality descriptions, one might speak of *validated personality descriptions*. These personality descriptions refer to important aspects of the total personality but do not attend to all of its major variables.

Measures of interests and of personality description are valuable tools for inferring the ability-value relationships of the individual. The complex interrelationships between abilities and values can be better understood, however, if one starts directly with ability and value measurements to avoid postulating constructs that are two levels removed from observable data. In this book, we view abilities and values as the major personality variables and interests and personality description as supporting data.

The individual's sets of abilities and values and the relationships among these abilities and values constitute the *personality structure.* When measurements of these abilities and values are stable, personality structure is said to be stable. Personality structure, however, does not describe the personality in action. When we consider how an individual utilizes abilities in the context of values, we require concepts in addition to those defining personality structure. As examples, quickness or slowness in utilizing abilities, level of activity, and endurance in responding are personality characteristics not typically included in the description of personality structure. These concepts characterize the individual's style of responding; taken together, they may be called *personality style.* Personality structure and personality style are both required to describe an individual's personality.

Not enough attention has been given to the description of personality style as manifested within normal limits. Some measured personality descriptions are, in part, attempts to describe personality style. They typically rely, however, on self reports of style rather than on actual observations. Data on style should be based on prolonged and continuous observation of the personality in action. Cumulative records of the type kept in school probably come closest to the kind of data on personality style that is needed. Ratings by persons who have observed an individual in many situations over a long period of time may also be useful. More than one source of data should be used to obtain validated descriptions of personality style.

The style, like the structure of personality, is expected to exhibit stability at physical maturity. Personality style can be said to be stable when repeated measurements show little change.

At this point it may be helpful to consider the development of personality, starting with the assumption that each individual has unique capabilities for responding. The practical limits of these capabilities with respect to variety (in kind), range (in number), and complexity (in interacting combinations) are largely determined by the interaction of heredity and environment. Response by an individual is contingent on appropriate capabilities and upon an environment that permits or stimulates the response. We can infer response capabilities from the individual's normative status as a member of a biological class (species and gender) and age group (developmental or maturational level) and from behavior, including response to stimulus conditions contrived to explore the limits of response capabilities (such as psychological tests).

The regular appearance of particular response capabilities at certain points in the life histories of several individuals allows the observer to describe an individual in terms of stages of behavioral development. The earliest responses appear in the maintenance of physiological functioning or result from direct stimulation. Later responses do not appear to be associated with the maintenance of physiological functioning or response to direct stimulation, but rather may be described as attempts by the individual to explore and to act on the environment. Responses are no longer limited to specific reactions to specific stimulation (elicited responses) but occur under varying conditions of stimulation (emitted responses).

The three principal stages of behavioral development are a *differentiation* stage, in which the individual tries out, develops, and expands response capabilities in terms of variety, range, and complexity; a period of *stability*, characterized by the crystallization and maintenance of a response repertoire; and a stage of *decline*, in which some response capabilities are affected by physiological changes associated with aging.

All response takes place in environmental settings, and most of it in social environments. During the differentiation stage, much of it takes place in familial and educational environments. During the stability period, much of it takes place in work environments. In the course of development, an individual experiences a variety of reinforcers. Most of these reinforcers are available in predominantly social and educational environments.

The developing personality can be described in terms of skills and needs (or abilities and values) at different points in the differentiation stage. At very early ages, an individual manifests the development of perceptual and motor skills and the dominance of physiological needs. As the individual increases mastery over the physical environment and learns to communicate with and to interact with other individuals, many skills and needs are exhibited. A corresponding set of abilities and values is developed. Figure 2.1 shows the inception of personality structure for the individual.

At some periods in the differentiation stage of behavioral development, the number of skills and needs increases or changes very rapidly (for example, when a child starts school or reaches puberty). These periods of sudden change are typically associated with marked changes in physical maturation and environmental stimulation. At physical maturity, the individual typically exhibits relatively

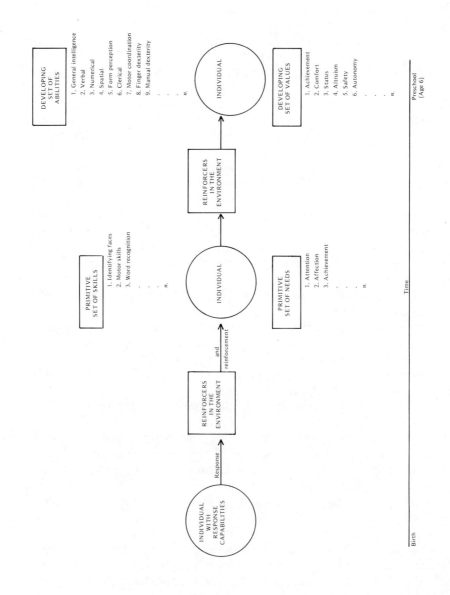

DEVELOPING
SET OF
ABILITIES

1. General intelligence
2. Verbal
3. Numerical
4. Spatial
5. Form perception
6. Clerical
7. Motor coordination
8. Finger dexterity
9. Manual dexterity
.
.
n.

PRIMITIVE
SET OF SKILLS

1. Identifying faces
2. Motor skills
3. Word recognition
.
.
n.

DEVELOPING
SET OF VALUES

1. Achievement
2. Comfort
3. Status
4. Altruism
5. Safety
6. Autonomy
.
.
n.

PRIMITIVE
SET OF NEEDS

1. Attention
2. Affection
3. Achievement
.
.
n.

INDIVIDUAL

INDIVIDUAL

REINFORCERS
IN THE
ENVIRONMENT

REINFORCERS
IN THE
ENVIRONMENT

INDIVIDUAL
WITH
RESPONSE
CAPABILITIES

Response

and
reinforcement

Birth

Time

Preschool
(Age 6)

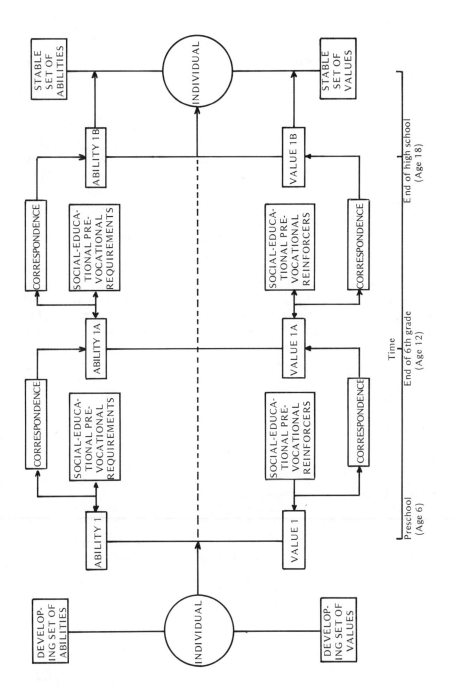

crystallized and stable abilities and values that represent the large variety of skills and needs. *Crystallization* refers to the retention of a particular set of abilities and values in the personality structure. *Stabilization* refers to the maintenance of abilities and values at relatively constant levels of strength and hierarchical ordering. Figure 2.2 illustrates the individuation of personality structure.

The process of crystallization and stabilization of both abilities and values is accompanied by the development of a unique personality style. With a crystallized and stable personality structure and style, the individual may be described as having a fully developed or mature personality. It is then possible to describe this mature personality in terms of measured abilities, values, and style. For most people, physical and psychological maturity are achieved at about the same time (Anastasi, 1958; Tyler, 1965). It is also at this time that most people begin their work experience.

With work experience, the individual encounters some new stimulus conditions and may develop some new skills and needs. In the initial period of work experience and with changes to new work environments, some change may be observed in an individual's skills and needs. The individual, however, maintains abilities, values, and style at stable levels even though some of them may not be highly involved in the work experience. Many abilities and values are relevant to work—that is, they are required and reinforced by it; others are related to nonwork activity. The *work personality* is defined in terms of those abilities, values, and style dimensions that have relevance for work.

REFERENCES

Anastasi, A. *Differential psychology.* (3rd ed.). New York: Macmillan, 1958.

French, J. W. *Manual for kit of selected tests for reference aptitude and achievement factors.* Princeton: Educational Testing Service, 1954.

Harman, H. H. *Modern factor analysis.* Chicago: University of Chicago Press, 1970.

Tyler, L. E. *The psychology of individual differences.* (3rd ed.). New York: Appleton-Century-Crofts, 1965.

3

The Work Personality

Before discussing how individuals interact with work environments, we need to describe the characteristics that individuals bring to the interaction. We have called these characteristics, taken collectively, personality, and have identified two major aspects of personality: structure and style. Personality structure refers to the individual's response capabilities and preferences for stimulus conditions. Personality style, on the other hand, refers to the individual's characteristic style of responding in bringing response capabilities and stimulus preferences into play in the interaction with the environment.

The dimensions that appear to be most important in the description of personality structure are abilities and values. As we discussed above, abilities provide a feasible and economic way to describe an individual's skills. By the same token, values provide a manageable way to describe an individual's needs.

When the concern is with the description of personality as it contributes to the understanding of work behavior, those abilities, values, and style dimensions that are most relevant must be identified. They describe the structure and style of the individual's unique work personality.

From a practical standpoint, the determination of the relevant abilities, values, and style dimensions in a work personality is made by both the employer and the employee. The employer specifies the behavior required to achieve the goals of the work organization, determines the stimulus conditions in which this behavior will take place, and sets up the reinforcements intended to stimulate and maintain appropriate behavior. We are, of course, aware of the fact that employer latitude in making these determinations is limited by the actions of government, organized labor, and competing work organizations.

In a very real sense, the employee also affects employer specifications of the work environment and its requirements. Employee requirements influence how the employer structures the work environment. The employees may accept, change, or reject the employer's specifications and working conditions. To recruit and hold workers, the employer must attend to employee satisfaction, which means the meeting of employee requirements. In this manner, employer and employee jointly determine the abilities, values, and style dimensions that will be found to be relevant in the work setting.

In making decisions about the most important ability dimensions in the work personality structure, we need to consider the major classes of work tasks that are found in some degree or combination in the many occupations that comprise the world of work. Building on the work of Fine (1955), the U.S. Department of Labor (1977) has adopted a system of classifying work tasks in terms of worker functions as they relate to data, people, and things. It is reasonable to think of the abilities that are required to perform these three classes of worker functions. In psychology these abilities might be referred to as symbolic abilities, interpersonal abilities, and sensorimotor abilities to identify the content of work skills required to deal with data, people, and things.

It is also useful to consider the basic psychological processes involved in work skills. These processes may be described as afferent, mediational, and efferent: afferent abilities are those that deal with the reception and interpretation of stimuli from the environment; mediational abilities refer to the individual's storing, processing, and transforming of information; and efferent abilities involve the individual's actions on the environment. All three processes are involved in skills that relate to all three content areas—data, people, and things.

Abilities, therefore, can be categorized in terms of both content and process. If the content categories are crossed with the process categories, nine ability areas important to functioning in work can be identified. These areas, with examples of basic ability dimensions, are shown in table 3.1.

What are commonly called *work skills* (such as fixing carburetors, typing, or selling) require the exercise or use of several different abilities in combination. For example, fixing carburetors draws largely on sensorimotor abilities. In this content area, it draws on

Table 3.1
EXAMPLES OF ABILITIES IN NINE CONTENT-PROCESS AREAS

	CONTENT		
PROCESS	Symbolic abilities (Data)	Interpersonal abilities (People)	Sensorimotor abilities (Things)
Afferent abilities (Input)	Verbal, numerical, and spatial perception	Person dynamics, group dynamics, and mass dynamics perception	Visual, auditory, tactual, kinesthetic, and form perception
Mediational abilities (Central processing)	Verbal, numerical, and spatial reasoning; memory for words, numbers, and space	Reasoning about person, group, and mass behavior; memory for person, group, and mass phenomena	Sensory judgment; mechanical reasoning; memory for objects and sensations
Efferent abilities (Output)	Verbal fluency; numerical computation; spatial manipulation; verbal, numerical, and spatial reporting; speaking	Communicating; persuading; leading, and following	Manual and finger dexterity; eyehand coordination; mechanical assembly; physical abilities (strength, endurance); inventing ability

abilities in the afferent, mediational, and efferent process areas. More specifically, visual, auditory, tactual, and form perception are used in combination with sensory judgment and mechanical reasoning and, finally, with manual and finger dexterity and eye-hand coordination. Some pioneering work in the identification of abilities used in the performance of complex skills (similar to work skills) has already been done by Fleishman (1954). More empirical studies need to be done to identify abilities central to the performance of the broad range of work skills required in our culture if we are to identify those abilities that are most important in describing an individual's work personality structure.

We have the technology to assess many of the abilities shown as examples in table 3.1. The task of assessment becomes problematic, however, because of the number of abilities that need to be assessed for an adequate description of work personality structure. Several abilities are required to describe a single work skill. Several (possibly hundreds of) work skills must be described if we are to assess the potential for the many different jobs an individual may be able to do. To assess an individual's abilities in a feasible and economic way, vocational psychologists developed multifactor test batteries (Super, 1958) that sample the kinds of abilities shown in table 3.1. These batteries focus on the assessment of between 9 and 15 ability dimensions, each of which may include one or several of the more basic abilities shown in table 3.1. However, the multifactor batteries focus largely on symbolic abilities, include some assessment of sensori-motor abilities, and do not assess interpersonal abilities. This latter content area is left mainly to observation and clinical judgment. Nevertheless, the multifactor test appears to be the best approach currently available for assessing ability dimensions in the work personality structure.

A good example of a multifactor test battery is the General Aptitude Test Battery (GATB) developed by the U.S. Department of Labor (1970). The GATB is designed to assess the following nine abilities (designated in the battery as aptitudes): G, general learning ability; V, verbal ability; N, numerical ability; S, spatial ability; P, form perception; Q, clerical ability; K, eye-hand coordination; F, finger dexterity; and M, manual dexterity. Although these nine ability measures obviously do not represent all of the content-process areas shown in table 3.1 (and the table itself does not exhaust all possible abilities), they do sample several major ability dimensions. These dimensions, in turn, represent combinations of several of the illustrative content-process areas. As examples, V, N, and S are symbolic abilities; K, F, and M are sensorimotor abilities; P and Q are afferent abilities; V and S are mediational abilities; and F and M are efferent abilities.

The ability coverage of the GATB, and the fact that it was care-fully standardized on large samples of workers employed in a wide range of occupations and validated extensively on more than a thousand occupations, make it one of the most useful among cur-rently available test batteries for the assessment of abilities in the work personality structure. It also has the attractive feature of being used to describe ability requirements of occupations (see the discus-sion of occupational aptitude patterns in chap. 4).

Value dimensions in the work personality structure may be identified from an analysis of work-related need dimensions. The Minnesota Importance Questionnaire (MIQ), developed by the Work Adjustment Project at the University of Minnesota, was designed to assess the following 20 needs relevant to work: ability utilization, achievement, activity, advancement, authority, company policies and practices, compensation, co-workers, creativity, independence, moral values, recognition, responsibility, security, social service, social status, supervision-human relations, supervision-technical, variety, and working conditions. The reliability and validity of the MIQ are described in the MIQ manuals (Gay, Weiss, Hendel, Dawis, & Lof-quist, 1971; Rounds, Henly, Dawis, Lofquist, & Weiss, 1981).

Factor analyses of MIQ data indicate that six factors can represent the 20 MIQ need dimensions. These factors may, therefore, be used as reference dimensions for the description of needs and may be called *value* dimensions. The six value dimensions are:

Achievement: the importance of an environment that encourages accomplishment

Comfort: the importance of an environment that is comfortable and not stressful

Status: the importance of an environment that provides recognition and prestige

Altruism: the importance of an environment that fosters harmony with and service to others

Safety: the importance of an environment that is predictable and stable

Autonomy: the importance of an environment that stimulates initiative.

Table 3.2 describes the six value dimensions in terms of the defining need scales and the MIQ statements for each need scale. The six

Table 3.2
DESCRIPTION OF VALUES BY NEED SCALE AND STATEMENT

VALUE	NEED SCALE	MINNESOTA IMPORTANCE QUESTIONNAIRE STATEMENT
Achievement	Ability utilization	I could do something that makes use of my abilities.
	Achievement	The job could give me a feeling of accomplishment.
Comfort	Activity	I could be busy all the time.
	Independence	I could work alone on the job.
	Variety	I could do something different every day.
	Compensation	My pay would compare well with that of other workers.
	Security	The job would provide for steady employment.
	Working conditions	The job would have good working conditions.
Status	Advancement	The job would provide an opportunity for advancement.
	Recognition	I could get recognition for the work I do.
	Authority	I could tell people what to do.
	Social status	I could be "somebody" in the community.
Altruism	Co-workers	My co-workers would be easy to make friends with.
	Moral values	I could do the work without feeling it is morally wrong.
	Social service	I could do things for other people.
Safety	Company policies and practices	The company would administer its policies fairly.
	Supervision-human relations	My boss would back up the workers (with top management).
	Supervision-technical	My boss would train the workers well.
Autonomy	Creativity	I could try out some of my ideas.
	Responsibility	I could make decisions on my own.

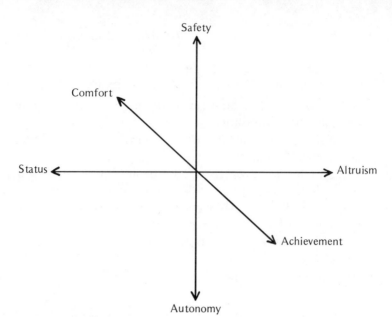

Figure 3.1. Three-dimensional arrangement of values.

values (reference dimensions) may be grouped according to source of reinforcement. If one looks at the six values as they are listed in the accompanying tabulation, it is possible to discern pairs of contrasting values. Figure 3.1 depicts these pairs of contrasting values as identified in a multidimensional scaling study of the MIQ values.

Source of reinforcement	Values	
Environmental	Safety	Comfort
Social	Status	Altruism
Self	Achievement	Autonomy

The MIQ appears to provide a broad coverage of work-relevant needs that, in turn, facilitate the description of the value dimensions of work personality structure. In addition, occupational reinforcer patterns (ORPs; see chap. 4) have been developed to describe work environments in MIQ terms.

Abilities and values, then, are seen as the major sets of dimensions for describing the work personality structure of an individual. These two sets of dimensions should be independent of each other and stable over time from the point when an individual reaches physical maturity. Research on abilities, as measured by the GATB, and on values, as measured by the MIQ, provides data in support of these expectations. These data are discussed in chapter 6, which summarizes

Work Adjustment Project research and other research relevant to the theory of work adjustment.

Work personality structure constitutes one major aspect of the work personality. The other major aspect is work personality style. Personality style takes account of how an individual with a particular personality structure will interact with an environment. The basic dimensions of personality style derive from the characteristics of responding—latency, intensity, pattern, and duration. For the work personality, the four basic dimensions of personality style shall be called *celerity, pace, rhythm,* and *endurance.*

Individuals differ in the speed with which they respond in interacting with the environment. Those who typically respond speedily are described as celerious, and an individual's typical latency of response may be measured along a dimension called celerity. In other words, celerity can be observed in terms of how quickly or slowly an individual responds in interacting with the environment.

The level of activity, reflecting the energy or effort expended by a responding individual, may be described on a dimension called pace. Individuals who habitually manifest a high level of activity can be described as high paced, whereas those who typically show a low activity level are low paced.

Habitual, or typical, pace is an average measure that does not account for variability in the level of activity. We cannot assume stability of pace for all individuals. It is, therefore, necessary also to consider a dimension of pace pattern called rhythm. Descriptive categories along this dimension include stable, cyclical, and erratic. Stable rhythm has minimal variability; cyclical rhythm has more variability, but in a predictable pattern; and erratic rhythm is variable without having a predictable pattern.

The length of time an individual continues to respond in interaction with the environment is a measure of endurance. The longer an individual continues to interact with the environment, the higher the individual's endurance.

The interrelationships among these dimensions of work personality style—celerity, pace, rhythm, and endurance—are illustrated in figure 3.2.

In figure 3.2, individual A is characterized by low celerity, low pace, stable rhythm, and high endurance. Individual B may be described as having moderate celerity, moderate pace, cyclical rhythm, and moderate endurance. Individual C has high celerity, high pace, erratic rhythm, and low endurance.

Since the dimensions of personality style discussed above are developed and exhibited over time, appropriate sources of data for the assessment of an individual's status with regard to them would

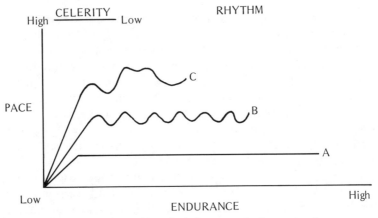

Figure 3.2. Interrelationships of celerity, pace, rhythm, and endurance.

include biographical data, cumulative records, school and work history information, and psychometric data over a time period. Clinical observation of current behavior in a variety of settings may also be utilized. Ratings of specific behaviors by persons who have observed the individuals over extended periods may supplement recorded data and clinical observations. The literature of vocational psychology and psychometrics has not attended to the development of measures of these specific dimensions of personality style. There is a need to study data from the sources mentioned to clarify the constructs themselves and to develop instruments to measure them. We will illustrate how this might be accomplished in the following paragraph.

We would expect the highly celerious individual to have a history that shows prompt or early completion of assignments, almost impulsive behavior, and tendencies toward emphasizing speed of response even at the expense of accuracy. Low celerity would be indicated by deliberateness of response, seeming procrastination, and longer latencies of response. Level of pace might be inferred from evidence of participation in a large number of activities or in activities requiring high energy expenditure, such as strenuous sports and much travel. High-paced individuals are characterized by an almost compulsive busyness and an inability to relax. Rhythm may be inferred from the constancy or inconstancy of the historical or observed pace indicators. Endurance might be judged on the basis of such evidence as completion of long-term projects, long tenure on jobs or in organizations, and lasting relationships with sports, hobbies, interests, and people.

The illustrations described above obviously provide only a few examples of the kinds of behavioral and historical data that may be useful in the assessment of these dimensions of personality style. Data from such conventional psychometric instruments as interest or personality inventories and ability tests may also be useful in the assessment of personality style. As examples, rapidity in completing self-report inventories or attitude scales may be an indicator of high celerity or high pace, whereas completion of repetitious psychometric tasks (such as the MIQ) may indicate endurance.

In this chapter, the work personality has been described in terms of its two major components, structure and style. The major dimensions of work personality structure are abilities and values, which are reference dimensions for skills and needs, respectively. The basic dimensions of work personality style are celerity, pace, rhythm, and endurance.

At this point we will turn to consider the nature and complexity of the work environment and then to describe it in terms of work personality. Description in similar terms of both work personality and work environment is a prerequisite to a more formal treatment of the process and prediction of work adjustment.

REFERENCES

Fine, S. A. A structure of worker functions. *Personnel and Guidance Journal,* 1955, *34,* 66-73.

Fleishman, E. A. Dimensional analysis of psychomotor abilities. *Journal of Experimental Psychology,* 1954, *48,* 437-454.

Gay, E. G., Weiss, D. J., Hendel, D. D., Dawis, R. V., & Lofquist, L. H. Manual for the Minnesota Importance Questionnaire. *Minnesota Studies in Vocational Rehabilitation,* XXVIII, 1971.

Rounds, J. B., Jr., Henly, G. A., Dawis, R. V., Lofquist, L. H., & Weiss, D. J. *Manual for the Minnesota Importance Questionnaire: A measure of vocational needs and values.* Department of Psychology, University of Minnesota, Minneapolis, 1981.

Super, D. E. (Ed.). *The use of multifactor tests in guidance.* Washington, D.C.: American Personnel and Guidance Association, 1958.

U.S. Department of Labor. *Dictionary of occupational titles* (4th ed.). Washington, D.C.: U.S. Government Printing Office, 1977.

U.S. Department of Labor. *Manual for the USES General Aptitude Test Battery.* Washington, D.C.: U.S. Government Printing Office, 1970.

4

The Work Environment

Before the rise of civilizations, work was not just an important aspect of life; it was a direct interaction with nature that was necessary for survival. The earliest work environments, then, were the natural habitats of those early humans. The tasks required were gathering food, hunting, and constructing shelter. As human groups developed, the first divisions of labor emerged; for example, the males hunted while the females took care of the children. The older individuals made decisions for the group. As groups competed for territory, the victors became masters and the vanquished became slaves who were required to perform the less desirable but necessary tasks. As human groups became larger, additional occupations with distinctive tasks developed—warriors, healers, and entertainers. The occupations became organized in a hierarchical fashion, and fields of work activity became recognizable. Work environments in this early structure, by fields and levels, had distinctive task requirements and working conditions.

With the coming of civilization, work environments became progressively less naturalistic and increasingly artifactual. Human societies became more orderly, more complex, and more capable of peaceful coexistence with other societies. Commerce among societies and migration of individuals between societies increased. Societies became interdependent for the products of work, which contributed to the further expansion of occupations and differently defined work environments. Individuals migrating from one group to another brought new skills that contributed to the work potential of the new group but that also required accommodation by the group. These developments led to increasing standardization of skills and work capabilities for specific occupations and relatively consistent definition of occupations and expectations about occupational work environments across groups.

With the advent of the industrial revolution, the number of occupations expanded enormously as a result of the development of human-machine interactions as production systems. The competition for markets and the need for large amounts of capital led to further expansion in the numbers of occupations, particularly in the business, commerce, finance, and transportation areas. The societal complications that resulted led to needs for more occupations in the areas of government, education, health, and social service. These developments also spurred the rapid growth of science and technology and led to highly specialized occupations in these areas. In turn, scientific advances produced more sophisticated work-related techniques and inventions, leading to our contemporary electronic and computer age and, of course, many additional occupations.

The many different occupations that now exist in our society offer more opportunities to utilize the skills of uniquely different individuals and offer greater potential for satisfying the differing needs of individuals. At the same time, the total number of occupations in the world of work has become too large and the relationships between them too complex for individuals to identify readily those occupations most likely to be consonant with their work personalities. Individuals need information that will enable them to enter the world of work, or to change jobs or occupations, in a way that will facilitate their own individual adjustment to work. They need to know which occupations have work environments that they can satisfy in terms of what they are able to bring to work and also which ones will satisfy what they want from the work environment. In short, individuals require a sophisticated classification system, work taxonomy, or occupational grouping system that will help them to obtain information about relatively small and manageable groups of occupations. Individuals can then focus on those groups that are consonant with their own work personality and that, therefore, represent optimal choices for work adjustment.

The work environment, the set of stimulus conditions in which work behavior takes place, has to be considered along with the work personality if one is to understand adjustment to work. Work environments are typically described only from the point of view of the employer. Such descriptions are usually expressed in such terms as work to be performed, tools and materials used, job title, and rate of compensation. This kind of description is based on an economic view of work in which the individual worker is seen largely as one of the factors in production. In such approaches the basic concept is the job. A *job* is usually defined as a group of similar positions in the employing organization. A *position* is a set of tasks performed by one worker. An *occupation* is a group of similar jobs found in several employing organizations. The focus in these definitions is on tasks to be performed, those tasks that are seen as necessary to attain the employer's objective.

Obviously, the focus on tasks to be performed is a necessary description of the work environment from a production standpoint. However, from the point of view of understanding adjustment to work, it is useful to translate task requirements into work-personality terms, or into terms that describe the abilities needed to perform the required tasks. For example, the task "adjust carburetor" can be described as requiring spatial ability and finger dexterity. The task "sell $1,000,000 in life insurance policies" can be viewed as requiring verbal, numerical, and interpersonal abilities.

Conventional work-environment description does not usually attend to how the work environment will meet the workers' needs and expectations. As examples, job descriptions for auto mechanics typically do not include information on the lack of social reinforcers, and job descriptions for life insurance agents do not usually describe the status and social service aspects of performing in the job.

Still another major omission from conventional, task-oriented descriptions is the lack of information on the impact workers can have in modifying work-environment characteristics. For example, a social worker may have considerable freedom in the choice of ways in which required tasks will be achieved, whereas an air traffic controller may not. Work environments should be described in terms that allow us to view them in relation to the work personality. Why it is desirable to do this will be shown in chapter 5.

Describing the work environment in work personality terms is a formidable task given the complexity of the world of work. This difficulty becomes readily apparent when one examines the Dictionary of Occupational Titles (U.S. Department of Labor, 1977), which contains descriptions for about twenty thousand jobs. These job descriptions are actually "average" or typical descriptions based on observations by job analysts of a number of positions for each particular job. Like people, jobs differ. In the same way that an understanding of individual differences is useful in studying work behavior, the study of work-environment differences may assist in understanding the complexity of the world of work.

To make the task of describing work environments in work personality terms manageable, one can think about jobs in terms of their similarities and commonalities. One basis for doing this is to examine the stimulus conditions surrounding response in the work environment. More specifically, these stimulus conditions may be categorized into two major classes: *cues,* which are stimulus conditions that signal for the worker what response is appropriate and when to respond; and *reinforcers,* which are stimulus conditions that are associated with the maintenance of response and the likelihood of future response.

Cues are stimulus conditions that are associated with skills and skillfulness. In the expression of a skill, cues trigger the appropriate response sequences. Level of skillfulness is linked, in part, to how quickly the worker perceives appropriate cues. Cues are also associated with reinforcers in that they signal which ones can be expected and at what level of strength.

Reinforcers are the stimulus conditions that are associated with needs. Needs are an individual's requirements for stimulus conditions if response is to be maintained. They derive from prior experiences of responding under a variety of stimulus conditions, and they are expressed by individuals as preferences for particular stimulus conditions. Effective reinforcers can be viewed as those that are responsive to the individual's needs. Many stimulus conditions and combinations of conditions in the work environment may serve as effective reinforcers. Some of these are established in the work environment by the employer and are intended to serve as effective reinforcers. They are often referred to as *rewards.* Examples include monetary compensation, certificates and other symbols of accomplishment, and fringe benefits. Some types of rewards are established in the form of *incentives,* such as bonuses or commissions that are contingent upon worker performance above the required base level. They are called incentives because the terms for reward are known in advance and can be expected by the worker.

Other stimulus conditions that operate as effective reinforcers may not be intended as rewards. They are effective because particular stimulus conditions in the work environment are consonant with the needs of particular individuals. For example, the production process may require an individual to work alone, a condition that is reinforcing if that worker has a need for autonomy or of not having to depend on others; or the work flow may require group interaction, which serves as reinforcement for a worker with a high affiliation need.

Similarities and commonalities of work environments may then be described in terms of the presence or absence, and level, of potential reinforcers. Their potential as reinforcers rests on their relationship to the needs of the workers. If the number of potential reinforcers identified in work environments proves to be unmanageable, reference dimensions that may be called *reinforcer factors* can be utilized to describe reinforcer patterns.

The similarities and commonalities in work environments may also be described in terms of skill requirements, as noted earlier. Even the simplest job requires several skills, and the total number of separate skills in the world of work is so large that some more economical form of description is needed. Since skills can themselves be described in terms of a smaller set of reference dimensions called abilities, it is more feasible to describe work environments in terms of their ability requirements.

This description of work environments in terms of both ability requirements and reinforcer patterns, which may be called the *work environment structure,* parallels the description of the work personality structure of individuals discussed earlier. In a similar manner, we can speak of *work environment style* in terms parallel to work personality style. For example, one might describe the work environment in terms of its requirements for celerity (speed of responding that is required), pace (level of activity required), rhythm (typical pattern of pace), and endurance (duration of responding that is required).

The following discussion shows how to use the description of work environment structure and style so that both work environment and the work personality can be described and measured on the same dimensions.

Work environment structure may be described in terms of two sets of dimensions, ability requirements and reinforcer factors, which correspond to the work personality structure dimensions of abilities and values. The reader will recall that these abilities may be measured using a multifactor ability test like the GATB and that values can be measured using an instrument like the MIQ. The work environment can be described in work personality terms by using these same dimensions to measure the characteristics of individuals employed in a particular work environment. The goal is to establish from these data the distinctive ability requirements and reinforcer pattern for a work environment, typically at the level of the job within a work organization or the occupation across work organizations. We identify those characteristic abilities and values that differentiate individuals in a specific job or occupation from those in other jobs and occupations. Multivariate techniques, such as multiple regression, multiple hurdles, and multiple discriminant function, are available to make this differentiation.

A good illustration of the establishment of ability requirements for occupations is found in the occupational aptitude patterns (OAPs) developed by the U.S. Department of Labor (1970). The process begins with job analysis to see that the same job (occupation) is being studied in different sites (both institutional and geographic). Many individuals working in the occupation are then administered the GATB. The three or four distinctive ability requirements are identified by their correlation with a criterion such as supervisor ratings or productivity, by the level of mean score and size of standard deviation, and by the rating of the importance of the ability to job performance. Cutoff scores are then determined for each of these abilities in a way that helps to identify individuals in the top and bottom halves of the distribution of criterion scores (supervisor ratings or productivity). Table 4.1 illustrates the OAPs that have been developed for several occupations.

Other approaches that establish ability requirements are Ghiselli's taxonomy of occupations based on analysis of the validity coefficients of occupational aptitude tests (1966) and the estimation methods of Viteles' Job Psychograph (1932); Paterson, Gerken, and Hahn's Minnesota Occupational Rating Scales (1941, 1953); and Desmond and Weiss' Minnesota Job Requirements Questionnaire (1970). The estimation methods allow ability requirements to be developed for many occupations in a relatively short period of time and with reasonable confidence in their applicability. The OAP approach allows use of the same instrument (the GATB) to obtain measurements of both abilities and ability requirements and the

Table 4.1
A SAMPLING OF OCCUPATIONS CLASSIFIED BY
OCCUPATIONAL APTITUDE PATTERNS (OAP)

OAP NUMBER	APTITUDE PATTERN[a]	REPRESENTATIVE OCCUPATIONS
1	GVQ	Copy writer, editor, writer, critic
2	GSP	Audiovisual specialist, fashion designer, photographer, illustrator
3	GV	Announcer, dramatic coach, drama teacher
8	GVNS	Biologist, botanist, soil conservationist, zoologist
14	KM	Farmworker, forest worker, logger
17	GNS	Architect, civil engineer, electrical engineer, industrial engineer
21	SMP	Carpenter, dental-laboratory technician, electrician, machinist
32	PKM	Cabinet assembler, die cutter, dry cleaner, upholsterer
34	KFM	Bindery worker, furnace tender, machine helper, packager
47	SM	Bus driver, chauffeur, driving instructor

Source: U.S. Department of Labor, *Manual for the USES General Aptitude Test Battery. Section II: Occupational Aptitude Pattern Structure* (Washington, D.C.: U.S. Government Printing Office, 1979).

[a]The aptitudes measured by the General Aptitude Test Battery are designated as G, general learning ability; V, verbal ability; N, numerical ability; S, spatial ability; P, form perception; Q, clerical ability; K, eye-hand coordination; F, finger dexterity; and M, manual dexterity.

basing of requirements on direct measurement of the workers' abilities.

The description of the work environment in need-value or reinforcer terms is illustrated by the development of occupational reinforcer patterns (ORPs) through the use of the Minnesota Job Description Questionnaire (MJDQ; Borgen, Weiss, Tinsley, Dawis, & Lofquist, 1968). The MJDQ presents the twenty need-reinforcer statements of the MIQ to raters who are asked to rate the work environment in terms of the relative presence or absence of the reinforcers described in the statements. The use of a multiple rank-order format for presenting the statements in blocks of five required the addition of a 21st need-reinforcer statement. Raters were selected for each occupation from immediate supervisors or incumbents. The scoring of the MJDQ is identical to that used for the ranked form of the MIQ, and it yields commensurate scores and profiles. The profiles or ORPs describe the relative presence or absence of reinforcers in the occupation. Expression of ORPs in the same terms (dimensions and scale) as the MIQ allows direct comparison of an individual's MIQ profile with the ORPs. Figure 4.1 illustrates the ORP for the occupation of carpenter.

Other approaches could be taken to the description of the reinforcer systems of work environments. For example, Super's Work Values Inventory (1970), England's Personal Values Questionnaire (1967), Rokeach's Survey of Values (1973), and the Allport, Vernon, and Lindzey Study of Values (1970) could be used as a basis for obtaining ratings or other measures of the reinforcer characteristics of work environments. We are not aware that these instruments have been used for this purpose. Other investigators have inferred need-satisfying characteristics of occupations from job satisfaction studies (e.g., Campbell & Pritchard, 1976; Herzberg, Mausner, & Snyderman, 1959; Schaffer, 1953) and from needs, interests, and personality data on individuals in different occupations (e.g., Holland, 1973; Roe, 1956).

Reinforcer systems might also be determined by using a method similar to the OAP approach, which measures the needs and values of individuals in different occupations and determines the patterns of needs and values that differentiate occupations from each other and that correlate with a criterion such as satisfaction. This method was used in a study by Weiss, Dawis, England, and Lofquist (1965).

There are, then, a number of ways in which work-environment structure may be described in work-personality terms—in terms of ability requirements and need/value reinforcer patterns. We can now combine these two sets of dimensions in a single descriptive system that cross-classifies occupations according to the two sets of dimensions. An initial attempt at establishing such a taxonomy is represented by the Minnesota Occupational Classification System (MOCS; Dawis & Lofquist, 1974). The system presents occupations in groups (taxons) identified by each occupation's membership in both a particular occupational aptitude pattern and a specific occupational reinforcer cluster (ORC). This taxonomic

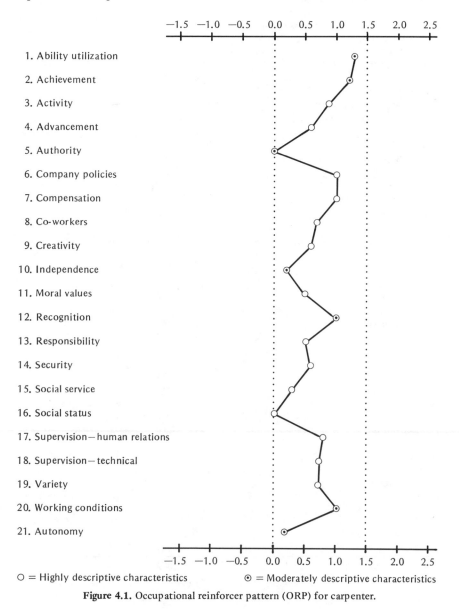

O = Highly descriptive characteristics   ⊙ = Moderately descriptive characteristics

Figure 4.1. Occupational reinforcer pattern (ORP) for carpenter.

Carpenter
(N = 39 supervisors)

OAP = 21

1965 DOT = 860.381
1977 DOT = 860.381-022

Descriptive characteristics

Make use of their individual abilities
Get a feeling of accomplishment
Have good working conditions
Receive recognition for the work they do
Do not tell other workers what to do
Do not plan their work with little supervision
Do not do their work alone

Occupations with similar ORPs

Air-conditioning mechanic
  (commercial and domestic)
Electrician
Elevator repairman
Furnace installer and repairman
Glazier (glass installer)
Maintenance man, factory or mill
Painter/paperhanger
Patternmaker, metal

Photoengraver (stripper)
Pipefitter
Plumber
Repossessor
Salesman, automobile
Sheet metal worker
Tile setter (ceramic)
Tool-and-die maker
Welder, combination

Summary Statistics

	Adjusted value	−1 SE	+1 SE	P	Q	Unadj. value
1. Ability utilization	1.31	1.24	1.39	.03	4.05	.67
2. Achievement	1.24	1.17	1.32	0.00	3.75	.60
3. Activity	.89	.77	1.02	.21	1.71	.25
4. Advancement	.61	.50	.72	.26	1.23	−.04
5. Authority	−.01	−.10	.08	.67	.02	−.65
6. Company policies	1.00	.92	1.08	.03	2.64	.35
7. Compensation	1.00	.90	1.10	.08	2.33	.35
8. Co-workers	.69	.60	.77	.05	1.67	.04
9. Creativity	.61	.52	.70	.15	1.44	−.04
10. Independence	.22	.11	.32	.62	.45	−.43
11. Moral values	.50	.37	.62	.15	.90	−.15
12. Recognition	1.01	.94	1.10	.05	2.72	.37
13. Responsibility	.55	.46	.64	.31	1.27	−.09
14. Security	.62	.48	.76	.38	1.04	−.03
15. Social service	.33	.22	.43	.38	.67	−.32
16. Social status	.05	−.07	.15	.49	.09	−.60
17. Supervision—human relations	.85	.76	.94	.10	2.04	.21
18. Supervision—technical	.72	.63	.81	.21	1.65	.07
19. Variety	.73	.64	.82	.28	1.69	.08
20. Working conditions	1.05	.97	1.14	.08	2.70	.40
21. Autonomy	.20	.09	.31	.69	.40	−.45
Adjusted neutral point	0.000	−.049	.048			
Unadjusted neutral point	−.645	−.695	−.598			

Figure 4.1—*Cont.*

system has the advantage of enabling one to identify appropriate occupational choices by entering the system with information about an individual's abilities, needs, or both. It also provides a way to learn about the ability requirements and need-reinforcer systems for a named occupation. The system, however, has the disadvantage of being limited in its occupational coverage by the numbers of available, empirically derived OAPs and ORCs. The 1974 MOCS was limited to the classification of 337 occupational and alternate titles. (Figure 4.2 illustrates a taxon from the 1974 MOCS.

A broader coverage of occupations is provided by the Minnesota Occupational Classification System II (MOCS II; Dawis, Lofquist, Henly, & Rounds, 1979/1982), which also describes work environment structure in terms of the two major axes of ability requirements and reinforcer system characteristics. Its broader occupational coverage is achieved by presenting the ability-requirement axis in terms of worker function levels with OAP information nested within the system in all cases where the OAPs are available. The description of worker function, taken from the Dictionary of Occupational Titles coding system, is presented in three ability requirement levels (high, moderate, average) for worker functions in the three separate fields of data, people, and things, resulting in twenty-seven ability requirement groups.

The second major axis for describing work environment structure involves six occupational-reinforcer clusters that are each described in terms of the most salient value reinforcers and their component need reinforcers. Available ORPs are nested within these clusters. The cross-classification of occupations according to the twenty-seven ability requirement groups and the six occupational-reinforcer clusters yields seventy-eight taxons that include information on 1,161 separate occupations. The number of taxons presented in MOCS II can be expanded over time to include several more as additional data on reinforcer systems become available for the description of other occupational-reinforcer clusters. The present taxonomy, however, is a much more useful system than the 1974 MOCS because of its broader coverage of levels and fields of work. Figure 4.3 shows a taxon from MOCS II, with the key to its interpretation described in figure 4.4.

Information on work environment style should also be included in the description of work environments. However, because the concept of work environment style (and of work personality style) is a recent development in work adjustment research, psychometrically adequate measures are not yet available. In their absence, we must resort to clinical judgments as the main source of information.

Structural Work	VIII-37
Occupational Group	Taxon

JOB REQUIREMENTS

				OAP 37						
				N 80 S 95 M 85						
ORP	DOT TITLE	GRP	DPT	HOC	INT	TEMP	PHYS	WTG	INV
1116	Painter	840	781	RCI	190	Y091	SLMH 346	319	KM
144	Carpenter	860	381	RIC	190	OY	LMH 2346	312	KM
1124	Pipe Fitter I	862	381	RIE	190	OY	LMH 2346	312	
1124	Plumber, Pipefitting								
1126	Plumber	862	381	RIE	190	OY	LMH 2346	312	KM
196	Maintenance Man, Factory or Mill	899	281	RIE	190	OY	LMH 2346	312	
196	Handy Man, Factory or Mill								
196	Plant-Maintenance Man								
196	Utility Repairman, Factory or Mill								

JOB REINFORCERS

ORC VIII
AU 1.30
Ach 1.24
Com 1.07
Sec 1.00
Au −.15

Things
Data-Things
Worker Functions

Figure 4.2. Taxon from the 1974 Minnesota Occupational Classification System.

To help obtain the most reliable clinical judgments, we may consider one of three assessment methods. The direct observation method requires job analysis that focuses on the interaction of the work environment with its workers, specifically in terms of celerity, pace, rhythm, and endurance. The observers are trained job analysts, supervisory personnel, or the workers themselves. Structured instruments may be developed to aid in the observation. Such instruments should focus on the presence or absence of observable environment behaviors: celerity might be observed in terms of the presence or absence of machine pacing or scheduled deadlines, or the presence or absence of a series of tasks that require immediate or quick response; rhythm might be indicated by the cyclical pattern of the tasks or the steady pace of the work.

The estimation method is applied to the description of work environment style by obtaining ratings from persons judged to be knowledgeable about that occupation. This method requires the development (including acceptable reliability and validity) of rating

REQUIREMENTS			REINFORCERS	
DATA	PEOPLE	THINGS	ACHIEVEMENT	COMFORT
MODERATE	AVERAGE	HIGH	HIGH	MODERATE
Compiling Computing	Speaking- signalling Serving Taking in- structions- helping	Setting up Precision working Operating- controlling	Ability utilization Achievement	Compensation

DOT Code	Occupational Title	OAP	ORC	ORP Vol., Page	
842.361-018	Plasterer	21	B	II	108
840.381-010	Painter	26	B	I	116
841.381-010	Paperhanger	21	B	I	116
842.361-010	Lather	26	B	II	82
860.381-022	Carpenter	21	B	I	44
860.381-046	Form Builder	21			
860.381-050	Joiner	21			
860.381-058	Shipwright	21			
860.381-066	Tank-Builder and Erector	21			
862.381-018	Pipe Fitter	21	B	I	124
862.381-022	Pipe Fitter, Diesel Engine II	21			
862.381-030	Plumber	21	B	I	126
861.381-018	Bricklayer	21	B	II	44
862.381-010	Aircraft Mechanic, Plumbing and hydraulics	26			
866.381-010	Roofer	26	B	II	114

Figure 4.3. Taxon 16B from Minnesota Occupational Classification System II.

TAXON 3 A

REQUIREMENTS			REINFORCERS		
DATA	PEOPLE	THINGS	ACHIEVEMENT	AUTONOMY	ALTRUISM
HIGH	HIGH	AVERAGE	HIGH	HIGH	MODERATE
Synthesizing	Mentoring	Feeding-	Ability	Responsibility	Social service
Coordinating	Negotiating	offbearing	utilization	Creativity	
Analyzing	Instructing	Handling	Achievement	Autonomy	

DOT Code	Occupational Title		OAP	ORC	ORP Vol., Page
045.107-010	Counselor [Counselor, School]		49	A	I 60

1. Taxon 3A is a listing of occupations having ability requirements pattern 3 and reinforcers typified by Cluster A.
2. Data, People, Things ability requirements are worker functions as defined in the *Dictionary of Occupational Titles* (4th ed.), 1977, pages 1369-1371.
3. Reinforcer dimensions are discussed in the following publications in the *Minnesota Studies in Vocational Rehabilitation* series:
   "An Inferential Approach to Occupational Reinforcement" (XIX, 1965)
   "The Measurement of Occupational Reinforcer Patterns" (XXV, 1968).
4. DOT Code and Occupational Title are as they appear for each occupation in the *Dictionary of Occupational Titles* (4th ed.).
5. Bracketed information provides more details about the nature of the occupational subgroup that supplied ORP/ORC data.
6. Occupational aptitude pattern, from the *Manual for the USTES General Aptitude Test Battery, Section II: Norms, Occupational Aptitude Pattern Structure*, 1979. Occupations are listed within each taxon in ascending order of OAP number.
7. Occupational reinforcer cluster identifies cluster membership for occupations used in the clustering of reinforcer patterns.
8. Occupational reinforcer pattern lists volume and page of the series *Occupational Reinforcer Patterns* in which the reinforcer pattern for the occupation appears. Volumes I-III of the series are available from Vocational Psychology Research, University of Minnesota.

Figure 4.4. Key to taxons of Minnesota Occupational Classification System II.

instruments analogous to the MJDQ but focused on the environmental style variables discussed above.

The inference method uses data on employees in a given work environment that describes them in terms of work personality style; the corresponding characteristics of work environment style are then inferred. For example, data indicating that a high percentage of the workers in the occupation are high on pace would lead to the inference that the work environment requires a high level of work activity.

Because each of the three methods is limited in some respects, we recommend strongly that at least two methods be used to arrive at a description of work environment style for a given occupation. In assessing the adequacy of knowledge of the expert raters when using the estimation methods, for example, one might compare results against those obtained with either the direct observation method or the inference method.

Early studies that describe work environments in terms of required temperaments and personality traits are relevant to our discussion of work environment style. As early as 1956, the U.S. Department of Labor published *Worker Trait Requirements for 4000 Jobs.* It included twelve temperament-requirement descriptions of occupations on dimensions such as REPSC, or situations involving repetitive or short-cycle operations carried out according to set procedures or sequences; and STS, or situations involving the precise attainment of set limits, tolerances, or standards. This set of temperament-requirement descriptions also included what we would now refer to as reinforcer characteristics. Examples include VARCH, or situations involving a variety of duties often characterized by frequent change; and ISOL, or situations involving working alone and apart in physical isolation from others, although activity may be integrated with that of others.

A form of this kind of information was included as worker-trait information in the description of work environments in the 1965 edition of the *Dictionary of Occupational Titles.* Unfortunately, there is little if any further work on this type of work-environment description, and the current (1977) edition of the DOT does not contain a worker-trait section.

The interest of psychologists in personality study has led to some work on the description of occupations in terms of the typical personalities of their members. As examples, Harrower and Cox (1942), Roe (1946, 1949, 1950, 1952), and Steiner (1948) studied occupations (predominantly professional) and described them in terms of the characteristic Rorschach signs in the responses of incumbents. These studies anticipated the current interest in describing work environments in work-personality terms, particularly in terms of reinforcer requirements and style dimensions.

Thus far we have focused on the meaning and importance of work in the total lives of individuals; have described central concepts in the development of an individual's personality; have discussed an approach to describing the work personality; and have discussed a way of describing the work environment in work personality terms. The task now is to provide a model that integrates all of this information in a way that the individual's adjustment to work can be better understood. As a first requirement, such a model should be empirically testable. The theory of work adjustment, presented in the next chapter, is proposed as one such model.

REFERENCES

Allport, G. W., Vernon, P. E., & Lindzey, G. *Manual: Study of values.* New York: Houghton Mifflin, 1970.

Borgen, F. H., Weiss, D. J., Tinsley, H. E. A., Dawis, R. V., & Lofquist, L. H. The measurement of occupational reinforcer patterns. *Minnesota Studies in Vocational Rehabilitation,* XXV, 1968.

Campbell, J. P., & Pritchard, R. D. Motivation theory in industrial and organizational psychology. In M. D. Dunnette (Ed.), *Handbook of industrial and organizational psychology.* Chicago: Rand McNally, 1976.

Dawis, R. V., & Lofquist, L. H. *Minnesota Occupational Classification System.* Work Adjustment Project, Department of Psychology, University of Minnesota, Minneapolis, 1974.

Dawis, R. V., Lofquist, L. H., Henly, G. A., & Rounds, J. B., Jr. *Minnesota Occupational Classification System II.* Vocational Psychology Research, Department of Psychology, University of Minnesota, Minneapolis, 1979/1982.

Desmond, R. E., & Weiss, D. J. Measurement of ability requirements of occupations. *Proceedings of the 78th Annual Convention of the American Psychological Association,* 1970, 149-150.

England, G. W. Personal value systems of American managers. *Academy of Management Journal,* 1967, *10,* 53-68.

Ghiselli, E. E. *The validity of occupational aptitude tests.* New York: Wiley, 1966.

Harrower, G. F., & Cox, K. J. The results obtained from a number of occupational groupings on the professional level with the Rorschach group method. *Bulletin of the Canadian Psychological Association,* 1942, *2,* 31-33.

Herzberg, F., Mausner, B., & Snyderman, B. B. *The motivation to work.* New York: Wiley, 1959.

Holland, J. L. *Making vocational choices: A theory of careers.* Englewood Cliffs, N.J.: Prentice-Hall, 1973.

Paterson, D. G., Gerken, C. d'A., & Hahn, M. E. *The Minnesota Occupational Rating Scales and Counseling Profile.* Chicago: Science Research Associates, 1941.

Paterson. D. G., Gerken, C. d'A., & Hahn, M. E. *Revised Minnesota Occupational Rating Scales.* Minneapolis: University of Minnesota Press, 1953.

Roe, A. A Rorschach study of a group of scientists and technicians. *Journal of Consulting Psychology,* 1946, *10,* 317-327.

Roe, A. Analysis of group Rorschachs of biologists. *Rorschach Research Exchange,* 1949, *13,* 25-43.

Roe, A. Analysis of group Rorschachs of physical scientists. *Journal of Projective Techniques,* 1950, *14,* 385-398.

Roe, A. Analysis of group Rorschachs of psychologists and anthropologists. *Journal of Projective Techniques,* 1952, *16,* 212-224.

Roe, A. *The psychology of occupations.* New York: Wiley, 1956.

Rokeach, M. *The nature of human values.* New York: Free Press, 1973.

Schaffer, R. H. Job satisfaction as related to need satisfaction in work. *Psychological Monographs,* 1953, *67,* (Whole No. 364).

Steiner, M. E. The use of projective techniques in industry. *Rorschach Research Exchange,* 1948, *12,* 171-174.

Super, D. E. *Work Values Inventory Manual.* Boston: Houghton Mifflin, 1970.

U.S. Department of Labor. *Dictionary of occupational titles* (4th Ed.). Washington, D.C.: U.S. Government Printing Office, 1977.

U.S. Department of Labor. *Manual for the USES General Aptitude Test Battery, Section II: Occupational aptitude pattern structure.* Washington, D.C.: U.S. Government Printing Office, 1979.

U.S. Department of Labor. *Worker trait requirements for 4000 jobs.* Washington D.C.: U.S. Government Printing Office, 1956.

Viteles, M. S. *Industrial psychology.* New York: Norton, 1932.

Weiss, D. J., Dawis, R. V., England, G. W., & Lofquist, L. H. An inferential approach to occupational reinforcement. *Minnesota Studies in Vocational Rehabilitation,* XIX, 1965.

PART II

Adjustment to Work

5

A Theory of Work Adjustment

In any scientific study, it is useful to have a theoretical framework to organize and evaluate prior research, to provide direction for future research, and to stimulate new ideas and concepts. Because the framework must be capable of generating empirically testable hypotheses, it should be stated in clearly defined terms that allow its major concepts to be operationalized and measurements to be taken to test these hypotheses.

The study of work adjustment, which has been the province of vocational psychology, focused for many years on the development of psychometric measures that were useful in the resolution of such problems related to work adjustment as vocational choice, personnel selection, work motivation, employee morale, and worker productivity. Research in this area, which tended to focus on solving the specific problem at hand, did not proceed from any integrating theoretical perspective. This resulted in the development of a number of psychometrically adequate measures that were useful in addressing work adjustment problems. Each measure produced a relatively independent body of research literature.

In recent years there has been increasing interest in attempts to integrate these disparate literatures. One way to do so is through the development and use of an overarching theoretical formulation. The theory of work adjustment (Lofquist & Dawis, 1969) is advanced as one such formulation. The theory grew out of the research of the Work Adjustment Project at the University of Minnesota. As early as 1960 (Scott, Dawis, England, & Lofquist), after reviewing the pertinent literature on various aspects of work adjustment, we realized that an integrating theory was necessary for a systematic inquiry into work adjustment. In 1964 (Dawis, England, & Lofquist), the first version of a theory was published; it was revised in 1968 (Dawis, Lofquist, & Weiss). An extended form of the theory was published in book form in 1969 (Lofquist & Dawis). Since that time, modifications and additions to the theory have appeared in several journal articles. The theory of work adjustment will be used here to integrate the concepts that have been discussed in the preceding chapters on the work personality and the work environment.

Before stating the theory of work adjustment in propositional form, it may be useful first to develop its central concepts. The theory of work adjustment is based on the concept of *correspondence between individual and environment*, which implies conditions that can be described as a harmonious relationship between individual and environment, suitability of the individual to the environment and of the environment for the individual, consonance or agreement between individual and environment, and a reciprocal and complementary relationship between the individual and the environment. Correspondence, then, is a relationship in which the individual and the environment are corresponsive (i.e., mutually responsive). Into this relationship, the individual brings requirements of the environment; the environment likewise has its requirements of the individual. To remain in the environment, the individual must achieve some degree of correspondence.

It is a basic assumption of the theory of work adjustment that *each individual seeks to achieve and maintain correspondence with the environment.* Achieving and maintaining correspondence with the environment are basic motives of human behavior.

There are several kinds of environments—home, school, work—to which an individual must relate. Achieving and maintaining correspondence with one environment may affect the correspondence achieved and maintained in other environments. *Work represents a major environment to which most individuals must relate.*

The individual brings certain skills to the work environment, which in turn provides certain rewards—wages, prestige, personal relationships to the individual. The individual's skills enable her or him to respond to the requirements of the work environment, and the rewards of the work environment enable it to respond to the requirements of the individual. When their minimal requirements are mutually fulfilled, the individual and the work environment are described as correspondent. In the case of work, then, *correspondence can be described as the individual fulfilling the requirements of the work environment and the work environment fulfilling the requirements of the individual.*

When an individual enters a work environment for the first time, behavior is directed towards fulfilling its requirements. The rewards of the work environment are also experienced. If a correspondent relationship with the environment is found, the individual seeks to maintain it. If not, the individual seeks to establish correspondence or, failing in this, to leave the work environment. There are many different kinds of work environments and many different kinds of individuals, and each work environment-individual relationship is idiosyncratic. In many cases, the initial relationship is not correspondent. In addition, both individuals and work environments are constantly changing. *The continuous and dynamic process by which the individual seeks to achieve and maintain correspondence with the work environment is called work adjustment.*

The achievement of minimal correspondence enables an individual to remain in a work environment. Remaining in the work environment, in turn, allows the individual to achieve more optimal correspondence and to stabilize the correspondent relationship. *This stability of the correspondence between the individual and the work environment is manifested as tenure in the job.*

As correspondence increases, the probability of tenure increases and the projected length of tenure increases as well. Conversely, as correspondence decreases, both the probability of remaining on the job and the projected length of tenure decrease. Tenure is the most basic indicator of correspondence. It can be said, therefore, that *tenure is a function of correspondence between the individual and the work environment.*

From the basic concepts of correspondence and tenure we can develop the concepts of satisfactoriness and satisfaction. If the individual has substantial tenure, it can be inferred that the requirements of the work environment are being fulfilled and that the work environment has been fulfilling the individual's requirements. The individual who fulfills the requirements of the work environment is termed a satisfactory worker. The individual whose requirements are fulfilled by the work environment is termed a satisfied worker. *Satisfactoriness and satisfaction indicate the correspondence between the individual and the work environment.* Satisfactoriness and satisfaction, then, are the basic indicators of the degree of success an individual has in achieving and maintaining correspondence with the work environment. Satisfactoriness is an *external* indicator of correspondence; it is derived or obtained from sources other than the individual worker. Satisfaction is an *internal* indicator of correspondence; it represents the individual worker's appraisal of the extent to which the work environment fulfills his or her requirements.

The theory may be informally stated as follows (see also the summary of the theory in the Introduction):

Work is an interaction between an individual and a work environment in which each has requirements of the other.

The work environment requires certain tasks to be performed and the individual brings skills to perform the tasks.

The individual, in exchange, requires compensation for work performance and additional conditions of work such as a safe environment, a comfortable place to work, congenial co-workers, a competent supervisor, and an opportunity to achieve.

As long as the environment and the individual continue to meet each other's requirements, their interaction is maintained.

When the requirements are not met, the individual or the environment moves to change or terminate the interaction.

The mutual responsiveness of the individual and the work environment to each other's requirements is a continuing process called *work adjustment.* The degree to which the requirements of either or both are met is described on a dimension called *correspondence.*

The basic motive of work behavior is seeking to achieve and maintain correspondence.

Two primary indicators of work adjustment are the *satisfaction* of the individual with the work environment and the satisfaction of the work environment with the individual, or the individual's *satisfactoriness.*

Both satisfaction and satisfactoriness are required for the individual to remain and be retained on the job. *Tenure* is the outcome of work adjustment.

The principal characteristics of the individual in relation to work adjustment may be collectively called the individual's *work personality.*

The work personality consists of at least two sets of characteristics: status characteristics (*personality structure*) and process characteristics (*personality style*).

Personality structure may be described in terms of the individual's *skills* and *needs* or in terms of the reference dimensions for skills (*abilities*) and the reference dimensions for needs (*values*).

Personality style describes the individual's typical ways of interacting with the environment (given a particular personality structure) on such dimensions as *celerity* (quickness or slowness in interacting with the environment), *pace* (level of activity typically exhibited in interaction with the environment), *rhythm* (typical pattern of pace in interaction with the environment), and *endurance* (duration of interaction with the environment).

The work environment may be described in terms commensurate with the description of work personality. *Work environment structure* may be described in terms of *skill requirements* and *need reinforcers* (classes of stimulus conditions the presence or absence of which is associated with satisfaction of needs). Work environment structure may also be described in terms of reference dimensions for skill requirements (*ability requirements*) and reference dimensions for need reinforcers (*reinforcer factors*). The characteristic patterns of ability requirements and of reinforcer factors for the work environment of an occupation may be respectively referred to as an occupational ability pattern and an occupational reinforcer pattern.

The style of the work environment may be described in terms of its requirements for *celerity* (speed of response), *pace* (level of activity), *rhythm* (typical pattern of pace), and *endurance* (duration of response).

Work adjustment can be predicted from the correspondence of the work personality and the work environment.

Using the preceding concepts, we can explore the problem of *predicting* work adjustment. Satisfactoriness and satisfaction can fluctuate with changes over time in both individuals and work environments. There are, however, minimum requirements of both individuals and work environments: minimum levels of satisfactoriness required of individuals and of satisfaction required by individuals. These minimum levels are best established by observing individuals who have remained in a work environment. The levels of satisfactoriness and satisfaction observed for a group of individuals with substantial tenure in a specific work environment establish the limits of satisfactoriness and satisfaction from which tenure can be predicted for other individuals (fig. 5.1).

Satisfactoriness and satisfaction can also be viewed as outcomes in the work adjustment process at various times during an individual's period of adjustment. In this sense, they are criterion measures of work adjustment that can be used to establish a methodology for the prediction of work adjustment from the assessment of work personalities in relation to work environments. The work personalities of individuals who fall within the limits of satisfactoriness and satisfaction for which substantial tenure can be predicted are inferred to be correspondent with the specific work environment. The different kinds of work personalities for which correspondence is inferred thus establish the limits for specific personality characteristics that are needed for adjustment to the specific work environment (fig. 5.2).

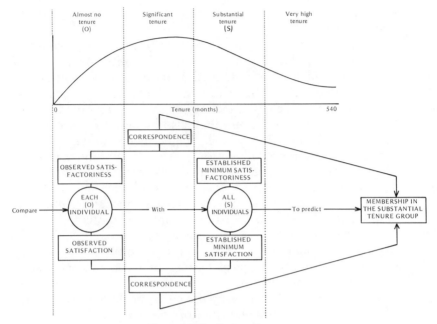

Figure 5.1. Prediction of tenure.

These limits can be used in estimating the degree of correspondence between other individuals and the specific work environment. The correspondence between work personality and work environment that is estimated in this fashion can be used to predict satisfactoriness and satisfaction.

Because satisfactoriness and satisfaction taken together can be used to predict tenure, the correspondence between work personality and work environment can also be used to predict tenure.

In chapters 2 and 3, we discussed the description and development of the work personality. We saw that the work personality can be described in terms of both its structure and style and that the major sets of variables in this description are the individual's abilities and values. These abilities and values go through a process of development and differentiation until a point of relative stability is reached. The theory of work adjustment is premised on the existence of a relatively stable work personality.

In chapter 4, the work environment was described in work personality terms, that is, as ability requirements as well as reinforcer patterns. Ability requirements are established from the study of satisfactory workers with substantial tenure, and reinforcer patterns are established from the study of satisfied workers with substantial tenure.

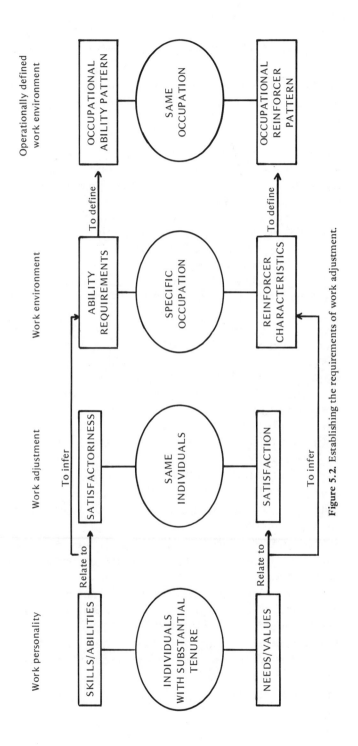

Figure 5.2. Establishing the requirements of work adjustment.

With the work personality and the work environment described in the same terms, and with the theory of work adjustment stated above, we can state the following formal propositions about work adjustment as a basis for research:

Proposition I. Work adjustment at any time is indicated by an individual's concurrent levels of satisfactoriness and satisfaction.

Proposition II. Satisfactoriness is a function of the correspondence between the individual's abilities and the ability requirements of the work environment, provided that the reinforcer pattern of the work environment corresponds to the individual's values.

Corollary IIa. Knowledge of the abilities of individuals and their satisfactoriness permits determination of the effective ability requirements of the work environment.

Corollary IIb. Knowledge of the ability requirements of the work environment and of an individual's satisfactoriness permits the inference of the individual's abilities.

Proposition III. Satisfaction is a function of the correspondence between the reinforcer pattern of the work environment and the individual's values, provided that the individual's abilities correspond to the ability requirements of the work environment.

Corollary IIIa. Knowledge of the values of individuals and their satisfaction permits the determination of the effective reinforcer pattern of the work environment.

Corollary IIIb. Knowledge of the reinforcer pattern of the work environment and of an individual's satisfaction permits the inference of the individual's values.

Proposition IV. Satisfaction moderates the functional relationship between satisfactoriness and ability-requirement correspondence.

Proposition V. Satisfactoriness moderates the functional relationship between satisfaction and value-reinforcer correspondence.

Proposition VI. The probability that an individual will be forced out of the work environment is inversely related to the individual's satisfactoriness.

Proposition VII. The probability that an individual will voluntarily leave the work environment is inversely related to the individual's satisfaction.

Combining propositions VI and VII, we have:

Proposition VIII. Tenure is a joint function of satisfactoriness and satisfaction.

Given propositions II, III, and VIII, this corollary follows:

Corollary VIIIa. Tenure is a function of correspondence between abilities and requirements and between values and reinforcers.

Proposition IX. Correspondence between work personality and work environment increases as a function of tenure.

These nine propositions in the theory of work adjustment have provided direction for the research done by the Work Adjustment Project. This research will be described in the context of a review of the research literature in the next chapter.

The prediction of work adjustment (fig. 5.3) can be affected by the manner in which an individual typically interacts with an environment given a particular work personality structure. In other words, it is also important to consider work personality style and work environment style, knowledge of which will improve the prediction of work adjustment. This may be stated formally as follows:

Proposition X. The correspondence between work personality style and work environment style moderates the prediction of work adjustment from the correspondence between work personality structure and work environment structure.

The preceding 10 propositions of the theory of work adjustment refer to the *prediction* of work adjustment; it now remains to describe the *process*. The major variables of this process shall be called *adjustment style dimensions.*

The dimensions of adjustment style may be derived from the concept of correspondence between an individual and a work environment. Correspondence describes not only the corresponsiveness or mutual responsiveness between individual and environment but also the degree of fit between work personality structure and work environment structure. Individuals with a very similar work personality structure may differ in the amount of correspondence they require of the work environment structure to remain in it. Tolerance of discorrespondence may be described on an adjustment style dimension of *flexibility*. For example, if two individuals prefer to work in a room with a temperature of 70 degrees, the more flexible individual may continue to work even if the temperature rises to, say, 85 degrees, or drops to 60 degrees. The less flexible individual would not be able to tolerate such changes and would not continue to work. Or, for a more psychological example, if two individuals

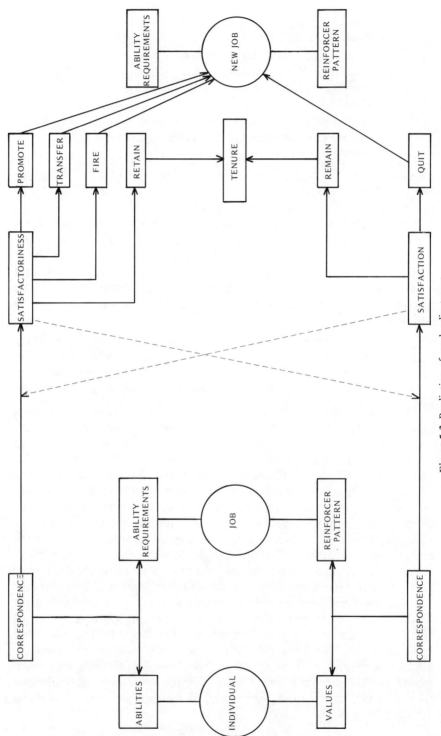

Figure 5.3. Prediction of work adjustment.

have a strong preference for working alone, the more flexible may tolerate some presence and interaction with other workers whereas the less flexible individual may not. The description of minimal correspondence for the prediction of tenure requires knowledge of an individual's flexibility.

If there is a need to increase correspondence with the environment, the individual may seek to change the environment or to change the way in which the work personality structure is expressed in the environment. When an individual responds by acting on the work environment to increase correspondence, the mode of adjustment may be described as *active*. When this kind of behavior is typical, the individual can be described as active. Individual differences in the likelihood of using this mode of adjustment may be described on an adjustment style dimension called *activeness*.

When an individual responds by changing the expression or manifestation of the work personality structure to increase correspondence, the mode of adjustment may be described as *reactive*. Individuals who typically exhibit this mode of behavior may be described as reactive, and the likelihood of using such behavior can be expressed on a personality style dimension called *reactiveness*. It is not expected that individuals will limit themselves exclusively to either the active or the reactive mode of adjustment but that both modes could be used.

In the examples of flexibility cited above, the less flexible individuals, if they adopted the active mode of adjustment, might readjust the thermostat, open or close windows, move to another room, complain about the presence of other workers, move to a solitary location, or request transfer to another job. On the other hand, these same (less flexible) individuals, if they adopted the reactive mode of adjusting, might drink hot or cold liquids, remove or put on clothing, endure and suffer through, concentrate on the work to exclude the perception of others, use daydreams and fantasies to escape from others, or rationalize the situation to themselves in order to endure the presence of others. Although these examples focus on possible behaviors of the less flexible individuals, the same kind of behaviors, indicative of activeness or reactiveness, might be observed for the more flexible individuals when their tolerance for discorrespondence is exceeded.

In the absence of instruments for measuring these three adjustment style dimensions, data on an individual's past history and experience can be used to assess the individual's standing on these dimensions. In the assessment of flexibility we may hypothesize that an individual who has a history that includes participation in a wide range of activities, experience in a wide range of situations, a successful work history over a wide range of jobs, and a heterogeneous group of friends will have a high level of flexibility. On the other hand, an individual with few or a very homogeneous group of friends, a narrow range of successful jobs or other activities, and exposure to a very narrow range of situations will have a low flexibility level.

We may hypothesize that the activeness of an individual is at a high level if there is evidence of, as examples, having held positions of leadership, having organized groups and activities, having developed new ways of doing things, and having taken the initiative in school, work, or community activities. Low-level activeness, on the other hand, would be indicated by a lack of initiative and innovativeness in an individual's history.

We may hypothesize that a high level of reactiveness is indicated by a history that includes abiding by the rules, carrying out assignments according to prescribed procedures, comfort or satisfaction in highly structured situations and groups, and loyal and continued participation in groups as a member rather than a leader. Low-level reactiveness would be evidenced by inability to participate in group situations, difficulty in following rules and prescribed procedures, and other evidences of isolationist tendencies.

Figure 5.4 illustrates the interrelationships among the three adjustment style dimensions designated as flexibility, activeness, and

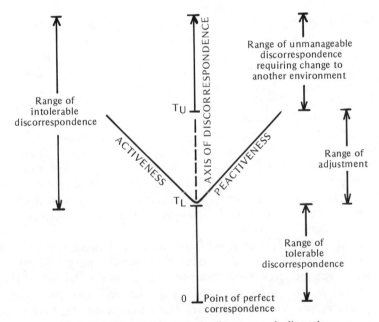

Figure 5.4. Relationships among adjustment style dimensions.

reactiveness. The individual's flexibility defines the distance from point 0 to point T_L (lower threshold) on the axis of discorrespondence; this distance also defines the range of tolerable discorrespondence. When discorrespondence exceeds the lower but not the upper threshold, the individual is in the range of adjustment; there, modes of adjustment can be described in terms of the independent dimensions of activeness and reactiveness. The length of time an individual remains in the range of adjustment describes the individual's *perseverance,* which in part depends on the effectiveness of the individual's mode of adjustment. Flexibility defines the distance from point 0 to point T_L, whereas perseverance defines the distance from point T_L to point T_U (the upper threshold on the axis of discorrespondence).

There are, then four adjustment style dimensions that are basic to describing behavior intended to achieve and maintain correspondence with the environment: flexibility (tolerance for discorrespondence with the environment before doing something to reduce the discorrespondence), activeness (reducing discorrespondence by acting to change the environment), reactiveness (reducing discorrespondence by acting on self to change expression of personality structure), and perseverance (tolerance of discorrespondence with the environment before leaving it, as indicated by length of stay).

Activeness and reactiveness may be thought of as adjustment modes, with flexibility determining when adjustment modes are to be used and perseverance determining the length of time they would be used.

One way to integrate the adjustment process aspects of the theory of work adjustment with its prediction aspects is to view work adjustment from a systems standpoint (Dawis & Lofquist, 1978). Figure 5.5 presents a systems conceptualization of the dynamics of work adjustment embodied in the theory of work adjustment.

The individual (I) is located in the upper left-hand corner and the work environment (E) is located in the lower right-hand corner. I comes to work with a set of needs and evaluates these against a set of expected reinforcers. If these reinforcers equal or exceed the needs, I feels satisfaction (SN) and proceeds to behave in the manner that I feels is expected (work behavior). I's work behavior consists mainly of task performance, which is then evaluated by E against the task requirements. If I's task performance meets or exceeds the task requirements, I is considered satisfactory, or as having achieved satisfactoriness (SS). This, in turn, results in organizational behavior that produces the reinforcement necessary to meet I's needs. I now can evaluate the actual reinforcers against needs and should continue to be satisfied and satisfactory until significant changes take place.

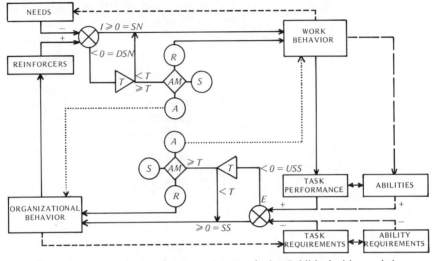

Figure 5.5. Work adjustment from a systems standpoint. Published with permission from the *Journal of Vocational Behavior,* 1978, *12.*
Copyright 1978 by Academic Press, Inc.

The main points in the system at which changes may affect the stable interaction are those involving needs, work behavior, task requirements, and organizational behavior. There is also the possibility of inaccurate evaluation on the part of *I* or *E.*

When *I* evaluates reinforcers as not meeting needs, *I* feels dissatisfaction (DSN). *I* has a tolerance for some dissatisfaction, but if it rises above *I*'s threshold (T), *I* will move to seek a better adjustment. *I* may use either or both of two adjustment modes (AM). *I* may accommodate to *E* by using a reactive mode (R) of adjustment, or *I* may act to change *E* by using an active mode (A). If these adjustments result in a tolerable level of dissatisfaction, *I*'s work behavior will be directed toward meeting *E*'s task requirements. If not, *I* will leave the work situation and separation (S) will occur.

When *E* evaluates *I*'s task performance as not meeting task requirements, *I* will be considered unsatisfactory (USS). *E* can tolerate some unsatisfactoriness, but if it exceeds *E*'s threshold (T), *E* will move to make the appropriate adjustments. *E* may accomodate *I* by being reactive (R), or *E* may take steps to effect a change in *I* by being active (A). If neither of these modes of adjustment by *E* achieves the desired effect, the only recourse for *E* is the separation (S) of *I* from the specific work situation (by transfer, demotion, promotion, or termination).

To forecast work adjustment, we need information on four components of the system shown in figure 5.5: needs, reinforcers, task performance, and task requirements. This information can be obtained on all components except task performance, which can be known only when the individual is behaving in the work situation. We thus substitute a measure of *potential* for task performance, which is abilities. Having made this substitution, it becomes more convenient for matching purposes to translate task requirements into ability requirements. These substitutions are shown on the right-hand side of figure 5.5.

The propositions in the theory of work adjustment are all reflected in the dynamic system shown in figure 5.5. The more recent derivation of adjustment style dimensions is also incorporated. In addition, the necessary intervening variables of individual work behavior and organizational behavior are introduced and integrated into the system to complete the description of the flow of the work adjustment process.

Using the concept of adjustment style and its dimensions (Dawis & Lofquist, 1976), we can further improve the prediction of work adjustment. The following additional propositions and corollaries are formulated to provide direction for future research:

> Proposition XI. The flexibility of the work environment moderates the functional relationship between satisfactoriness and ability-requirement correspondence.
>
> Proposition XII. The flexibility of the individual moderates the functional relationship between satisfaction and value-reinforcer correspondence.
>
> Proposition XIII. The probability that the work environment will use adjustment modes is inversely related to the individual's satisfactoriness.
>
>> Corollary XIIIa. Knowledge of this probability associated with the individual's satisfactoriness permits the determination of the work environment's flexibility threshold.
>
> Proposition XIV. The probability that the individual will use adjustment modes is inversely related to the individual's satisfaction.
>
>> Corollary XIVa. Knowledge of this probability associated with the individual's satisfaction permits the determination of the work environment's flexibility threshold.
>
> Proposition XV. The probability that the work environment will act to remove the individual is inversely related to the perseverance level of that work environment.
>
>> Corollary XVa. Knowledge of this probability associated with the work environment's perseverance permits the

determination of the work environment's perseverance threshold.

Proposition XVI. The probability that the individual will act to leave the environment is inversely related to the perseverance level of that individual.

Corollary XVIa. Knowledge of this probability associated with the individual's perseverance permits the determination of the individual's perseverance threshold.

Given Propositions VIII, XV, and XVI, it follows that:

Proposition XVII. Tenure is a function of satisfactoriness, satisfaction, and the perseverance levels of the individual and of the work environment.

The total set of propositions suggests research hypotheses that may be tested to determine the usefulness of the theory in understanding work adjustment. The present set of propositions is premised on existing knowledge about work personalities and work environments; this knowledge is, in turn, limited by the current methods used to describe work personalities and work environments. Work adjustment is very complex, and additional research findings and improved methods may suggest other propositions.

REFERENCES

Dawis, R. V., England, G. W., & Lofquist, L. H. A theory of work adjustment. *Minnesota Studies in Vocational Rehabilitation,* XV, 1964.

Dawis, R. V., & Lofquist, L. H. Personality style and the process of work adjustment. *Journal of Counseling Psychology,* 1976, *23,* 55-59.

Dawis, R. V., & Lofquist, L. H. A note on the dynamics of work adjustment. *Journal of Vocational Behavior,* 1978, *12,* 76-79.

Dawis, R. V., Lofquist, L. H., & Weiss, D. J. A theory of work adjustment (a revision). *Minnesota Studies in Vocational Rehabilitation,* XXIII, 1968.

Lofquist, L. H., & Dawis, R. V. *Adjustment to work.* New York: Appleton-Century-Crofts, 1969.

Scott, T. B., Dawis, R. V., England, G. W., & Lofquist, L. H. A definition of work adjustment. *Minnesota Studies in Vocational Rehabilitation,* X, 1960.

6

Research on Work Adjustment

INSTRUMENTATION FOR THE THEORY

Before applying a theory with confidence, we need to assess its validity in accounting for existing data in the literature and to test it by conducting research. The theory of work adjustment specifies the variables that have to be measured in this research: work personality variables (abilities, needs and values, personality style, adjustment style) and work environment variables (ability requirements, reinforcer systems, environment style). These variables were defined and discussed in chapters 2 through 5, and measures of them were described.

The theory also specifies the indicators of work adjustment (satisfactoriness, satisfaction, and tenure) and requires that correspondence between work personality and work environment be measured. The conceptual definition and measurement of these variables is discussed below.

Satisfactoriness is a concept that arose out of the fact that employers and employing organizations have certain goals, the attainment of which requires the coordinated performance of groups of people. The proper coordination of these groups is accomplished by breaking the total required performance into sets of tasks, one set for each employee, and promulgating rules to govern the performance of each set of tasks in relation to the performance of all other sets of tasks. In time, similar sets of tasks and similar sets of rules are standardized or become standard for most employing organizations. Standardization permits the employing organization to evaluate each employee in terms of some desired standard of performance or in terms of comparison with the performance of other employees, past or present, on the same set of tasks. This evaluation constitutes the satisfactoriness of the employee.

In other words, from the standpoint of satisfactoriness, the work environment of an individual is defined by the series of tasks that must be performed and the set of rules that must be followed. The behavior of the individual within this defined environment is the basis for the satisfactoriness evaluations.

In a sense, when hiring an individual the employing organization "pays" for a standardized set of work behaviors. Satisfactoriness refers more directly to the standardized set of work behaviors required of the employee than to that employee's contribution toward the attainment of the employing organization's larger goals. Therefore, the assessment of satisfactoriness focuses on measurements of the extent to which the employee meets task requirements and conforms to rules.

In most employing organizations, the assessment of satisfactoriness takes the form of employee performance appraisal, which typically utilizes a rating form completed by supervisory personnel. No single rating form is in common use; each employing organization develops its own forms for jobs to be rated. For purposes of research, therefore, it is desirable to develop a measure that can be used across employing organizations and across jobs to allow the theory to be tested under comparable conditions in a variety of work environments.

An example of a measure of satisfactoriness that may be used in research across organizations and jobs is the Minnesota Satisfactoriness Scales (MSS; Gibson, Weiss, Dawis, & Lofquist, 1970), which was developed following a search of the literature to identify the kinds of information that might indicate satisfactoriness. Examples of such indicators are quantity and quality of work; job suitability; promotability; meriting a pay raise; and frequency of absences, lateness, accidents, and disciplinary actions. Experimental rating forms were constructed to incorporate items that sampled these kinds of indicators. Supervisor ratings were obtained for almost 1,000 employees working in skilled, nonskilled, blue collar and white collar occupations. Preliminary analyses of these data indicated that two factors accounted for the common variance in most employee groups: a performance factor, with loadings on such items as quality of work, promotability, and meriting a pay raise; and a conformance factor, with loadings on such items as frequency of absences, lateness, and accidents.

Revisions of the experimental scales resulted in the development of the MSS as a rating questionnaire with 28 items designed to assess the satisfactoriness of an individual as an employee. For most of the items, which are presented in question form, the rater is asked to compare the employee with other members of the work group and to indicate the employee's standing on a 3-point scale such as "not as well (good)," "about the same," or "better"; or "less," "about the same," or "more." Other items ask the rater to make a decision on such items as giving the employee a pay raise or promotion to a position of more responsibility. The final item asks for an overall rating of the employee's satisfactoriness by indicating in which fourth of the distribution of other people doing the same work the employee would fall.

The MSS is scored on five scales: general satisfactoriness, performance, conformance, dependability, and personal adjustment. Internal consistency reliabilities for these scales (obtained on several different worker groups) range from .69 to .95, with a median of .87. The validity of the MSS has been demonstrated against a criterion of job tenure in a study of more than fifteen hundred workers (Anderson, 1969). Discriminant validity is indicated by analyses of correlations between the MSS and the Minnesota Satisfaction Questionnaire, which showed that the variance shared by the two instruments ranged from only 2 to 10% for different occupational groups.

Other investigators (e.g., Campbell, Dunnette, Lawler, & Weick, 1970) have distinguished between the criterion variables of performance and effectiveness. Performance refers to the evaluation of the employee's behavior on the job; effectiveness refers to the employee's contribution to the organization's objectives. An instrument like the MSS might be used to measure performance-criterion variables, whereas effectiveness is typically measured by such productivity indicators as sales volume and number of units produced. Effectiveness criteria may be influenced by factors not under the employee's control such as level of competition and other market factors, level of technology, and socially influenced limitations on productivity. Other problems in the measurement of productivity as a criterion include low reliability (e.g., Rothe, 1946a, 1946b, 1947, 1951) and numerous sources of invalidity (e.g., Hardin, 1951; Heron, 1952a, 1952b).

Other indicators associated negatively with the criterion of effectiveness include absences, accidents, and turnover. These indicators appear to be attractive in a face validity sense and to be objective and easily measured; there are, however, unsuspected problems in definition, data collection, and use. For example, Vander Noot, Kunde, and Heneman (1958), in a survey of 620 manufacturing firms, found a large variation in the computation of absence rates, with seventeen different formulas being used to compute rates. This variation appears to result from differing organizational needs and objectives.

Inasmuch as effectiveness criteria relate more to organizational objectives, they do not really reflect the individual's personal and unique contributions. The theory of work adjustment focuses more on individual performance (satisfactoriness) than on productivity. For the purpose of instrumenting the theory, the MSS appears to be the more appropriate measure of satisfactoriness.

Satisfaction in work has been defined in a number of ways in the literature. For Hoppock (1935), it is the individual's overall feeling about the job as expressed in liking or disliking. Schaffer (1953), Maslow (1954), and Roe (1956) view satisfaction in terms of meeting human needs. For Vroom (1964), satisfaction results from the product of the valence of work outcomes and the perceived instrumentality of the job in producing these outcomes. Katzell (1964) sees satisfaction as an affective response on a pleasurable-displeasurable dimension that results from discrepancy between the amount of the stimulus that is experienced and how that stimulus is valued. Smith, Kendall, and Hulin (1969) consider job satisfaction to be affective responses to different facets of the job situation that result from the perception of what is expected as fair and reasonable as compared with what is experienced, given the available alternatives. For Locke (1976), job satisfaction is a pleasurable or positive emotional state resulting from the appraisal of how well one's job situation fulfills one's values, taking into account the congruence of these values with one's needs.

In the theory of work adjustment (Dawis, Lofquist, & Weiss, 1968), satisfaction is the result of the worker's appraisal of the extent to which the work environment fulfills the individual's needs. This view and those of the other investigators cited above are essentially similar and complementary, although they may differ in their emphases. From the several definitions, job satisfaction might be defined as a pleasurable affective condition resulting from one's appraisal of the way in which the experienced job situation meets one's needs, values, and expectations. Conversely, job dissatisfaction is an unpleasant affective condition resulting from the perception that the experienced job situation fails to meet one's needs, values, and expectations.

Several instruments are available to measure job satisfaction (Robinson, Athanasiou, & Head, 1969). Some early instruments include those developed by Hoppock (1935), Kerr (1948), Brayfield and Rothe (1951), Baehr (1953), Morse (1953), Johnson (1955), and Twery, Schmid, and Wrigley (1958). Of these Hoppock's Job

Satisfaction Blank (JSB), a four-item measure of overall satisfaction, remains the most used. Each item presents the respondent with seven statements describing a continuum from extreme dissatisfaction to extreme satisfaction, and the respondent checks the one statement that best represents his or her feelings about the job. Reliability of the JSB is reported to be in the .80s.

More recently developed and frequently used measures of job satisfaction include the Cornell Job Descriptive Index (JDI; Smith, Kendall, & Hulin, 1969) and the Minnesota Satisfaction Questionnaire (MSQ; Weiss, Dawis, England, & Lofquist, 1967). The JDI consists of five scales, containing from nine to eighteen items, that measure satisfaction with work, supervision, pay, promotion, and co-workers. The items consist of word or phrase descriptions of these five job facets. The respondent checks whether or not the items describe the job. Satisfactory reliabilities are reported for the JDI.

The MSQ consists of 100 items designed to assess satisfaction with 20 separate aspects of the work environment (called work reinforcers) that pertain to 20 psychological needs. These 20 needs are ability utilization, achievement, activity, advancement, authority, company policies and practices, compensation, co-workers, creativity, independence, moral values, recognition, responsibility, security, social service, social status, supervision-human relations, supervision-technical, variety, and working conditions. The respondent rates each item on a 5-point scale ranging from Not Satisfied (the aspect is much poorer than expected) to Extremely Satisfied (the aspect is much better than expected.) The MSQ manual reports reliability and validity data indicating that the instrument is appropriate for use in both research and practice. For research on the theory of work adjustment, the MSQ is particularly appropriate because it was designed to measure dimensions of job satisfaction that parallel dimensions of needs as measured by the Minnesota Importance Questionnaire (MIQ).

Tenure is simply defined as the length of time an individual remains in a work environment. Because it is an indicator of work adjustment and also a result of adequate adjustment to work, tenure reflects acceptable levels of both satisfactoriness and satisfaction. It is the work-adjustment indicator that is easiest to observe and measure accurately, although in practice we typically rely on reports of tenure or on recorded information. Since one must wait for some time before a measure of tenure can be obtained, reliance is often placed on the shorter-term indicators of satisfactoriness and satisfaction.

There are at least three kinds of tenure: position or job tenure, or the time spent in a particular position; organizational tenure, or the time spent in an organization irrespective of the positions held; and occupational tenure, or the time spent in a specific occupation irrespective of organizational membership or positions held. Research on work adjustment most often uses position or occupational tenure.

In vocational psychology, occupational tenure is frequently used as a criterion. For example, Strong (1943) used occupational tenure as a criterion in selecting individuals to include in occupational reference groups for the occupational scales of the Strong Vocational Interest Blank. He also used occupational tenure to validate the scales in his 18-year follow-up study (Strong, 1955). In the well-known studies of the British National Institute for Industrial Psychology (Cherry, 1974; Hunt & Smith, 1945) occupational tenure was a criterion used to evaluate the effectiveness of vocational guidance. Thorndike and Hagen (1959) used occupational tenure and position tenure as two of seven criteria in their study *10,000 Careers.* In industrial-organizational psychology, position tenure is frequently used to study turnover as it relates to job satisfaction, morale, training, and management policies and practices (e.g., Porter & Steers, 1973).

Organizational tenure has not typically been used as an outcome criterion in research in vocational psychology. It is, however, beginning to attract attention as a useful dependent variable, as in organizational commitment studies (Farris, 1971; Rabinowitz & Hall, 1977). Position or job tenure is, from the standpoint of the theory of work adjustment, the most unambiguous tenure outcome measure because it is a direct consequence of the individual's interaction with one specific work environment. On the other hand, position tenure is typically limited to a shorter period and is, therefore, less representative of overall career adjustment than is occupational tenure. Studies of job satisfaction and tenure obviously use position tenure, whereas studies of career satisfaction use occupational tenure. Both kinds of tenure should be included as outcome criteria in the broadest study of work adjustment.

RESEARCH ON THE THEORY OF WORK ADJUSTMENT

We will present research on the theory of work adjustment in two parts: first, research relevant to the formal propositions of the theory; second, other research that contributes to the explication and application of the theory. The theory is presented in operational terms in figure 6.1.

Research on Propositions

1. Proposition I states that work adjustment at any time is indicated by an individual's concurrent levels of satisfactoriness and satisfaction.

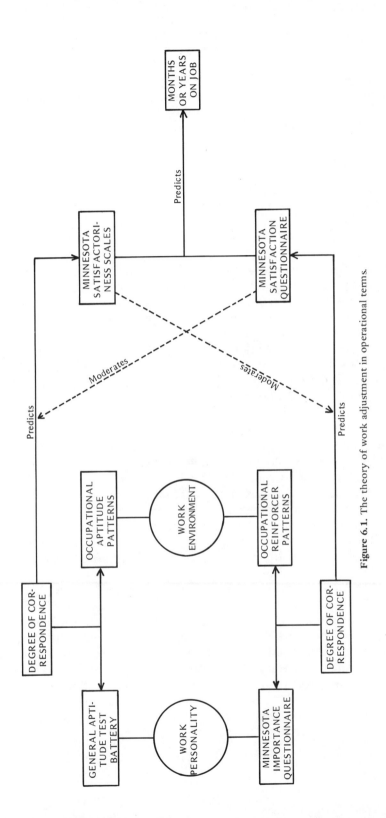

Figure 6.1. The theory of work adjustment in operational terms.

Table 6.1
CORRELATION BETWEEN SATISFACTORINESS AND SATISFACTION

GROUP	NUMBER IN GROUP	MAXIMUM CANONICAL CORRELATION COEFFICIENT
Janitors and maintenance workers	209	.13
Assemblers	68	.31
Machinists	199	.24
Office clerks	186	.17
Salespersons	165	.11
Engineers	317	.20
Total	1,144	.12

Source: D. J. Weiss, R. V. Dawis, L. H. Lofquist, and G. W. England, Instrumentation for the theory of work adjustment, *Minnesota Studies in Vocational Rehabilitation,* XXI, 1966.

This proposition leads to the expectation of relative independence of measured satisfactoriness and satisfaction. The data in table 6.1, which shows the correlations between sets of satisfactoriness and satisfaction scores for six occupational groups, confirm this expectation.

These correlations indicate that the variance common to satisfactoriness and satisfaction is no more than 10% for any of the occupational groups. Similar results were reported in Carlson, Dawis, England, and Lofquist (1963). These findings support the requirement implied in Proposition I that satisfactoriness and satisfaction should be independent indicators of work adjustment. Studies in the applied psychology literature of the relationship between job performance (satisfactoriness) and job satisfaction also support the relative independence of these two indicators of work adjustment (e.g., Brayfield and Crockett, 1955; Pervin, 1968).

2. Proposition II states in part that satisfactoriness is a function of the correspondence between the individual's abilities and the ability requirements of the work environment. When satisfactoriness is predicted from ability test scores, as in the typical selection situation, the closeness of the predicted satisfactoriness to the observed satisfactoriness is a measure of the correspondence between the individual's abilities and the ability requirements of the work environment. This relationship of closeness may be expressed technically by a correlation coefficient. Table 6.2 shows the correlation coefficients obtained for four occupational groups, which support the proposition. Studies in the applied psychology literature that demonstrate significant relationships between abilities and other measures of satisfactoriness, such as supervisor ratings of job performance, and grades achieved in occupation training programs (e.g., Ghiselli, 1966; U.S. Department of Labor, 1970), also confirm the validity of Proposition II. This proposition is also the basic premise for test validation procedures.

Table 6.2

CORRELATION BETWEEN PREDICTED AND OBSERVED SATISFACTORINESS

GROUP	DEVELOPMENT		CROSS-VALIDATION	
	NUMBER IN GROUP	COEFFICIENT OF CORRELATION	NUMBER IN GROUP	COEFFICIENT OF CORRELATION
Machinists and assemblers (I)	133	.48	118	.20*
Clerks (I)	93	.35	83	.27*
Clerks (II)	83	.37	93	.18*
Engineers (I)	152	.42	151	.05
Engineers (II)	151	.48	152	.05
Janitors and maintenance workers (I)	82	.45	97	.20*
Janitors and maintenance workers (II)	97	.33	82	.38**

Note. Double cross-validation study, using reciprocal averages prediction, based on unpublished data from the Work Adjustment Project, Department of Psychology, University of Minnesota. A large group was randomly divided into two groups to enable independent calculation and comparison of correlations for separate groups.

*Significant at the .05 level.

**Significant at the .01 level.

3. A corollary of Proposition II states that knowledge of the abilities and satisfactoriness of individuals permits determination of the effective ability requirements of the work environment. This statement is substantiated by the considerable body of work on the development of occupational aptitude patterns (U.S. Department of Labor, 1970). Other studies designed to develop selection test batteries, as for personnel selection and scholastic admission, have established test cutoff scores that, in turn, effectively describe the ability requirements of the relevant environment and lend further support to this corollary.

4. Proposition III states in part that satisfaction is a function of the correspondence between the reinforcer pattern of the work environment and the individual's values. Values, as we have seen, serve as reference dimensions for needs and are derived from need measurement. Research to date in the Work Adjustment Project has focused on need-reinforcer correspondence and satisfaction. When satisfaction is predicted from need scores, the closeness of the predicted satisfaction to the observed satisfaction is a measure of the correspondence between the individual's needs and the reinforcer pattern of the work environment. The data in table 6.3 lend support to Proposition III, and additional studies of needs-reinforcer correspondence and satisfaction have shown similar results (Betz, 1969; Elizur & Tziner, 1977; Lichter, 1980; Rounds & Dawis, 1975; Salazar, 1981). For example, the study of Elizur and Tziner found a

Table 6.3

CORRELATION BETWEEN PREDICTED AND OBSERVED SATISFACTION

GROUP	DEVELOPMENT		CROSS-VALIDATION[a]	
	NUMBER IN GROUP	MULTIPLE CORRELATION COEFFICIENT	NUMBER IN GROUP	COEFFICIENT OF CORRELATION
Assemblers, long tenure (I)[b]	99	.59*	98	.38*
Assemblers, long tenure (II)[b]	98	.60*	94	.44*
Assemblers, short tenure	75	.63*	40	.42*
Laborers, short tenure	88	.59		
Laborers, long tenure	77	.63*	40	.22
Managers	90	.56	44	.01
Nurses, full-time (I)	212	.46*	211	.32*
Nurses, full-time (II)	211	.55*	212	.27*
Nurses, part-time (I)	169	.50*	171	.26*
Nurses, part-time (II)	171	.54*	169	.24*
Nurses, supervisory (I)	99	.70**	99	.48**
Nurses, supervisory (II)	99	.68**	99	.30**
Packers, male	68	.64		
Packers, female	34	.92*		
Secretaries	80	.64**	42	.26
Social workers, female	70	.66**	40	−.09

Source. Unpublished data from the Work Adjustment Project, Department of Psychology, University of Minnesota.

[a]Correlation obtained on a new sample.

[b]Whenever possible, a large group was randomly divided into two groups to enable independent calculation and comparison of correlations for separate groups.

*Significant at the .05 level.

**Significant at the .01 level.

canonical correlation of .84 between job satisfaction scores on 20 work aspects and the difference scores obtained between vocational needs and job rewards on the same 20 work aspects.

5. A corollary of Proposition III states that knowledge of the values of individuals and their satisfaction permits the determination of the effective reinforcer pattern of the work environment. Support for this corollary is found in studies that parallel the development of the United States Employment Service's occupational aptitude patterns by inferring the reinforcer pattern of an occupation (or other defined environment) from the correlation of need (value) and satisfaction scores.

6. Proposition IV states that satisfaction moderates the functional relationship between satisfactoriness and ability-requirement correspondence. In a Work Adjustment Project study, the prediction of satisfactoriness from ability test scores was found to be more accurate for groups of individuals with high satisfaction scores than for those with low satisfaction scores (table 6.4). Additional evidence

Table 6.4

CORRELATION BETWEEN ABILITIES AND SATISFACTORINESS

GROUP	NUMBER IN GROUP	SATISFACTORINESS MEASURE	
		PRODUCTIVITY	SUPERVISOR EVALUATION
Total male group	169	.43*	.44*
High satisfaction	56	.63*	.69*
Middle satisfaction	57	.48	.52
Low satisfaction	56	.42	.34
Total female group	183	.26*	.27*
High satisfaction	61	.63*	.34
Middle satisfaction	61	.29	.33
Low satisfaction	61	.42	.38

Source. Unpublished data from the Work Adjustment Project, Department of Psychology, University of Minnesota.

*Significant at .05 level.

in support of Proposition IV may be found in a study by Locke, Mento, and Katcher (1978). They found that ability predicted performance more effectively when groups were homogeneous in their motivation than when the groups were heterogeneous with respect to motivation. It seems reasonable to view satisfaction as an indicator of motivation. In another study, Ivancevich (1976) found that measured satisfaction moderated the prediction of a variety of job performance criteria from scores on the Employee Aptitude Survey and that levels of prediction differed for different types of satisfaction.

7. Proposition VII states that the probability that an individual will voluntarily leave the work environment is inversely related to the individual's satisfaction. Taylor and Weiss (1972) attempted to predict individual job termination from measured satisfaction (using the MSQ) and from four additional biographical items (age, number of dependents, education, and sex). They found that only satisfaction resulted in hit rates (correct identification of job leavers) above the base rate in both development and cross-validation groups. This study lends some support to Proposition VII of the theory. Additional support may be found in extensive reviews of studies of employee turnover (e.g., Muchinsky & Tuttle, 1979; Porter & Steers, 1973) that have shown that job satisfaction is consistently negatively related to turnover in a wide variety of occupational groups. If absenteeism can be viewed as a beginning form of voluntary departure from a job, these same reviews also show a consistently negative relationship with job satisfaction.

8. Proposition VIII, which combines propositions VI and VII, states that tenure is a joint function of satisfactoriness and satisfaction.

Table 6.5
PERCENTAGE OF STAYERS AND LEAVERS AT TIME 2 BY
SATISFACTION-SATISFACTORINESS GROUPS AT TIME 1

MEASURES	GROUP	N	PERCENTAGE STAYERS	PERCENTAGE LEAVERS
Intrinsic satisfaction	Dissatisfied-unsatisfactory	187	64	36
and general satisfactoriness	Dissatisfied-satisfactory	210	64	36
	Satisfied-unsatisfactory	215	68	32
	Satisfied-satisfactory	186	74	26
Intrinsic satisfaction	Dissatisfied-unsatisfactory	197	62	38
and performance	Dissatisfied-satisfactory	201	64	36
	Satisfied-unsatisfactory	206	67	33
	Satisfied-satisfactory	195	74	26
Extrinsic satisfaction	Dissatisfied-unsatisfactory	184	64	40
and general satisfactoriness	Dissatisfied-satisfactory	216	62	38
	Satisfied-unsatisfactory	218	72	28
	Satisfied-satisfactory	181	75	25
Extrinsic satisfaction	Dissatisfied-unsatisfactory	191	60	40
and performance	Dissatisfied-satisfactory	209	61	39
	Satisfied-unsatisfactory	212	69	31
	Satisfied-satisfactory	187	78	22

Anderson (1969), in a 2-year longitudinal study of 809 individuals in seven occupational groups, found that individuals who were both satisfied and satisfactory at time 1 were significantly more likely to have remained in the job at time 2 than were individuals who were either dissatisfied or unsatisfactory or both. Table 6-5 presents partial data from the Anderson study. These data support propositions VIII and VII as well as Proposition VI, which states that the probability that an individual will be forced out of the work environment is inversely related to the individual's satisfactoriness. In the Anderson data, Proposition VI appears to be supported for the satisfied groups but not for the dissatisfied groups.

9. Proposition IX, which states that correspondence between work personality and work environment increases as a function of tenure, requires longitudinal study. One is in progress as part of a continuing Work Adjustment Project follow-up of vocational counseling clients. Indirect evidence of the validity of this proposition is found in studies of changes in abilities and interests with tenure on the job. For example, Bentz (1953) found significant changes in intelligence test scores of Sears Roebuck executives after an 8-year interval. Strong (1955), in his classic study *Vocational Interests 18 Years after College*, reported changes in interest scores in the direction of more similarity to the appropriate occupational group (table 6.6).

Table 6.6
INTEREST SCORES OF BUSINESS MANAGERS

SCALE	NO.	TEST		RETEST		DIFFERENCE BETWEEN TEST AND RETEST[a]	
		OWN GROUP	NON-GROUP	OWN GROUP	NON-GROUP	OWN GROUP	NON-GROUP
Production manager	36	42.2	34.0	51.3	36.9	9.1	2.9
Personnel manager	26	37.7	31.9	44.6	35.0	6.9	3.1
Sales manager	23	39.9	32.7	47.1	31.9	7.2	—0.8
President	16	38.1	31.7	43.1	34.6	5.0	2.9
Public administrator	9	38.6	32.3	50.2	40.5	11.6	8.2
All business managers	110	39.8	32.7	47.5	35.4	7.7	2.7

Note: Reprinted from E. K. Strong, Jr., *Vocational interests 18 years after college* (Minneapolis: University of Minnesota Press, 1955), p. 86.

[a]All differences are significant at the .01 level except that of —0.8.

Wiener and Klein (1978), in a study of the relationship between job satisfaction and the congruence of vocational interests with present occupation, found that the relationship was significant for samples of long-tenured individuals but not significant for short-tenured samples. The differences in correlations (between job satisfaction and interest congruency) for the long and short tenured groups were statistically significant.

Research on Adjustment Style

The expanded theory of work adjustment presented in chapter 5 states additional propositions and corollaries that deal with the more recent concepts related to the adjustment style dimensions of the work personality. Research efforts to date have focused on the construct validity of the adjustment style measures of flexibility, activeness, and reactiveness.

Cheung (1975) was able to develop threshold measures of flexibility (tolerance of discorrespondence) by using the Thurstone method of categorical judgment and the methods of signal detection theory. She found that it was possible to use these measures to separate high- and low-flexible groups and that these groups differed in adjectival self-description in the expected directions. In a multitrait, multimethod study of flexibility, activeness, and reactiveness, Humphrey (1980) found evidence of convergent and divergent validity for all three constructs. He also found that a measure based on self-reported life experiences appeared to have more promise as the basis for instrument development than a hypothetical work-situation questionnaire or a self-description checklist.

The Work Adjustment Project is developing instruments to use in assessing the adjustment style dimensions of flexibility, activeness, reactiveness, and perseverance. One of these is a Life Experiences Questionnaire (LEQ) that obtains self-report information on life experiences reflecting tolerance for discorrespondent situations (flexibility, perseverance), actions to change environmental situations (activeness), and actions taken to change expression of one's personality (reactiveness). Another of these instruments is a Work Situation Questionnaire (WSQ) that presents response choices to an individual for coping with each of a number of different work environment problems. The problems were selected to allow for the appropriateness of either an active or a reactive response choice, depending upon the particular individual's adjustment mode preference. The response choices, representing active and reactive modes of adjustment, were selected to be equally attractive and to be mentioned with equal frequency by subjects in a free-response situation. Both the LEQ and the WSQ have received preliminary validation against self-report ratings on the adjustment style dimensions.

One promising approach to validating these adjustment style measures involves testing the new propositions in the theory of work adjustment that relate to adjustment style. For example, one might identify occupations that clearly require workers who are active (or reactive), assess the satisfaction and satisfactoriness of the workers in each group, and correlate scores on the adjustment style measures with levels and combinations of satisfaction and satisfactoriness. One would expect higher levels of satisfaction and satisfactoriness for workers whose adjustment style scores correspond with the characterization of the occupation.

Another way to assess adjustment style dimensions might involve the inference of style characteristics from the configuration of scores on existing personality measures for satisfied and satisfactory workers in environments clearly describable as requiring active or reactive workers.

Research on Needs, Values, and Reinforcers

A survey of the literature on the concept of values reveals a number of emphases in definition. Most researchers, however, agree that what is important to the individual is central in the definition of values (e.g., Allport, Vernon, & Lindzey, 1970; England & Lee, 1974; Katzell, 1964; Locke, 1976; Rokeach, 1973; and Super, 1973). Values, as importance dimensions, are conceptualized in the theory of work adjustment as reference dimensions for the description of needs. Needs are preferences for reinforcers expressed in terms of the relative importance of each reinforcer to the individual. Reinforcers, in turn, are stimulus conditions that follow upon and are associated with the maintenance of responding, or work behavior.

The MIQ, as a measure of needs, operationalizes these concepts by asking an individual to assess the relative importance of 20 work reinforcers that were previously identified as contributing significantly to satisfaction in work. The concept of values as reference dimensions for needs developed out of studies of the underlying structural organization of needs, principally through the use of factor analysis.

Studies of the factor structure of the MIQ show that needs can be organized around six dimensions. Four factor analyses of MIQ data were prepared for 1,621 vocational rehabilitation clients, 3,033 employed workers, 419 college students, and a heterogenous group of 5,358 individuals that included the three groups above plus 285 vocational-technical school students (Gay, Weiss, Hendel, Dawis, & Lofquist, 1971). A principal factor solution was used, with squared multiple correlations as communality estimates and orthogonal rotation to a varimax criterion. Similar results were obtained for each of the four groups. The factor structure for the largest group is summarized in table 6.7.

Table 6.7
VARIMAX FACTOR LOADING MATRIX FOR TOTAL GROUP ($N = 5,358$)

MINNESOTA IMPORTANCE QUESTIONNAIRE SCALE	I	II	III	IV	V	VI	VII	h^2
Ability utilization	−.16	.38	−.21	−.25	−.56	−.11	.00	.60
Achievement	−.18	.28	−.20	−.34	−.56	−.17	−.03	.61
Activity	−.27	.07	−.67	−.14	−.19	−.11	.04	.59
Advancement	−.37	.33	−.08	.03	−.41	−.37	−.12	.58
Authority	−.21	.54	−.17	−.04	−.02	−.40	.06	.53
Company policies and practices	−.64	.14	−.09	−.33	−.12	−.07	−.09	.58
Compensation	−.49	.13	−.20	.01	−.09	−.34	−.29	.50
Co-workers	−.22	.05	−.37	−.44	−.07	−.28	−.06	.46
Creativity	−.10	.77	−.12	−.19	−.22	−.05	−.02	.70
Independence	−.16	.22	−.58	−.01	−.05	−.12	−.04	.43
Moral values	−.22	.08	.03	−.47	−.05	−.00	−.04	.28
Recognition	−.33	.28	−.19	−.05	−.32	−.45	−.05	.54
Responsibility	−.11	.79	−.20	−.13	−.19	−.14	−.03	.75
Security	−.44	−.09	−.42	−.03	−.20	−.26	−.23	.54
Social service	−.03	.18	−.28	−.51	−.22	−.06	.11	.44
Social status	−.14	.21	−.23	−.13	−.12	−.55	−.00	.45
Supervision-human relations	−.74	.21	−.12	−.18	−.05	−.10	.05	.66
Supervision-technical	−.70	.13	−.24	−.17	−.12	−.11	.14	.63
Variety	−.08	.34	−.56	−.16	−.05	−.17	.01	.49
Working conditions	−.49	−.00	−.41	−.12	−.16	−.25	−.24	.58
Contribution of factor	2.71	2.26	2.03	1.16	1.21	1.28	.27	10.91
Proportion of common variance	.25	.21	.19	.10	.11	.12	.02	1.00
Proportion of total variance	.14	.11	.10	.06	.06	.06	.01	.51

Source. E. G. Gay, D. J. Weiss, D. D. Hendel, R. V. Dawis, and L. H. Lofquist, Manual for the Minnesota Importance Questionnaire, *Minnesota Studies in Vocational Rehabilitation*, XXVIII, 1971.

Table 6.8

VARIMAX FACTOR LOADING MATRIX FOR TOTAL MALE GROUP ($N = 1,609$)

MINNESOTA IMPORTANCE QUESTIONNAIRE SCALE	FACTOR						
	I	II	III	IV	V	VI	h^2
Ability utilization	.21	.31	.14	.22	.60	.16	.59
Achievement	.16	.17	.13	.35	.62	.27	.66
Activity	.28	.06	.66	.07	.20	.12	.58
Advancement	.41	.22	.08	−.14	.37	.51	.64
Authority	.16	.45	.13	.03	.03	.47	.47
Company policies and practices	.71	.10	.04	.36	.11	.11	.66
Compensation	.41	.04	.20	−.07	.05	.53	.50
Co-workers	.31	.06	.31	.42	.03	.33	.48
Creativity	.04	.78	.11	.23	.23	.07	.73
Independence	.12	.24	.60	.01	.03	.14	.45
Moral values	.18	.09	−.10	.50	.09	.00	.31
Recognition	.17	.21	.15	.06	.35	.60	.59
Responsibility	.10	.78	.21	.15	.17	.21	.77
Security	.52	−.13	.43	−.16	.19	.28	.62
Social service	.08	.24	.21	.59	.18	.01	.49
Social status	.08	.13	.17	.17	.11	.68	.55
Supervision-human relations	.71	.19	.07	.26	.12	.19	.66
Supervision-technical	.70	.08	.24	.19	.13	.11	.62
Variety	.04	.38	.51	.13	.02	.20	.46
Working conditions	.54	−.02	.41	.01	.06	.34	.58
Contribution of factor	2.77	2.00	1.83	1.36	1.27	2.17	11.40
Proportion of common variance	.24	.18	.16	.12	.11	.19	1.00
Proportion of total variance	.14	.10	.09	.07	.06	.11	.57

Source. D. J. Seaburg, J. B. Rounds, Jr., R. V. Dawis, and L. H. Lofquist, *Values as second order needs* (Paper presented at the 84th annual meeting of the American Psychological Association, Washington, D.C., September 1976).

Factor I appears to represent the importance of safety in a predictable work environment, factor II reflects the importance of autonomy, factor III appears to describe a preference for comfort in the work environment, factor IV reflects the importance of opportunities for altruism, factor V indicates preferences for an environment that permits achievement and accomplishment, and factor VI appears to describe the importance of opportunities for status; factor VII, which is meaningless in terms of content, is a residual factor.

The generalizability of this MIQ factor structure was determined by performing a second series of factor analyses using MIQ data for 9,377 vocational rehabilitation clients (Seaburg, Rounds, Dawis, & Lofquist, 1976). The subjects were divided into eight subgroups defined by sex-group membership and the age groups of 16-18, 19-25, 26-45, and 46-71 years. The same factor analysis procedures as those described above were used. The resulting factor structures were similar for age groups within sex but differed slightly between

Table 6.9

VARIMAX FACTOR LOADING MATRIX FOR TOTAL FEMALE GROUP ($N = 1,674$)

MINNESOTA IMPORTANCE QUESTIONNAIRE SCALE	FACTOR						
	I	II	III	IV	V	VI	h^2
Ability utilization	.22	.35	.22	.11	.58	.17	.59
Achievement	.24	.25	.09	.24	.56	.32	.61
Activity	.08	.14	.67	.28	.17	.15	.61
Advancement	.18	.18	.30	−.07	.27	.58	.56
Authority	.13	.51	.11	.10	−.01	.42	.47
Company policies and practices	.71	.10	.20	.03	.13	.22	.63
Compensation	.25	.06	.26	.05	−.04	.62	.52
Co-workers	.22	.10	.18	.58	−.02	.32	.53
Creativity	.16	.76	−.05	.12	.23	.03	.68
Independence	.06	.34	.44	.11	.07	.16	.35
Moral values	.41	.08	−.16	.14	.07	−.05	.23
Recognition	.12	.24	.08	.10	.30	.65	.60
Responsibility	.12	.78	.09	.11	.17	.17	.71
Security	.16	−.11	.61	.05	.06	.44	.61
Social service	.11	.19	.13	.50	.26	−.01	.38
Social status	.04	.18	.15	.27	.11	.57	.46
Supervision-human relations	.72	.13	.14	.05	.07	.23	.62
Supervision-technical	.61	.06	.34	.07	.12	.21	.56
Variety	−.04	.42	.32	.39	.05	.15	.46
Working conditions	.33	.01	.49	.14	.05	.43	.56
Contribution of factor	2.04	2.16	1.87	1.08	1.06	2.51	10.72
Proportion of common variance	.19	.20	.17	.10	.10	.23	.99
Proportion of total variance	.10	.11	.09	.05	.05	.13	.53

Source. D. J. Seaburg, J. B. Rounds, Jr., R. V. Dawis, and L. H. Lofquist, *Values as second order needs* (paper presented at the 84th annual meeting of the American Psychological Association, Washington, D.C., September 1976).

the sexes in each age group. Two additional factor analyses were completed for 1,609 males (table 6.8) and 1,674 females (table 6.9), including in each sex group at least 400 individuals for each of the original four age groups.

These factor structures were very similar to that shown for the earlier study in table 6.7. The negative loadings in factors I, III, IV, V, and VI in table 6.7 are an artifact of the analysis that can be reversed by reflecting the dimension to obtain positive loadings. The size of the factor loadings, positive or negative, provides the significant information about the identification of the factor dimensions. Six dimensions in tables 6.7-6.9 appear to provide adequate description of the organization of the 20 MIQ needs. These six dimensions may be regarded as value dimensions following the definitions presented above.

The availability of value dimensions as reference dimensions provides a more parsimonious approach to the description of the reinforcer preferences of the individual. The factor analyses show convincingly that six dimensions are enough to describe the common variance represented in the 20 MIQ need dimensions. They also specify basic need commonalities that may suggest areas of importance associated with, or indicative of, a particular value beyond those assessed by the MIQ. For example, the safety value assessed by the MIQ touches on the importance of company policies and practices and of immediate supervision. More complete assessment, however, might reveal other reinforcers in the job situation that contribute to a predictably safe environment for the individual, such as stability of management, size and reputation of the company, and position of the company in the marketplace over the years.

Multidimensional scaling studies conducted by the Work Adjustment Project staff (Rounds, unpublished, 1976) demonstrate that the six values found in the research cited above can be further organized along three dimensions as shown previously in figure 3.1 (page 30). The six values are grouped into three sets of polar opposites: altruism vs. status, achievement vs. comfort, and autonomy vs. safety.

A number of studies have investigated the relationship of biographical data to needs and values as measured by the MIQ. The expectation that there is a relationship is derived from the assumption in the theory of work adjustment that the work personalities of individuals develop from their response and reinforcement histories, that is, their experiences with responding in certain ways and under different conditions of reinforcement in social, educational, and work settings.

Gray (1974), using 8th and 10th grade students as subjects, studied the relationship of reported school and outside activities to needs as measured by the MIQ. She also examined the relationship of participation in activities to the development of needs by obtaining a second measurement of needs in a 2-year follow-up study. Gray reported reliable but modest relationships between activities and needs at both times.

Fruehling (1980) studied the relationship of student-reported biographical information to MIQ-measured needs for a national sample of high school students in grades 8 through 11. She found many significant zero order correlations in expected directions,, although few relationships generalized across grades or between sexes.

In a further analysis of the Fruehling data, Eberly (1980) studied the multivariate relationships between rationally developed biographical data scales designed to tap six vocational values and the same values measured by the MIQ. Working with data for eight groups (four high school grade levels and both sexes), she found significant predictions (linear multiple regression) for 34 of the 48 possible relationships.

Engdahl (1980) studied the factor structure of biographical data obtained in the Fruehling study and examined its relationship to vocational needs and values as measured by the MIQ. His factor analysis yielded 27 interpretable biographical factors that were shown to be consistent with previous studies in the literature. Using these factors to develop biodata-factor scales, he was able to predict 18 of the 20 MIQ needs and all 6 of the MIQ values for male, female, and total high school student groups. On cross-validation, 15 of the 18 needs and all 6 values were predicted successfully.

Using college sophomores as subjects, Meresman (1975) studied the relationship of biographical information to MIQ measured vocational needs. For development groups he found significant bivariate and multivariate relationships with all twenty MIQ scales. However multivariate relationships for only three of the scales held up on cross validation.

Rounds, Dawis, and Lofquist (1979) studied life history correlates of vocational needs, as measured by the MIQ, for a sample of 290 female adults. A weighted biographical information form was developed to predict scores on each of the 20 MIQ need scales. It was possible to predict MIQ scale scores from the biographical data items. Using a double cross-validation design, statistically significant validity coefficients were obtained for 19 of the 20 MIQ scales, ranging from .13 to .47, with a median of .35. The prediction equations for females did not generalize to a male sample. In additional unpublished Work Adjustment Project research, MIQ scale scores for males were successfully predicted from biographical data. We may thus conclude that needs as measured on the MIQ can be predicted from biographical data for both sexes. The prediction equations (item weightings) differ for the sexes, however, suggesting that the development of needs for each sex derives from different experiences with reinforcement.

Eberly, Rounds, Dawis, and Williams (1976) studied the vocational needs of neuropsychiatric patients, rehabilitation clients, and college students (all male and between the ages of 20 and 22 years) to determine whether their assumed different reinforcement histories had resulted in differential reinforcer preferences (needs) as measured by the MIQ. Differences in reinforcement histories were assumed from the statuses of the groups: the neuropsychiatric group consisted of Vietnam veterans now hospitalized, the rehabilitation group consisted of vocational rehabilitation clients who had experienced a disability but were not hospitalized, and the college group consisted of students who were not veterans and had no apparent disabilities. The mean profiles for the three groups were highly similar in shape; however, significant mean differences were found for these groups on 13 of the 20 MIQ scales. The scale scores were generally highest for the neuropsychiatric group and next highest for the rehabilitation group. These results suggest that traumatic experiences may heighten the importance of reinforcers without affecting the rank order of preferences.

Although Rounds et al. (1979) found sex differences in the development of needs from experienced reinforcement, other data indicate that there are no significant sex differences in the perception of reinforcers in work environments. Flint (1980) studied the perception of reinforcers in 12 occupations that were male dominated, female dominated, or not sex dominated by sampling equal numbers of male and female raters employed in each occupation. He found that highly similar (and at times practically identical) occupational reinforcer patterns were generated from the ratings of each sex group in an occupation. Correlations between male and female profiles (ORPs) ranged from .91 to .98, which compares favorably with the median random split group reliability for ORPs of .91 (Borgen, Weiss, Tinsley, Dawis, & Lofquist, 1968).

Perceptions of work reinforcers yield a factor structure that appears to parallel the organization of need-reinforcer preferences into the six-value structure described earlier. Shubsachs, Rounds, Dawis, and Lofquist (1978) performed factor analysis of data from 6,000 raters on reinforcer patterns for 109 occupations that approximated the distribution of the U.S. employed labor force. The data were best represented by three factors identified as a self-reinforcement factor, an environmental/organizational reinforcement factor, and a reinforcement via altruism factor. These factors were found to correspond respectively to the achievement-autonomy-status, safety-comfort, and altruism need factors (values) of the MIQ. This study presents evidence to confirm the validity of the construct of values as reference dimensions for needs and extends the usefulness of the construct to the description of reinforcers in work environments in terms of reinforcer factors that parallel values.

The six-value system for representing reinforcers in the work environment has provided a basis for developing a taxonomy of work environments. Dawis, Lofquist, Henly, and Rounds (1979/1982) constructed the Minnesota Occupational Classification System II (MOCS II) by clustering 1,100 occupations into 78 taxons according to similarity of reinforcer patterns and ability-requirement patterns. The six-value system provides a feasible and meaningful basis for differentiating among occupational groups in terms of their distinctive reinforcer characteristics.

The critical validation of measures of needs, values, and reinforcers lies in the successful prediction of satisfaction from the correspondence of an individual's needs and values with her or his work environment reinforcers. Weiss, Dawis, England, and Lofquist (1965) reported that average satisfaction for a high-need, high-reinforcement group was significantly higher than that for a high-need, low-reinforcement group, whereas average satisfaction for a high-need, low-reinforcement group was significantly lower than that for a low-need, low-reinforcement group.

In another study, of 134 managers, 117 truck drivers, 122 secretaries, and 198 nurses, the same investigators reported significant cross-validated correlations ranging from .23 to .48 between need-reinforcer correspondence and satisfaction.

Betz (1971) studied 105 female cashiers, checker markers, and sales clerks and found significant correlations between job satisfaction and need-reinforcer correspondence, ranging from .32 to .45 using different indices of correspondence. Lichter (1980), in a study of clients of a vocational assessment clinic followed up after a period of 1 to 2 years, found a correlation of .37 between need-reinforcer correspondence and satisfaction for a total group of 223 males and females. The correlation for males under 30 was .41; for males 30 and over, .41; for females under 30, .39; for females 30 and over, .24. The first three group correlations were significant at the .05 level. Rounds (1981) found correlations ranging from .14 to .55 (with a median of .33) between need-reinforcer correspondence and satisfaction 1 to 2 years after counseling for 116 female and 106 male clients.

The prediction of satisfaction from need-reinforcer correspondence was further supported by a study by Salazar (1981) in the Republic of the Philippines. She reported correlations of .18 to .34 for a group of 69 graduates of a counselor training program who subsequently obtained positions in educational institutions.

Understanding of the construct of vocational needs can be extended by examining the relationship of vocational needs to other personality dimensions. As an example, Thorndike, Weiss, and Dawis (1968) used canonical correlation to study the relationship between needs as measured by the MIQ and interests as measured by the Strong Vocational Interest Blank (SVIB; Strong, 1943). They found maximum canonical correlations of .78 (for a student group) and .74 (for a rehabilitation group). These canonical correlations are high enough to indicate that needs and interests measured in these ways belong in the same domain of personality variables. They are not high enough, however, to indicate that these instruments are measuring the same construct (i.e., needs and interests are not the same construct).

Sloan (1979) studied the relationship between vocational needs as measured by the MIQ and personality characteristics as measured by the Minnesota Multiphasic Personality Inventory (MMPI; Hathaway & McKinley, 1967). Using data on eight large groups of rehabilitation clients (M/F × young/older × physically disabled/psychiatrically disabled). She related MIQ need/value scores to MMPI scores for 13 clinical scales, 13 content scales, and 8 special scales. Among other things, she found multiple correlations in the neighborhood of .2 to .4 between subsets of MIQ scales predicting MMPI scales and vice versa. These correlations were low, but they were significant and replicated across groups. This study indicates that needs and values as measured by the MIQ and personality dimensions as measured by the MMPI are related but not measures of the same constructs. In other words, each kind of assessment contributes additional unique information to knowledge of the work personality.

In an interesting validation of MIQ responses using experimental methodology, Stulman (1974) compared preferences for creativity and independence reinforcers as measured by the MIQ with expressed and behavioral preferences for experimental conditions that presented different levels of creativity and independence as reinforcers. He found that the expressed and behavioral preferences for working under prescribed vs. permissive conditions, combined with working alone vs. working with others, consistently reflected the MIQ scores on creativity and independence that were obtained from the subjects 2 weeks prior to the experiment. This study supports the feasibility of studying work reinforcers in the experimental laboratory.

In this chapter we have briefly reviewed research relevant to the theory of work adjustment. Research on the structure of work personality and work environment provides a solid foundation for the continuing study of work adjustment. Obviously, more work needs to be done to refine the existing assessment instruments and to expand their coverage. Research on styles of adjustment, work personality, and work environment is in the early stages. Experimental forms for rating style dimensions are included in Appendix A. When adequate assessment instruments for these style dimensions are available, research on the ongoing work adjustment process can be undertaken with more assurance of theoretically meaningful results.

The theory of work adjustment may be applied to the professional practice of counseling, training, and environmental design. In the practice of counseling, the emphasis is on enhancing an individual's understanding of self and the environment and of facilitating courses of action that promise optimal adjustment. In the practice of training, the emphasis is on the development of skills needed to achieve and maintain adjustment. In the practice of environmental design, the emphasis is on structuring or restructuring the environment to increase the likelihood of adjustment by individuals.

In the next five chapters, we will discuss specific ways in which the theory can be applied. Our primary focus will be on practice related to work. However, application to nonwork problems will also be treated.

REFERENCES

Allport, G. W., Vernon, P. E., & Lindzey, G. *Manual: Study of Values.* Boston: Houghton Mifflin, 1970.

Anderson, L. M. *Longitudinal changes in level of work adjustment.* Unpublished doctoral dissertation, University of Minnesota, 1969.

Baehr, M. E. A simplified procedure for the measurement of employee attitudes. *Journal of Applied Psychology,* 1953, *37,* 163-167.

Bentz, V. J. A test-retest experiment on the relationship between age and mental ability. *American Psychologist,* 1953, *8,* 319-320.

Betz, E. L. Need reinforcer correspondence as a predictor of job satisfaction. *Personnel and Guidance Journal,* 1969, *47,* 878-883.

Betz, E. L. *Occupational reinforcer patterns and need-reinforcer correspondence in the prediction of job satisfaction.* Unpublished doctoral dissertation, University of Minnesota, 1971.

Borgen, F. H., Weiss, D. J., Tinsley, H. E. A., Dawis, R. V., & Lofquist, L. H. The measurement of occupational reinforcer patterns. *Minnesota Studies in Vocational Rehabilitation,* XXV, 1968.

Brayfield, A. H., & Crockett, W. H. Employee attitudes and employee performance. *Psychological Bulletin,* 1955, *52,* 396-424.

Brayfield, A. H., & Rothe, H. F. An index of job satisfaction. *Journal of Applied Psychology,* 1951, *35,* 307-311.

Campbell, J. P., Dunnette, M. D., Lawler, E. E., III, & Weick, K. E., Jr. *Managerial behavior, performance, and effectiveness.* New York: McGraw-Hill, 1970.

Carlson, R. E., Dawis, R. V., England, G. W., & Lofquist, L. H. The measurement of employment satisfactoriness. *Minnesota Studies in Vocational Rehabilitation,* XIV, 1963.

Cherry, N. Do career officers give good advice? *British Journal of Guidance and Counseling,* 1974, *2,* 27-40.

Cheung, F. M. *A threshold model of flexibility as a personality style dimension in work adjustment.* Unpublished doctoral dissertation, University of Minnesota, 1975.

Dawis, R. V., Lofquist, L. H., Henly, G. A., & Rounds, J. B., Jr. *Minnesota Occupational Classification System II.* Vocational Psychology Research, Department of Psychology, University of Minnesota, Minneapolis, 1979/1982.

Dawis, R. V., Lofquist, L. H., & Weiss, D. J. A theory of work adjustment (a revision). *Minnesota Studies in Vocational Rehabilitation,* XXIII, 1968.

Eberly, R. E. *Biographical determinants of vocational values.* Unpublished doctoral dissertation, University of Minnesota, 1980.

Eberly, R. E., Rounds, J. B., Jr., Dawis, R. V., & Williams, R. *Vocational needs of three adult male groups: Neuropsychiatric patients, rehabilitation clients, and college students.* Unpublished research paper, Work Adjustment Project, Department of Psychology, University of Minnesota, 1976.

Elizur, D., & Tziner, A. Vocational needs, job rewards, and satisfaction: A canonical analysis. *Journal of Vocational Behavior*, 1977, *10*, 205-211.

Engdahl, B. E. *The structure of biographical data and its relationship to vocational needs and values.* Unpublished doctoral dissertation, University of Minnesota, 1980.

England, G. W., & Lee, R. The relationship between managerial values and managerial success in the United States, Japan, India, and Australia. *Journal of Applied Psychology*, 1974, *59*, 411-419.

Farris, G. F. A predictive study of turnover. *Personnel Psychology*, 1971, *24*, 311-328.

Flint, P. L. *Sex differences in perceptions of occupational reinforcers.* Unpublished doctoral dissertation, University of Minnesota, 1980.

Fruehling, R. T. *Vocational needs and their life history correlates for high school students.* Unpublished doctoral dissertation, University of Minnesota, 1980.

Gay, E. G., Weiss, D. J., Hendel, D. D., Dawis, R. V., & Lofquist, L. H. Manual for the Minnesota Importance Questionnaire. *Minnesota Studies in Vocational Rehabilitation*, XXVIII, 1971.

Ghiselli, E. E. *The validity of occupational aptitude tests.* New York: Wiley, 1966.

Gibson, D. L., Weiss, D. J., Dawis, R. V., & Lofquist, L. H. Manual for the Minnesota Satisfactoriness Scales. *Minnesota Studies in Vocational Rehabilitation*, XVII, 1970.

Gray, B. L. *A longitudinal study of extracurricular activities, vocational needs, and individual need stability during adolescence.* Unpublished doctoral dissertation, University of Minnesota, 1974.

Hardin, E. *Measurement of physical output at the job level.* Research and Technical Report 10. Industrial Relations Center, University of Minnesota, 1951.

Hathaway, S. R., & McKinley, J. C. *Minnesota Multiphasic Personality Inventory: Manual for administration and scoring.* New York: Psychological Corporation, 1967.

Heron, A. The establishment for research purposes of two criteria of occupational adjustment. *Occupational Psychology*, 1952, *26*, 78-85. (a)

Heron, A. A psychological study of occupational adjustment. *Journal of Applied Psychology*, 1952, *36*, 385-387. (b)

Hoppock, R. *Job satisfaction.* New York: Harper, 1935.

Humphrey, C. C. *A multitrait-multimethod assessment of personality styles in work adjustment.* Unpublished doctoral dissertation, University of Minnesota, 1980.

Hunt, E. P., and Smith, P. Vocational psychology and choice of employment. *Occupational Psychology*, 1945, *19*, 109-116.

Ivancevich, J. M. Predicting job performance by use of ability tests and studying job satisfaction as a moderating variable. *Journal of Vocational Behavior*, 1976, *9*, 87-97.

Johnson, G. H. An instrument for the measurement of job satisfaction. *Personnel Psychology*, 1955, *8*, 27-37.

Katzell, R. A. Personal values, job satisfaction, and job behavior. In H. Borow (Ed.), *Man in a world at work.* Boston: Houghton Mifflin, 1964.

Kerr, W. A. On the validity and reliability of the Job Satisfaction tear ballot. *Journal of Applied Psychology*, 1948, *32*, 275-281.

Lichter, D. J. *The prediction of job satisfaction as an outcome of career counseling.* Unpublished doctoral dissertation, University of Minnesota, 1980.

Locke, E. A. The nature and causes of job satisfaction. In M. D. Dunnette (Ed.), *Handbook of industrial and organizational psychology.* Chicago: Rand McNally, 1976.

Locke, E. A., Mento, A. J., & Katcher, B. L. The interactions of ability and motivation in performance. An exploration of the meaning of moderators. *Personnel Psychology*, 1978, *31*, 269-280.

Maslow, A. H. *Motivation and personality.* New York: Harper, 1954.

Meresman, J. F. *Biographical correlates of vocational needs.* Unpublished doctoral dissertation, University of Minnesota, 1975.

Morse, N. C. *Satisfactions in the white-collar job.* Ann Arbor: University of Michigan, 1953.

Muchinsky, P. M., & Tuttle, M. L. Employee turnover: An empirical and methodological assessment. *Journal of Vocational Behavior*, 1979, *14*, 43-77.

Pervin, L. A. Performance and satisfaction as a function of individual environment fit. *Psychological Bulletin*, 1968, *69*, 56-68.

Porter, L. W., & Steers, R. M. Organizational, work, and personal factors in employee turnover and absenteeism. *Psychological Bulletin*, 1973, *80*, 151-176.

Rabinowitz, S., & Hall, D. T. Organizational research on job involvement. *Psychological Bulletin*, 1977, *84*, 265-288.

Robinson, J. P., Athanasiou, R., & Head, K. B. *Measures of occupational attitudes and occupational characteristics.* Survey · Research Center, University of Michigan, Ann Arbor, 1969.

Roe, A. *The psychology of occupations.* New York: Wiley, 1956.

Rokeach, M. *The nature of human values.* New York: Free Press, 1973.

Rothe, H. F. Output rates among butter wrappers: I. Work curves and their stability. *Journal of Applied Psychology*, 1946, *30*, 199-211. (a)

Rothe, H. F. Output rates among butter wrappers: II. Frequency distributions and an hypothesis regarding the "restriction of output." *Journal of Applied Psychology*, 1946, *30*, 320-327. (b)

Rothe, H. F. Output rates among machine operators: I. Distributions and their reliability. *Journal of Applied Psychology*, 1947, *31*, 484-489.

Rothe, H. F. Output rates among chocolate dippers. *Journal of Applied Psychology*, 1951, *35*, 94-97.

Rounds, J. B., Jr. *The comparative and combined utility of need and interest data in the prediction of job satisfaction.* Unpublished doctoral dissertation, University of Minnesota, 1981.

Rounds, J. B., Jr., Dawis, R. V., & Lofquist, L. H. Life history correlates of vocational needs for a female adult sample. *Journal of Counseling Psychology*, 1979, *26*, 487-496.

Salazar, R. C. *The prediction of satisfaction and satisfactoriness for counselor training graduates.* Unpublished doctoral dissertation, University of Minnesota, 1981.

Schaffer, R. H. Job satisfaction as related to need satisfaction in work. *Psychological Monographs*, 1953, No. 364.

Seaburg, D. J., Rounds, J. B., Jr., Dawis, R. V., & Lofquist, L. H. *Values as second order needs.* Paper presented at the 84th annual meeting of the American Psychological Association, Washington, D.C., September 1976.

Shubsachs, A. P. W., Rounds, J. B., Jr., Dawis, R. V., & Lofquist, L. H. Perception of work reinforcer systems: Factor structure. *Journal of Vocational Behavior*, 1978, *13*, 54-62.

Sloan, E. B. *An investigation of relationships between vocational needs and personality.* Unpublished doctoral dissertation, University of Minnesota, 1979.

Smith, P. C., Kendall, L. N., & Hulin, C. L. *The measurement of satisfaction in work and retirement.* Chicago: Rand McNally, 1969.

Strong, E. K., Jr. *Vocational interests of men and women.* Stanford, Calif.: Stanford University Press, 1943.

Strong, E. K., Jr. *Vocational interests 18 years after college.* Minneapolis: University of Minnesota Press, 1955.

Stulman, D. A. *Experimental validation of the independence and creativity scales of the Minnesota Importance Questionnaire.* Unpublished doctoral dissertation, University of Minnesota, 1974.

Super, D. E. The Work Values Inventory. In D. G. Zytowski (Ed.), *Contemporary approaches to interest measurement.* Minneapolis: University of Minnesota Press, 1973.

Taylor, K. D., & Weiss, D. J. Prediction of individual job termination from measured job satisfaction and biographical data. *Journal of Vocational Behavior*, 1972, *2*, 123-132.

Thorndike, R. L., & Hagen, E. *10,000 careers.* New York: Wiley, 1959.

Thorndike, R. M., Weiss, D. J., & Dawis, R. V. The canonical correlation of vocational interests and vocational needs. *Journal of Counseling Psychology,* 1968, *15,* 101-106.

Twery, R., Schmid, J., & Wrigley, C. Some factors in job satisfaction: A comparison of three methods of analysis. *Educational and Psychological Measurement,* 1958, *18,* 189-202.

U.S. Department of Labor. *Manual for the USES General Aptitude Test Battery.* Washington, D.C.: U.S. Government Printing Office, 1970.

Vander Noot, T., Kunde, T., & Heneman, H. G., Jr. Comparability of absence rates. *Personnel Journal,* 1958, *36,* 380-382.

Vroom, V. H. *Work and motivation.* New York: Wiley, 1964.

Weiss, D. J., Dawis, R. V., England, G. W., & Lofquist, L. H. An inferential approach to occupational reinforcement. *Minnesota Studies in Vocational Rehabilitation,* XIX, 1965.

Weiss, D. J., Dawis, R. V., England, G. W., & Lofquist, L. H. Manual for the Minnesota Satisfaction Questionnaire. *Minnesota Studies in Vocational Rehabilitation,* XXII, 1967.

Weiss, D. J., Dawis, R. V., Lofquist, L. H., & England, G. W. Instrumentation for the theory of work adjustment. *Minnesota Studies in Vocational Rehabilitation,* XXI, 1966.

Wiener, Y., & Klein, K. L. The relationship between vocational interests and job satisfaction: Reconciliation of divergent results. *Journal of Vocational Behavior,* 1978, *13,* 298-304.

PART III

Application of the Theory

7

Vocational Counseling

COUNSELING FOR WORK ADJUSTMENT

Application of the theory in work-related counseling includes its use in counseling for career choice, counseling for adjustment to present job, and counseling for job change. In all of these uses, the theory provides a framework for conceptualizing the problem in terms of the interaction between person and environment. It also suggests the information that is important for describing both the person and the environment, descriptions that are needed to forecast the outcome of the person's satisfaction, satisfactoriness, and tenure. The required information about an individual involves skills, abilities, and needs/values; about an environment, ability requirements and reinforcer characteristics. In chapters 3 and 4, we discussed measures of these sets of variables—for example, the General Aptitude Test Battery (GATB), the Minnesota Importance Questionnaire (MIQ), occupational aptitude patterns (OAPs), and occupational reinforcer patterns (ORPs). However, other measures and instruments may be used.

Career Counseling

The choice of a career is undoubtedly one of the most important decisions made by an individual. Despite this truth, many people make their choice without knowing enough about their career potential or the opportunities for satisfaction that different careers offer. Ideally, the individual should know what characteristics are relevant for the career, both for satisfying the demands of the job and for meeting the requirements the individual has of the job. This knowledge, in turn, requires the individual to know what a career (job, occupation) expects from the worker and what it offers for meeting the individual's requirements for a satisfying career.

An individual can become informed about work-relevant characteristics through vocational assessment, in the form of systematic appraisal of that individual's vocational characteristics. The individual must also have access to occupational information in terms that can be related to the assessed work-relevant characteristics.

The theory of work adjustment provides one model for individual assessment. It also provides a methodology that describes careers in direct relation to the assessment information and a procedure that forecasts the likelihood of the individual's work adjustment in a particular career.

Career counseling in the framework of the theory of work adjustment might proceed as follows: A client has no preference for a particular career but wants to explore the most appropriate choices. The counselor begins by describing the counseling process and the use of the work adjustment model to determine the appropriateness of various career possibilities. The counselor makes clear to the client that the model provides information for discussion, but that the choice of a career is the responsibility of the client. The counselor's major role is to help in the assessment and decision-making process. The counselor explains the rationale for focusing the vocational assessment on skills, abilities, and needs/values and describes the assessment instruments that are available. The client is then asked to complete a biographical form to give information about work-relevant characteristics as reflected in past and present activities.

A psychometric test battery is then administered to the client. The battery includes a measure of multiple abilities, such as the GATB, and a measure of multiple needs or values, such as the MIQ. To provide an independent assessment of the client's work-relevant characteristics, the counselor estimates from the biographical information the probable levels and patterns of the client's abilities and needs/values for the same dimensions that are being measured psychometrically. These estimates can be based on a clinical appraisal of the biographical information or on empirically derived scoring keys from research that relates biographical items to measured abilities and needs/values. The counselor could also use another estimate of measured scores based on clinical judgments from the initial interview.

After completing the psychometric battery, the client can be asked to estimate the levels and patterns of his or her measured abilities and needs/values before seeing the psychometric results. The counselor can now interpret the results of the psychometric assessment. The client's estimates may be used as starting points for discussion, by exploring the convergence and divergence of estimated and measured scores. The counselor's estimates from biographical data may be used to confirm the psychometric results. In case of discrepancy, the counselor should explore possible explanations with the client. The purpose of comparing client and counselor estimates with measures of abilities and needs/values scores is to validate the assessment information by using various data sources.

The counselor may now wish to explore the client's perceptions of the meaning of the pattern of needs and values and to ask whether it agrees with the client's perception and experience. The counselor will also explore the client's perception of the accuracy of the assessed pattern of abilities. If client perceptions of her or his needs/values and abilities are at variance with the assessment data that the counselor has interpreted, additional psychometric measurements (for example, ability measures such as the Employee Aptitude Survey or the Flanagan Industrial Tests) may be considered. For needs and values, other measures might include the Work Values Inventory or the Occupational Values Inventory. When variance between client perception and psychometric assessment persists, or where the variance is between psychometric measures of the same characteristics, the counselor and client may wish to explore specific experiences with ability utilization or with need reinforcement in past behavioral environments, especially work environments.

Interest and personality trait measures may serve as useful adjuncts to the exploration of the work personality by the counselor and the client. Interests are preferences (liking or disliking) for activities, and personality trait measures are assessments of the likelihood of particular behavior. Both interests and personality traits are viewed, in the theory of work adjustment, as reflections and derivatives of ability-value relationships. Counselors who subscribe to this view may want to clarify assessed abilities and values by administering interest and personality trait measures such as the Strong Campbell Interest Inventory, the Kuder Occupational Interest Survey, the Minnesota Multiphasic Personality Inventory, or the California Psychological Inventory.

After discrepancies have been clarified and the client is satisfied with the interpretation of the assessment data, the counselor may determine the adequacy of the client's understanding of his or her work personality by asking the client to summarize what has been learned about levels and patterns of skills, abilities, needs, and values. If the client's understanding is accurate, the focus in the counseling process should shift to the relation of work personality characteristics to work environments. The counselor must know about work and work environments and have access to a taxonomic system that provides ways of determining correspondence between the client's unique work personality and specific work environments. In the context of the theory of work adjustment, the counselor would use the Minnesota Occupational Classification System II (MOCS II) as an appropriate taxonomy for career counseling.

Because MOCS II classifies work environments (occupations) according to the two major axes of ability requirements and reinforcer-system characteristics (see chap. 4), the counselor may enter the taxonomic system by using information on the client's abilities or on the client's needs and values. The system may also be entered by using occupational titles that are suggested by the counselor's clinical appraisal of the assessment data. A taxonomy like MOCS II allows the counselor and client to narrow the range of occupations to a few groups that seem appropriate for optimal work adjustment.

Working with leads provided by the taxonomy, the client, assisted by the counselor, can explore other detailed job information, such as kinds of work activities (as described in *Dictionary of Occupational Titles*, U.S. Department of Labor, 1977), compensation rates and job opportunities (for example, as given in *Occupational Outlook Handbook*, U.S. Department of Labor, 1982), and training requirements (as described in publications of professional and trade organizations). At this point, the counselor should shift the initiative in exploration to the client to test motivation and to reinforce the principle that the career decision is the responsibility of the client. For example, "homework" tasks may be assigned to the client, such as locating additional information about target occupations, visiting work environments or schools, and interviewing incumbent workers.

When the exploration is completed, client and counselor begin the process of narrowing possible career choices to the most optimal ones in terms of likely work adjustment (optimal satisfaction and satisfactoriness). This process can be approached from both an actuarial-prediction standpoint and a clinical-prediction standpoint. Both approaches are needed because the best decision is likely to flow from some combination of actuarial and clinical components. Although the actuarial approach is demonstrably more reliable, it does not consider all the relevant information. A clinical component in the decision making, based on both the client's subjective appraisal and the counselor's clinical experience, is necessary to account for the uniqueness of the client.

In the final stages of the counseling process, the counselor has a responsibility as a professional psychologist to encourage the client to consider the actuarial prediction data; however, the decision itself is the responsibility of the client. The important outcome is for the client to make the decision on the basis of the best data available and to be willing to live with it. Once the career decision is made, the counselor should provide the client with a written summary of the assessment information and the resulting decisions.

The career planning procedures described above assume that the individual client has the freedom and capability to follow through on the best career choices. Obviously, in the real world there are many very real constraints that limit the client. Realistic career planning must also attend to such factors as financial resources, availability of training, individual and family mobility, and family and societal expectations.

The career counseling process described above is summarized in Table 7.1.

Job Adjustment Counseling

When an employed client complains about lack of challenge in the job, dissatisfaction with working conditions, unhappiness with "psychic" rewards, feeling "burned out," or the need for midcareer change, the counselor is presented with a family of problems that might be labeled job adjustment problems. These problems differ from problems related to career choice in that they are client perceptions that arise from actual experience in work. The counselor's first task is to determine whether the negative feelings that are expressed have a substantive basis and how serious they are. The theory of work adjustment offers a framework for the counselor to use in exploring the basis and extent of the problem.

First, the counselor determines the nature of the client's work personality and learns about the client's current work environment. This assessment can be done, in part, by using the procedures and instruments described in the section on career counseling. When describing the work environment, however, the focus is on the current job situation rather than on identifying several potentially correspondent work environments.

This first stage in job adjustment counseling focuses on the degree of personality-environment correspondence as a way to forecast the possible attainment of work adjustment (satisfaction, satisfactoriness, and tenure). If the forecast favors work adjustment, the problem may rest with inaccurate client perception arising from insufficient information about the work environment, problems outside of work that spill over into the work environment, underdeveloped skills, or misunderstood needs. The counselor's role may then center around improving client understanding of self (work personality) and the work environment.

Table 7.1 **CAREER COUNSELING PROCESS**

PROCESS OBJECTIVES	COUNSELOR INTERVENTIONS	PROGRESS MARKERS	ADJUSTMENT INDICATORS	CAREER OUTCOMES
Establish relationship	Communicates warmth, acceptance, interest	Client relaxed & communicating		
	Clarifies presenting problem by appropriate use of questions & of selective reinforcement	Client describes need for career planning & career aspirations		
	Describes theory of work adjustment approach & the counseling process	Client summarizes major concepts in work adjustment approach		
	Describes major ability & need/value dimensions and interests; describes assessment procedures; assures confidentiality of info	Client agrees to a schedule for assessment & subsequent interviews		
Obtain background data	Describes importance of biodata & experiences	Client completes biodata forms & reviews them with counselor	Increase in client's vocationally relevant talk, indicates active participation	
	Estimates client abilities & needs/values from interviews and biodata			
Obtain psychometric assessment data	Administers psychometric instruments; notes client behavior during testing	Client returns for testing; client behavior during testing indicates proper motivation		
Interpret vocational assessment data	Compares counselor estimations with psychometric data to resolve discrepancies	Client returns for scheduled counseling interviews		
	Assists client in interpretation of psychometric data using client estimations as background information	Client completes a self-estimation of ability & need levels		
	Explains meaning of pattern of needs/values	Client asks questions about meaning of patterns, levels of abilities, & needs/values; client indicates understanding through ability to summarize counselor interpretations		

Counselor goal	Counselor action	Client response	Indication	Client outcome
Describe work personality	Synthesize assessment, biographical, & clinical data to describe total work personality	Client relates past experiences to observed needs/values pattern; Client participates in synthesizing activity	Client acceptance of description of work personality structure indicated by questions about its relation to occupations & careers	Client understanding of self in vocational terms
Relate work personality to work environments	Relates client work personality to possible work environments, assisting client in use of work taxonomy information	Client works with taxonomic info & explores additional job info as homework	Client completion of homework indicates serious commitment to career choice process	Client understanding of work environments in relation to self
Facilitate career choice process	Works with client to narrow choices to a cluster of occupations	Client makes tentative choices & explores (by interview or observation) the actual job environment; Client narrows vocational choices		
Facilitate career decision making	Summarizes work adjustment likelihood on both actuarial & clinical basis	Client makes decision on optimal career	Client choice of appropriate educational career track or job cluster indicates successful counseling process	Client satisfaction with career choice
Follow up on educational progress or obtaining a job	Requests follow-up survey data	Client responds to follow-up	Client placement in appropriate education, training, or job placement attests to motivational impact of counseling; Placement consonant with actuarial & clinical forecasts	Continued client satisfaction with choice
Follow up after several months of employment	Requests client assessment & MSQ & (with permission) MSS data	Client accedes to employer follow-up with MSS; client completes MSQ	Satisfaction Satisfactoriness	Continuing progress in a career
Follow up in the long-term	Requests client information on current job & future plans	Client responds to request for follow-up data	Client expresses satisfaction; client in appropriate job	Tenure demonstrated on appropriate job (or jobs within appropriate career ladder)

If the forecast is unfavorable for work adjustment, the counselor's role may center first on ascertaining whether the client's expression of work personality can be changed or whether the current job environment can be modified. The goal in either case is to increase correspondence.

If increasing correspondence (to forecast work adjustment) appears to be infeasible, the client and counselor have two alternatives. One is to explore how to compensate for the inadequate person-environment correspondence by increasing correspondence outside of the work environment itself. For example, inadequate ability utilization in the work environment may be compensated by appropriate community activities, hobbies, or additional part-time work. Insufficient reinforcement for needs such as social service and moral values might be compensated by volunteer work, religious activities, and youth work. The other alternative is to plan for a change in job or career.

Counseling for Job Change

Planning for job change entails a search for job environments within the same occupation (perhaps in different organizations or localities) that are likely to be more correspondent. Finding other compatible environments within the same occupation allows the client to capitalize on previous work experience when applying for work. In planning for job change, other factors obviously must be considered, such as financial ability, family considerations, and loss of seniority and fringe benefits. If planning for a career change is necessary, the counseling procedures and strategies described in the previous section may be used.

There are large individual differences in the accuracy of client perceptions, in the real circumstances underlying perceived problems, and in client tolerance for discorrespondence with work environments and its consequences for total life adjustment. From the data now available, it is unlikely that all or most individuals should be expected to experience midlife crisis or burn-out. Job adjustment counseling based on the theory of work adjustment focuses on assessment of the individual's unique problem and on an individualized, data-based solution.

VOCATIONAL REHABILITATION COUNSELING

Because work is an important and large part of most people's lives, vocational rehabilitation counseling remains an integral part of the rehabilitation process. Assisting individuals who are handicapped to find or to return to employment that is both productive and satisfying requires more than a knowledge of physical and medical limitations. The vocational rehabilitation counselor must also know how to assess the vocational potential of the client and the likelihood of vocational satisfaction. Knowledge of physical and medical limitations, or vocational expectations based on disability group membership, do not by themselves allow the counselor to attend effectively to individual differences in work potential among clients.

The theory of work adjustment can be applied to rehabilitation counseling in several ways. It can provide a way to conceptualize disability in psychological terms that add vocationally relevant information to the basic medical and physical information about the client. It can also help to identify and specify the kinds of information needed for a vocational assessment of the client. It can suggest procedures that might be used in counseling. The theory also describes work environments in psychological (nonphysical, nonmedical) terms that relate to an individual's work adjustment. Finally, it can suggest outcome criteria to evaluate the effectiveness of vocational rehabilitation counseling.

Work adjustment, in our theory, is the outcome of the interaction between the individual and the work environment. The significant individual characteristics in this interaction are abilities and values, which describe the structure of the work personality. This structure, for physically mature individuals, is relatively stable. It is also different for each individual, having developed from that individual's unique response and reinforcement history; this is true for both handicapped and nonhandicapped individuals. Within the handicapped population, individuals who are congenitally handicapped and those whose handicap results from trauma or disease processes have a relatively stable and unique work personality. Possible exceptions to this generalization might be found in individuals whose handicap results from progressive disease conditions that affect vocationally relevant abilities.

Proceeding from the theory of work adjustment, we base our approach to disability and work on the premise that, for counseling purposes, a discussion of the influence of a disabling condition is more meaningful when the emphasis is placed on the effect of the trauma or disease condition on job-relevant abilities. This emphasis includes the effect of the trauma or disease condition on vocational needs and values when changes in the needs and values are accompanied by significant changes in job-relevant abilities. Thus, describing the impact of a disabling condition on an individual in work adjustment terms may not be the same as describing it in medical diagnostic terms.

The example that follows views disability in the context of work adjustment. Two individuals, both bookkeeping machine operators, have scores at the 90th and 70th percentiles, respectively, on the clerical perception scale (Q) of the GATB. Although both of these scores are within the range for which satisfactory performance as a bookkeeping machine operator is predicted in terms of the job's OAP (U.S. Department of Labor, 1979), individual A is likely to be an extremely satisfactory worker, whereas individual B will probably be only marginally satisfactory. Both individuals suffer a loss of visual acuity as a result of an industrial accident. Residual visual acuity is 20/100 for individual A and 20/60 for individual B. After visual loss, individual A drops to the 70th percentile on Q, while individual B drops to the 55th percentile. In terms of medical diagnostic measurements, as well as absolute loss of measured clerical ability, individual A is more severely disabled. When reference is made, however, to prediction of job performance based on OAPs, it is found that individual B has fallen markedly below the level on Q for which satisfactory work performance as a bookkeeping machine operator would be predicted, whereas individual A remains within the necessary limits of correspondence between ability and job requirement. Thus, in work adjustment for this specific job, individual B is more severely disabled and less likely to be able to readjust to the job. This example illustrates the utility of viewing disability with a focus on work adjustment.

The following definitions describe disability in the terminology of the theory of work adjustment and provide the framework around which a psychology of disability and work can be developed. *Disability* may be defined literally as ability loss (dis-ability). It is a significant decrease in the level of one ability or more in the ability set. A significant decrease is one for which there are changes in ability-requirement correspondence that alter the effective range of correspondence needed for work adjustment in specific occupations. Decreases in level of ability may be measured in relation to ability levels before trauma or to levels held by workers employed in the specific occupation.

Disabling conditions are changes or limitations in physical and bodily functions that can, but do not necessarily, have a significant effect on an individual's ability levels. That is, an individual may have a disabling condition without being disabled in work adjustment if that condition does not result in a significant decrease in the level of job-relevant abilities.

Severity of disability may be measured on a scale reflecting the magnitude of ability loss. Some measures include amount of ability loss from the original pattern of ability levels (magnitude of loss);

amount of resultant decrease in satisfactoriness in a specific job (effect of loss); reduction of number of job-requirement patterns potentially available to the individual (effect of loss); and time required to transfer, develop, or adapt skills from remaining abilities to compensate or substitute for lost skills and abilities, when this is deemed necessary to achieve optimal adjustment to work. Reference is made here to the ease or difficulty with which the individual is able to adapt or shift to other behaviors that will facilitate work adjustment.

Permanence of disability might be described in terms of ability levels remaining lower than the predisability levels after maximum treatment. *Progressive* disability is defined as a continuing decrease in ability levels over a series of successive measurements, with increasing restriction on work adjustment possibilities. *Congenital* disabling conditions result in abilities that are similar to those of the average individual but are perhaps more limited in range and pattern and that occur perhaps at lower levels. These abilities result from social-educational experiences in the same fashion as for "normal" individuals. The individual is not disabled in the sense of experiencing a decrease in ability levels as a result of trauma, although a disabling condition has been experienced.

Needs and values, which are major variables in the theory of work adjustment, are not part of these definitions of disability. The assessment of needs and values is important in counseling with both handicapped and nonhandicapped individuals. Their importance in the assessment of disability would appear, however, to be limited to those cases in which ability assessment is directly affected. For example, if an individual exhibited marked change (from high to low) in the level of ability utilization need, the counselor may be unable to make an accurate assessment of posttrauma abilities.

Vocational rehabilitation counseling helps an individual to learn about skills, abilities, needs, and values, and it explores the ability requirements and reinforcers available in jobs and occupations so that appropriate vocational decisions can be made. Counseling success may be evaluated in terms of measured work adjustment on follow-up or counselee choice of objectives that are consonant with the prediction of work adjustment.

The vocational rehabilitation counselor who views disability in the conceptual framework of the theory of work adjustment may wish to consider the following procedural steps:

1. Obtain background information relevant to the medical description of the disabling condition, the reasons for referral, and the counselee's expectations of the counseling.

At this point, the counselor obtains information about the circumstances surrounding referral for vocational rehabilitation counseling. The counselor needs to know how the counselee, the physician, and other rehabilitation workers view the disabling condition and its implications for work. Such information may be useful in anticipating how the counselee is likely to respond in the initial interviews.

The counselor also seeks information about the disabling condition viewed within the context of the individual's treatment history. Relevant background information may be found in the medical diagnostic records, including the description of the traumatic incident; the medical treatment record; available social history information; the counselee's cumulative record in school; any previous counseling records; and available test results.

2. Establish an initial accepting relationship and involve the counselee in the process of data gathering.

The counselor involves the counselee as an active participant in the search for additional data on the work personality that are useful in making predictions of work adjustment. A detailed biographical history and previous psychometric information provide useful data.

3. Construct a model of the pretrauma work personality.

The counselor estimates the counselee's levels and pattern of abilities and needs/values before the occurrence of the disabling condition. A model of the pretrauma work personality must be constructed to establish a base or comparison level against which to view posttrauma abilities, needs, and values and against which the effects of rehabilitation treatment and counseling can be assessed.

4. Consult with medical experts on medical treatment goals and plans and on environmental limitations, if any, for this individual.

The medical information sought at this point is that which is relevant to the individual's disabling condition, general functioning, and physical capacities.

5. Establish, by psychometric assessment, present levels of abilities, needs, and values.

The counselor measures abilities, needs, and values in the same terms used to construct the model of the pretrauma work personality.

6. Evaluate psychometrically the progress that is made in rehabilitation by comparing pretrauma and posttreatment levels of abilities, needs, and values in relation to posttrauma levels.

Changes in ability levels and in needs and values may be studied by retesting during the course of the broader rehabilitation process. This broader process may include medical treatment, physical therapy, psychotherapy, occupational therapy, and work adjustment training. From data on changes during the rehabilitation process, the counselor can assess the effects of additional treatment both in raising measured abilities and changing needs and values.

7. Assist the counselee in gaining knowledge of abilities, needs, and values.

    The counselor interprets psychometric information to the counselee to promote understanding and acceptance of the posttrauma work personality.

8. Determine which jobs, across levels and fields of work, have ability measurements that correspond to the counselee's ability pattern.

    Determine which jobs, across levels and fields of work, have reinforcer systems that correspond to the counselee's need/value pattern.

    Determine which jobs meet required correspondence levels for both ability requirements and reinforcer patterns, for the purpose of predicting work adjustment.

    These counselor tasks will be aided by making use of the information contained in the MOCS II.

9. Screen the jobs for which employment success would be predicted against the medical evaluations of the capacity of this counselee to do the physical tasks involved in the jobs and to perform in the physical environments in which they are located.

10. Help the counselee to select jobs that match his or her ability and need/value patterns.

    The counselor brings to the counselee's attention those jobs for which the ability and need/value correspondences are predictive of work adjustment. The section Job Adjustment Counseling contains suggestions of techniques that may help the counselee to understand her or his work personality and to relate it to prospective jobs for which work adjustment (satisfaction and satisfactoriness) seems most likely.

When disability and vocational rehabilitation counseling are approached in terms of the theory of work adjustment, several criteria of the effectiveness of counseling are available at various points in the rehabilitation process. The following are examples:

> Increases in counselee use of abilities as treatment and counseling progresses; this may be reflected by increased ability levels.

Counselee progress in, and satisfaction with, a course of training for an occupation for which work adjustment is predicted.

Counselee choice of an occupation for which work adjustment is predicted.

Counselee satisfactoriness in meeting selection standards and obtaining a job for which work adjustment is predicted.

Counselee adjustment (satisfactoriness plus satisfaction) in a job held for a significant period of time (e.g., 6 months) where the correspondence for both the abilities and the needs/values was appropriate.

Tenure in a job or in an occupation for which work adjustment was predicted.

UNEMPLOYMENT COUNSELING

In the modern day world of work, losing one's job is a reality that must be faced by many people. The impact of job loss can be psychologically severe. Psychological consequences include loss of self-esteem, loss of identity, and depression. Detailed discussions of the psychological effects of unemployment may be found in, among others, Bakke (1934, 1940), Friedmann and Havighurst (1954), Roe (1956), and *Work in America* (1973). Unemployed individuals may need the assistance of a counselor to work through the personal impact of job loss.

One of the best ways to help is to provide counseling that highlights the individual's potential for reemployment and, at the same time, attends to the individual's psychological needs. To do this, the counselor needs a system that translates the counselee's skills and previous experiences into appropriate job possibilities. The theory of work adjustment is one such system. Using it, the counselor can adopt one of three strategies.

First, the counselor and counselee can determine the levels and patterns of satisfactoriness and satisfaction for the lost job if there was substantial job tenure, or for the modal occupation if tenure on the lost job was brief. If both satisfactoriness and satisfaction were adequate, MOCS II can be used to locate potential reemployment possibilities in the taxon that includes the previous job or modal occupation. The search for additional appropriate job possibilities can be extended to adjacent taxons. This approach generates a list of possible jobs that have ability requirements and reinforcer systems similar to the lost job in which the worker was optimally adjusted to work (i.e., satisfactory and satisfied). Counselor and counselee can check this list of job possibilities for such hiring factors as specialized training, certification, and experience requirements and for such labor market factors as geographic location, number of openings, and pay rates. Focusing on the generation of a list of possible occupations and directing counselee's energies to exploring and narrowing the list may well provide effective therapy for the psychological trauma of unemployment while initiating concrete steps toward solution of the economic problem.

Second, if assessment of satisfactoriness and satisfaction in the lost job or modal occupation indicates one or the other was inadequate, the counselor and counselee can proceed by addressing that problem. If satisfactoriness was inadequate and satisfaction was adequate, the counselee's ability levels and pattern should be assessed. Given knowledge of the ability levels and pattern, the counselor and counselee can explore occupations with reinforcer systems similar to the lost job but requiring different (and more appropriate) ability levels and patterns. This exploration is facilitated by entering MOCS II via the Occupational Reinforcer Cluster (ORC) Value Index to locate appropriate taxons with differing ability requirement characteristics.

MOCS II might also be entered on the basis of the assessed abilities, using the Ability Requirements Index or the OAP index if the GATB was used for assessment. The taxons located in this fashion will then be examined for appropriateness of their reinforcer systems.

Both these approaches produce a list of possible occupations for reemployment. The counselee can then proceed to the tasks of exploring, narrowing, and choosing optimal reemployment possibilities.

If satisfactoriness was adequate but satisfaction was not, counselor and counselee should assess the counselee's need/value levels and pattern. With this information, MOCS II may be entered for taxons with ability requirements similar to the lost job. These taxons are then evaluated for appropriateness of their reinforcer systems for the individual.

It is also possible to proceed from assessed needs and values to appropriate taxons and then to locate those occupations having the appropriate ability requirements. Both approaches will generate a list of possible occupations for counselee consideration.

The two strategies described above capitalize on information from the lost job or modal occupation. Their use may bring the immediate generation of reemployment possibilities, with the added virtue of focusing the counselee's attention on his or her assets for employment. This process may have the salutary effects of minimizing trauma and motivating the counselee to take concrete actions.

The third strategy is applied when the assessment of both satisfactoriness and satisfaction of the counselee in the lost job or modal occupation shows them to be inadequate. The counselor and counselee will then wish to proceed with career counseling as if initial career choices were to be made. Procedures for career counseling have been described above. In these cases, however, the counselor must be aware of, and deal with, the psychological consequences of unemployment.

REFERENCES

Bakke, E. W. *The unemployed man.* New York: Dutton, 1934.

Bakke, E. W. *The unemployed worker.* New Haven: Yale University Press, 1940.

Friedmann, E. A., & Havighurst, R. *The meaning of work and retirement.* Chicago: University of Chicago Press, 1954.

Roe, A. *The psychology of occupations.* New York: Wiley, 1956.

Special Task Force to the Secretary of Health, Education, and Welfare. *Work in America.* Cambridge, Mass.: The MIT Press, 1973.

Super, D. E. The structure of work values in relation to status, achievement, interests, and adjustment. *Journal of Applied Psychology,* 1962, *42,* 231-239.

U.S. Department of Labor. *Dictionary of occupational titles.* (4th ed.). Washington, D.C.: U.S. Government Printing Office, 1977.

U.S. Department of Labor. *Manual for the USES General Aptitude Test Battery, Section II: Occupational aptitude pattern structure.* Washington, D.C.: U.S. Government Printing Office, 1979.

U.S. Department of Labor. *Occupational outlook handbook, 1982-83.* Washington, D.C.: U.S. Government Printing Office, 1982.

8

Personal Counseling

Many clients seen in vocational counseling need assistance with problems that require personal counseling. The model used in the theory of work adjustment provides a way to view such problems as marital difficulties, family conflicts, psychological stress, addictive behavior, self-denigration, and dependency. The work adjustment model is useful to counselors because it provides for systematic analysis to identify the critical factors and dynamics that underlie the difficulty.

Because many of these problems are interpersonal, treatment for them through the work adjustment model requires that a person or persons be regarded as the "environment" for the client. The following sections illustrate how the model can be used to conceptualize problems in personal counseling.

MARRIAGE COUNSELING

One can view each partner in a marriage relationship as the primary environment for the other. It then becomes apparent that the model presented in figure 5.3 can be modified to focus on marital rather than work adjustment and, if applied bilaterally (in both directions from the perspective of each partner), can be used to describe marital adjustment. Figure 8.1 illustrates such a marital adjustment model.

In the model, marital satisfaction is shown as a function of the correspondence between a partner's needs/values and the reinforcers provided by the other partner. Similarly, marital satisfactoriness is shown as a function of the correspondence between a partner's

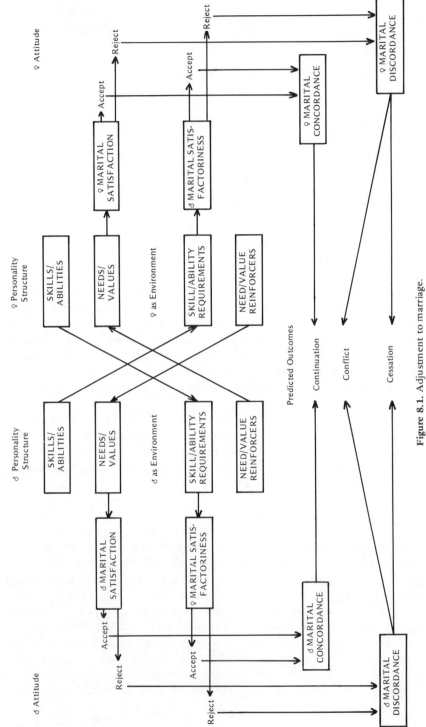

Figure 8.1. Adjustment to marriage.

skills/abilities and the other partner's skill/ability requirements. Where correspondence is at an adequate level, a partner is positively predisposed, or is accepting of the other partner. Conversely, where correspondence is inadequate, the partner has a negative (rejecting) attitude. Each partner holds an attitude of acceptance or rejection of the other partner on the basis of the partner's satisfaction or the other partner's satisfactoriness, or both. These attitudes reflect the perceived degree of correspondence/discorrespondence; in other words, the greater the correspondence the stronger the attitude of acceptance and, conversely, the greater the discorrespondence, the stronger the attitude of rejection.

Marital concordance is the condition that prevails when a partner's attitudes are accepting of the other partner in terms of both satisfaction and satisfactoriness. Discordance results when a partner's attitude is rejecting of the other partner for reasons either of satisfaction or satisfactoriness, or both. When both partners are concordant, continuation of the marriage relationship is predicted. When either partner or both are discordant, conflict in or cessation of the relationship is predicted. The likelihood and severity of conflict in the relationship are predicted to vary in one of three ways: Conflict is least likely and least severe when both partners are satisfied and satisfactory (concordant). Conflict is more likely when one or both partners are dissatisfied than when one or both are unsatisfactory; in other words, satisfaction is more powerful than satisfactoriness in the marriage relationship. Conflict is most likely and most severe when both partners are dissatisfied and unsatisfactory (discordant).

This model of the marriage relationship is useful in diagnosis. It provides an analytic framework and specifies the important factors to consider. For example, if a partner is dissatisfied, one would examine the needs of that partner against the reinforcers provided by the other partner; if a partner judges the other to be unsatisfactory, one would examine not only the skills of the other partner but also the requirements of the first partner. The model can be used to identify specific sources of conflict and factors to be assessed.

To use the model effectively, the counselor should have a rubric for assessing those skills and needs most relevant to the marriage relationship. Such assessment can be done psychometrically (using psychological instruments) or clinically (using interview and biographical data). Having a rubric for assessment ensures systematic analysis. The ability and value structures presented in the theory of work adjustment provide one basis for such a rubric. For example, the six values measured by the MIQ (achievement, comfort, status, altruism, safety, and autonomy) may be used to generate a list of specific needs and reinforcers that are relevant to the marital relationship.

Although the model may appear, to some, to oversimplify adjustment in marriage, its usefulness requires attention to a number of conditions that qualify its application. Marital satisfaction and satisfactoriness are based on perceptions of needs, skills, reinforcers, and requirements rather than on the objective status of these factors. When dissatisfaction arises from perceived lack of reinforcement, for instance, the counselor will want to determine the objective reality of the reinforcers to determine whether the problem lies in reality or perception.

Individuals also differ in the amount of correspondence that they require for satisfaction and satisfactoriness. The same objective degree of correspondence may be adequate for one individual (or couple) but not for another. Each individual has a threshold of tolerance for discorrespondence, or an individual level of flexibility. Couples may also have rather similar or different levels of individual flexibility.

As in adjustment to work, adjustment in marriage is a continuous process of maintaining adequate correspondence. A fuller understanding of this process requires more than the structural matching model shown in figure 8.1. Both conflict resolution and continued adjustment are better described when information on adjustment style variables is added. The description of conflict resolution is enhanced by knowledge of the adjustment modes (activeness, reactiveness) likely to be used by the marriage partners and the likely receptivity of each partner to these modes.

The relative importance of satisfaction and satisfactoriness in determining marital concordance/discordance may vary with the cultural background of the partners. Similarly, the relevance of skills, needs, requirements, and reinforcers to marriage will be couple specific and may be group specific. Group is used here to include race, national origin, class, sex, age, religion, and geographic location.

Finally, the model does not account directly for influences on marital adjustment that derive from sources outside of the immediate partner relationship. However, these influences will be reflected indirectly through some modification of the needs and requirements of the partners and the levels of correspondence achieved.

Family Counseling

The work adjustment model may be adapted to help the family counselor in diagnosis, or in the identification, location, and description of problems. As in working with adjustment in marriage, the model provides a framework for analysis and specifies important factors to consider.

The adapted model would treat the individuals involved both as personalities and as environments in a set of personality-environment interactions. Personalities are described in terms of skill and need— what they bring to others in the family and what they expect from the others who serve as primary environments. Environments are described in terms of skill requirement and need reinforcement— what the environment expects (requires) and what it offers to satisfy needs. Because each family member can be regarded either as personality or environment, family interrelationships may be treated as partnerships in much the same way as they are in the marriage relationship.

The first task in using such a model is to identify the person with the presenting problem, who is then treated as a primary partner (with a definable personality) who interacts with another family member (or other members) as the primary environment and partner. The interaction is reciprocal, with each partner (or collective partner) behaving as a personality and serving as the environment for the other. The interaction is also dynamic in that a continuous process of reciprocal behavior by both partners is needed to maintain the level of correspondence required for satisfactory and satisfying family adjustment, as perceived by both partners in the relationship.

The following examples show various ways to identify the individual or individuals to be treated (in the model) as the primary environment for the person with the presenting problem. The father or mother, if there is clear evidence of a strongly patriarchal or matriarchal family structure, may be selected as the primary environment (and the primary personality interacting with the individual with the presenting problem as that person's environment). The other parent and siblings may be treated as much less central to problem analysis and solution. Similarly, one parent may be seen as the primary environment, with the other parent and children treated as important enough as parts of the environment to require reshaping of the description of the parent as environment.

Two strong parents (both dominating individuals) might together be treated as the primary environment; or the description may be combined and reshaped, if necessary, as in the second example given above.

The total remaining family, excluding the individual with the presenting problem, might be seen (in the model) as combining to define the environment for that person. The model may have to be used more than once to describe several family interactions using different pairs of individuals as the primary environments and personalities in interaction with each other.

The individual with the presenting problem is simply the person brought to the attention of the family counselor as a "problem" for the family. At this point, this individual is a problem only in the context of family expectations and as the initial focal point for the analysis of relationships among the family members.

These examples illustrate some of the decisions that underlie an effective identification of focal points for assessing skills, needs, requirements, and reinforcers for use in the analytic model to explore family discordance and to suggest counseling strategies. In making these decisions, the counselor depends upon inferences from data in behavioral records, biographical information, and interviews.

When the primary identifications have been made, the individuals as personalities and as environments can be described psychometrically or clinically using instruments and rubrics adapted from those used to apply the theory of work adjustment. Other instruments may be used or adapted if they describe the relevant dimensions in such a correspondence model of family interaction.

The model described does, of course, have its limitations. For example, factors outside the family environment may significantly affect family relationships. The model focuses only on the family itself. Within its limitations, however, the model does provide a framework for analyzing family interrelationships. It focuses on individual family members and their perceptions of skills, needs, requirements, and reinforcers. It also stresses perceptions of environments, rather than limiting environmental descriptions to only their objective physical and social properties. It attends to individual differences rather than to uniform application of particular theory-based causes or explanations, or particular preferred therapeutic approaches.

STRESS COUNSELING

Stress is a popular topic, with a flood of literature relating to its management. Other literature tells us to expect certain events in life to be stressful, such as job burn-out and midlife crisis. We believe that stress has been much overused to explain problems of adjustment. It is also difficult to define stress in terms that allow observation and objective description. This difficulty with the definition of stress sometimes leads to circular explanations. For example, particular periods in life produce stress and, therefore, if you are entering that period and having difficulty adjusting, you must be experiencing stress. These explanations are not really useful to the counselor.

Some definitions of stress are so broad that they seem to encompass almost all problems, normal or abnormal, that one can experience in life. It becomes difficult to operationalize stress in ways that would allow the orderly study of causes and processes, with subsequent diagnosis and treatment. Other definitions suffer from their narrowness. For example, those that refer to specific and delimited applications of noxious stimuli (like electric shock) in the laboratory are convenient for experimental design and useful in research (e.g., on animal learning), but these definitions are not directly transferable to human life experiences with stress.

An earlier, promising conceptualization of stress viewed it as the result of disturbed homeostatic balance; however, there was insufficient detail about the significant components involved in the balanced state or on the ways to observe and measure the components. Starting from a homeostatic view, we may use some of the concepts of the theory of work adjustment to define the significant components of stress in observable and measurable ways.

The homeostatic condition may be thought of as the state of corresponsiveness between an individual and an environment. Each meets the requirements of the other, resulting in adjustment for the individual and lack of stress. This corresponsiveness is specific to identifiable environments, such as work, marriage, family, school, and social community. To observe and measure the state of corresponsiveness, we must describe both the specific environment and the individual in the same, commensurate terms. One way to do this is illustrated by the operationalization of the theory of work adjustment as described in chapter 5.

Psychological (as opposed to physiological) stress can be defined, using this corresponsiveness approach, as an intervening psychological state inferred from an antecedent condition of discorrespondence (imbalance) and consequent behavior directed toward reducing the discorrespondence (reestablishing balance). The indicators of stress (dissatisfaction with and unsatisfactoriness in specific environments like work, school, and home) may be found in the consequent behaviors (such as aggressive action directed toward the environment, other persons, or self, or withdrawal from contact with the environment—being absent or noncommunicative). The existence of stress would be confirmed by examination of the antecedent conditions through objective analysis of the kinds and degrees of discorrespondence and the determination of the person's perception of a discorrespondent state of affairs that may or may not be objectively substantiated.

An objective analysis might take the form of assessing discorrespondence between the individual's abilities and the ability requirements of the environment, or between the environment's reinforcers and the reinforcer requirements (needs) of the individual. Stress might result when the ability requirements significantly exceed the abilities or when the reinforcer requirements exceed the environmental reinforcers. The subjective analysis of antecedent conditions can parallel the objective analysis, but it consists of self-report data (perceptions). Both the antecedent and the consequent conditions are needed to define stress when using the corresponsiveness approach.

The preceding discussion should help to clarify the definitional problem and provide a way to judge whether specific environments are likely to be more stressful than others. However, individuals differ in their tolerance for discorrespondence—their flexibility— and one should avoid ascribing stress to individuals simply on the basis of their exposure to a given environment or their membership in an occupational group.

When people seek counseling to deal with perceived stress, or when people are referred for counseling because they are unable to cope with stress, the counselor may have to deal first with the presenting symptoms by using accepted techniques such as behavioral counseling. The sources of stress, and a longer range solution, could be approached by viewing stress as a class of adjustment problems definable in terms of concepts like those in the theory of work adjustment. Stress may refer to a class of more urgent problems that, except for degree of experienced distress, do not differ in form from less urgent, more typical, adjustment problems. There may thus be no justification for investing stress with the surplus meaning that one finds in popular writing on the subject. From an adjustment standpoint, psychological stress is not necessarily dysfunctional; it can serve to motivate. One might even view stress as the stimulus for creative problem solving.

This discussion deals with psychological stress, and it is further limited to the use of concepts from the theory of work adjustment to define and analyze stress. It does not deal with physiological or physical stress.

ADDICTION COUNSELING

The concepts embodied in the theory of work adjustment may provide additional insights into the problems and treatment of addictive behavior (e.g., alcoholism, drug dependence). Although we are not proposing a new theory of addictive behavior or a new method of treatment, we believe that these concepts can sharpen diagnosis and treatment strategies.

It is assumed that most people undergoing counseling or treatment for addictive behavior are doing so because of behavioral consequences that are judged as disruptive and harmful to their families, the larger society, or themselves. They are, in theory of work adjustment terms, not adjusted to the environments in which they behave. Adjusted behavior requires correspondence of the individual and the environments. In addictive behavior, the discorrespondence manifests itself in lack of satisfactoriness, wherein the individual fails to meet the requirements of the environments (the family, the employer, society at large).

The following assertions have not been tested empirically; they derive logically from the theory and may be viewed as hypotheses. If addictive behavior is maintained, the individual and the environment may be discorrespondent from the standpoint of satisfactoriness (i.e., not meeting social task requirements), but they must be correspondent from the standpoint of satisfaction (i.e., needs and values are being reinforced by the social environments). This suggests the desirability of assessing the individual's needs and values; assessing the reinforcer systems of the relevant environments; and determining the linkages between the reinforcers and the social task requirements (the presence of reinforcers that satisfy needs and values but are not linked to the performance of social task requirements).

In reinforcer terms, as related to needs and values, alcoholism may be maintained in three ways. First are the self-reinforcers, or the feelings of achievement and accomplishment, of autonomy and creativity, and of being in control (responsibility). In many cases, these feelings are delusions, but in others they are not. Other examples of self-reinforcements are the hedonistic feeling of pleasure and comfort and the feelings of safety and lack of stress that are engendered by reduction of anxiety. Second are the social reinforcers, such as status in a social group, a form of safety through conformity with the role models in a social group, and identification and camaraderie with the members of the social group (a form of altruism). Third are the environmental reinforcers, or the institutionalized reinforcement that is not contingent on satisfactory task performance (in work or social environments). For example, pay, security, and status may be automatically achieved without reference to satisfactoriness of performance. To the extent that the environment minimizes the adverse consequences of unsatisfactory task performance associated with addiction, the environment inadvertently reinforces the addiction.

Counseling and treatment of addiction might then include the assessment of individual needs and values, environmental reinforcers, and exploration with the individual of the meaning of reinforcer preferences and the manner or mode in which needs and values are satisfied. This exploration can lead to a search for alternative effective reinforcers that do not also appear to maintain addictive behavior. The strategy of extinguishing dysfunctional reinforcement and substituting appropriate reinforcers requires an individually reengineered reinforcer system that should, of course, involve the individual's understanding, acceptance, and participation.

The ability information that is used in the theory of work adjustment may help in the design of treatment. For example, therapy that is heavily based on verbal communication may be most effectively utilized when the level of verbal usage is matched with the individual's level of verbal ability. Individuals with high numerical abilities may be easier to influence if counseling and treatment include quantitative information. Cognitive therapy may be more effective for individuals high in data abilities than for individuals high in things abilities. In other words, abilities and ability patterns may serve as moderator variables affecting the success of the counseling and treatment approach.

Another set of moderator variables may be found in the adjustment and personality style dimensions described in the theory. For example, environmental manipulation may be more appropriate for persons high on activeness, whereas approaches designed to assist the individual in changing attitudes may be more effective with persons high on reactiveness. Treatment that focuses on quick and immediate actions may work better with highly celerious individuals; long-term treatment may be ineffective with low-endurance individuals. Changing to new environments may be more effective with individuals high on flexibility.

These examples of possible applications of the theory of work adjustment to addiction counseling emphasize the individuality of each client and the consequent need to attend to individual differences. Although particular therapists and counselors are likely to adopt a particular theory or treatment approach for use with a large number of individuals, within-group individual differences will be large and the individuality of each will need to be considered in the application of the overall theoretical approach. The concepts and variables in the theory of work adjustment provide one means of doing this.

COUNSELING FOR SELF-ESTEEM

A common problem encountered by counselors is variously described as low self-esteem, lack of self-esteem, self-denigration, poor ego strength, and low estimation of self-worth. In working with these problems, the counselor may first wish to ascertain the accuracy or basis of the negative self-concept. The clients' descriptions of the bases for such feelings may be vague or incomplete. In other cases, the clients may have inaccurate perceptions of their capabilities or of the ways in which the environment is responding to them. There will, of course, be cases where the clients' perceptions are accurate.

In helping clients to explore their negative feelings about self, the counselor may wish to use the theory of work adjustment as a framework for the client's description of his or her personality and the environmental contexts in which it operates. Following this exploration with the client, the counselor can objectively assess the same personality and environmental variables to provide the data-based criteria against which accuracy of client perceptions can be evaluated.

If the perception is inaccurate, the counselor can seek to improve accuracy by helping the client learn how he or she is seen by the environment. If the perception is accurate, the counselor will have to help the client to deal with this reality. Counseling strategies might include focusing on strengths and assets and minimizing liabilities through the identification of more correspondent environments in which the client can operate.

Feelings of low self-esteem are probably more common than most of us realize. They become counseling concerns when they result in poor work and social adjustment or interfere with attempts to maintain and improve adjustment. This discussion is not directed toward extreme cases of self-denigration with pathological symptoms.

Another way in which to view negative self-esteem from the perspective of the theory of work adjustment is to consider these negative evaluations of self as dissatisfaction resulting from a lack of correspondence between needs and the perception of reinforcers for these needs. The needs of primary concern here are those requiring self or social reinforcers. For example, high-strength preferences for reinforcers associated with the ability utilization, achievement, creativity, and responsibility needs may be matched with the perception of inability to use abilities, to accomplish something, to try out one's own ideas, or to control what is done. With social reinforcers, preferences for those associated with status, recognition, advancement, and social service may occur with the perception of inability to achieve status, recognition, advancement, or to help others. In these examples, the origin of the low self-esteem is the individual's perceived incapability of self, not the environment. The counselor may first want to determine the accuracy of the perception of incapability. If it is inaccurate, objective assessment information (that is reliable and valid) may modify and correct the client's perceptions; if it is accurate, some program of skills acquisition that includes mechanisms of self-reinforcement may be considered.

If the high-strength preferences (needs) are actually not reinforced in the environment, the origin of the low self-esteem is to be found in the environmental reinforcer system. In such cases, the individual's perceptions are accurate, and the counselor may either work with the client toward changing the environmental conditions or work to find more appropriate environments.

If the low self-esteem appears to arise from the client's inaccurate perception of the environmental conditions (and this is independent of the client's perception of incapability), objective (reliable, valid) assessment information that describes the relevant environments may correct the misperceptions.

COUNSELING FOR DEPENDENCY

We do not agree with the view that all, or even most, individuals should become "independent." We do believe that dependency can be seen as a problem in particular cases when it results in an individual failing to reach a level of accomplishment that is consistent with potential, or when it imposes undue hardship on others. In these instances, counseling might begin by exploring the high-strength reinforcer preferences of the individual and the operative reinforcers in the individual's environments. This exploration should help to identify the need-reinforcer combinations that maintain the dependent behavior. An assessment of the individual's abilities and the ability requirements of the relevant environments should provide information on how much of the dependency is unwarranted and how much change can reasonably be expected in terms of ability to perform tasks independently. Given these sets of information, the counselor may then wish to work with the client on the acquisition of skills appropriate to the client's potential and likely to be reinforced in ways that are both strongly preferred by the individual and different from those that appear to maintain the dependency.

Under special circumstances, individuals may find themselves thrust into environments that they cannot leave and do not yet fully understand, but where they are required to function at a level that can be described as dependent. In such instances, the individual must demonstrate a high degree of flexibility (tolerance for discorrespondence) in order to survive. Examples include immigrants or people thrust into new settings, such as prisons and hospitals. Decreased dependency becomes possible with lowered flexibility (lowered tolerance of discorrespondence), the acquisition of additional skills required for independence, and the desire to be less dependent. The condition of desiring to be less dependent is included to emphasize the fact that dependency is not always undesirable and that the client's wishes for change or lack of change should be taken into account.

9

Adjustment to Retirement

It is a well-known fact Americans are an aging population. With improved health care and nutrition, more Americans are living longer. The numbers of retired persons are increasing even though legislation has raised the mandatory retirement age. Retirement is an event that most of us will have to face, one that occasions an abrupt change in the environments in which we function and in our attendant life styles. The management of changes brought about by retirement requires planning for both economic and psychological adjustment. Our impression is that a good deal of attention is given to financial planning with much less emphasis on psychological planning.

At retirement, an individual's personality and behavior patterns are typically very stable in structure, style, and manifest content (habits, schedules, activities, and expectations). Much of this stability presumably derives from long-term interactions with preretirement environments, especially work environments, which are dominant for several reasons.

Work is the activity that occupies most of an individual's waking hours. As Roe (1956) pointed out, work is the single situation likely to provide the most satisfaction of human needs. Work, in large part, determines an individual's self-concept (Super, 1957). It also affects the individual's social status (Gross, 1964); is seen as important for mental health (Menninger, 1964); and is a factor in longevity (Palmore, 1969). These reasons suggest that leaving work for retirement requires planning for the replacement of the role that work plays in the individual's life. This planning, which must be done on an individual basis, can be facilitated by using the theory of work adjustment to conceptualize the individual-work relationship that will be lost and to devise strategies for identifying suitable replacements to compensate for the loss brought about by retirement.

When the theory is used, a key objective of the planning process for most individuals will be the maintenance of individual-environment correspondence in the retirement period at tolerable levels, or levels not too different from those experienced in work. The assumption here is that most individuals, over their work lives, achieved an acceptable level of correspondence with their work environments. Because this correspondence with work maintained the individuals and had a significant impact on their lives, we suggest that the best way to retire is to continue to "work" in similar nonwork environments.

In planning for retirement, the counselor will first examine the individual's correspondence with the work environment to determine the significant elements in the correspondence (i.e., what skills/abilities and needs/values and style characteristics were salient) and the levels of satisfactoriness and satisfaction they produced. This examination can be done psychometrically using the dimensions and instruments developed for application of the theory of work adjustment. It can also be approximated by clinical inference from interviews, biographical information, and information about the individual's work environments. According to the theory, it should also be possible to infer the individual's personality characteristics from knowledge of the work-environment characteristics and the individual's levels of satisfactoriness and satisfaction. Similarly, the counselor can infer the characteristics of the work environment from the individual's personality characteristics and the tenure and reported satisfactoriness and satisfaction in the work environment. The purpose of these approaches is to understand the individual's level of work adjustment and the elements central to it.

Having developed an understanding (with the individual) of the work personality—principally in terms of response capabilities, reinforcer preferences, and response style—the counselor's next task is to identify suitable retirement environments for which continued correspondence can be predicted. Suitable environments are those in which task requirements are appropriate and need/value reinforcement is likely. In the theory of work adjustment, these environments include activities permitted in environments as well as those prescribed by environments. The counselor and the client should seek to identify broad groupings of environments to allow for the possibility of combinations of environments leading to correspondence and to allow for client choice from a range of alternatives.

The search for suitable environments focuses outside of the typical world of work. At least three major obstacles must be faced in this search: one is the limitations imposed by the client's financial status, another is the client's mobility or lack of it, and the third is the lack of systematically organized information on available nonwork environments. Ideally, this information should be available in descriptive terms that allow comparison with the client's personality. It should also be organized to facilitate the identification of clusters or families of nonwork environments—a taxonomy of retirement environments based on major personality dimensions (analogous to work environment systems like MOCS II). The individual should also be able to choose environments without being restricted by financial considerations.

The counselor and client might take several steps to identify suitable retirement environments:

1. Develop a list of available nonwork environments that are feasible in terms of geography, accessibility, and financial considerations. Examples would include specific "jobs" in volunteer agencies, churches, governmental settings, hospitals, and professional, trade, and social organizations. These specific jobs should be listed by titles that reflect in a general way the cluster of primary tasks to be performed in a particular setting; examples include church secretary, mayor (in a small community), political campaign manager, fund raiser, head of a community planning or study group, and performer and singer in a community theatre.

2. Narrow the list by ranking the environments in order of feasibility of access (entry) and sorting them into broad categories of client interest (high, medium, or low). Choose a manageable number of the most feasible environments that are also in the high or medium interest categories.

   The selected environments can then be rated in terms of personality structure dimensions (ability requirements and reinforcer systems). A standard rating form might provide a 5-point scale (anchored for high and low at the ends and medium in the middle) that rates each job for ability requirements for working with data, people, and things and that rates reinforcer systems in terms of the six values of achievement, comfort, status, altruism, safety, and autonomy. Both counselor and client can rate the selected environments. The counselor might make use of available occupational information (*Dictionary of Occupational Titles* or ORPs) by locating job titles analogous to the retirement jobs. The client might base ratings on observations of the jobs and interviews with job incumbents. The two sets of ratings can then be compared to arrive at a more reliable set of environmental descriptions. Discrepancies in counselor-client ratings may clarify client perceptions and expectations about the retirement environments and may indicate the need for more information.

3. Compare the client's personality structure with the retirement environment structures to locate the most correspondent job environment or combination of environments. Such comparisons will permit the estimation of likely satisfaction and satisfactoriness in particular retirement environments.

4. Consider other life-style factors that might moderate the choice of the retirement environments, such as likely consequences for husband-wife or family relationships, daily schedules, use of weekends, manner or style of dress, and time away from home.

If the counselor and the client find that it is not possible to identify a suitable environment or environments for retirement, they may then pursue one of two different approaches. The first involves acting on the environment to create the suitable retirement jobs. The second involves acting on the individual. Acting on the environment to create suitable retirement jobs can proceed in two different directions. The counselor and client might construct a new retirement job by putting together a number of correspondent minienvironments (each consisting of one or a few tasks together with their associated reinforcer systems) to form a new job that corresponds much better than existing jobs to the client's salient abilities and values. For example, the client might do limited amounts of volunteer work in several organizations with differing selected task requirements and reinforcers in each activity. The goal here is for the combined whole to provide adequate correspondence to the client's personality, which would not be the case for any of the separate retirement jobs previously explored.

If this approach is not feasible, it may be necessary to construct a new retirement job if the client or others can provide the resources to do so. For example, the client may be able to set up a retirement environment similar in its major aspects to the client's preretirement work. The retired business executive may manage a small business on a time-limited basis or may serve as an uncompensated consultant to public groups. A retired truck driver might offer a cross-country tour bus service, for expenses only, to charitable organizations. A retired high school language teacher might set up a part-time service offering language instruction for travelers and business people for a nominal fee. A carpenter might design special furniture and equipment for the handicapped and older people.

Designing new environments can take the form of building on and enlarging hobbies, crafts, and nonwork talents. A person who worked in retail sales and engaged in craft hobbies might establish a small shop offering craft products. A person in a social service job who enjoyed contact with people and also had musical talent might set up classes for group instruction in the area of talent. A journalism professor whose hobby was gardening might write books or free-lance articles on various aspects of the hobby. Perhaps, in choosing hobbies, people should consider the possible contributions they might make to retirement jobs.

An approach to acting on the individual to accommodate to available environments for retirement might require several steps. The first is identifying the available environments that come closest to being correspondent. By analyzing the skill requirements and rein-forcer systems in these environments, the counselor can identify which aspects are not correspondent (e.g., levels or kinds of skills missing, and needs that will not be reinforced).

Client and counselor can then explore training that is likely to raise skill levels or develop new skills that will meet requirements. For unmet needs, the counselor can identify other needs in the same value group that would be reinforced and help the client to accept somewhat less than the ideal situation. They can explore the satis-faction of unmet needs by engaging in new activities, such as hob-bies. Throughout, the counselor works with the client to focus more strongly on needs that are reinforced as a means of compensating for the lack of some reinforcers, and helps the client to accept the unavailability of those that are missing.

The drastic change in environment that occurs with retirement will, in many cases, require accommodation by the individual. The focus of adjustment is the search for environments that are very similar to those in which the individual was adjusted in work. Be-cause the retirement environments are not likely to be ideally corre-spondent, counselors may well be engaged in counseling toward client accommodation, in addition to the environmental assessment and identification activities described above.

If we accept the approach to psychological adjustment in retire-ment that is suggested by the theory of work adjustment, it becomes obvious that counseling and planning for retirement should begin some years before it happens. A good time to begin is that point in a work career at which an individual has achieved work adjustment, as reflected in substantial tenure and continuing satisfaction and satisfactoriness. Early planning for retirement will allow the identifi-cation of appropriate retirement environments to be completed soon enough to test out their suitability. It will also allow time to acquire any new skills that are needed and to experience new reinforcers that satisfy old (established) needs.

Many people do not have retirement counseling available to them, or they may not wish outside help in planning. These people may still use the framework of the theory of work adjustment in self-planning. They can focus on the same personality dimensions and engage in the same process of identification of suitable retirement environments. They are not likely, however, to have the assessment instruments that are available to counselors. As a result, they will have to estimate their levels and patterns of abilities and values. Abilities might be inferred from experiences of satisfactorily meeting task requirements in work and nonwork activities; values may be inferred from the reinforcer systems they have found to be satisfying in work and nonwork settings. The theory indicates the important ability and value dimensions for which estimates are necessary. In making estimates by inference, one should follow the practice of convergent validation that is used in professional test construction, in which estimates are based on information from several independent sources.

The self-planner may also use other procedures described earlier, such as rating environments for possibility and suitability, trying out potential environments, constructing new ones, acquiring new skills, and identifying new reinforcers likely to be satisfying. The basic criteria for identifying suitable retirement environments remain the same: tenure (is this an environment that will wear well over time?), satisfaction (will this environment provide happiness?), and satisfactoriness (are these activities within my capabilities?).

More research is needed that focuses on overall psychological adjustment to retirement. In recent years, research on aging has increased significantly and has contributed very useful knowledge about the aging process and its specific effects on a number of psychological variables. This research should be taken into account in planning for retirement. Even more research is needed if the purpose of retirement planning is to effect the best overall psychological adjustment to retirement and not simply to focus on more narrowly defined objectives. If one wishes to apply the theory of work adjustment model to retirement planning (either counselor-assisted or self-planning), research is needed in areas and directions such as those suggested in the following paragraphs.

Comprehensive surveys of available retirement environments (including nonwork or avocational environments) should be conducted. Information from these surveys should include details about frequency of availability of specific environments, geographic distribution, continuity or likely duration of the environment, possible obstacles to admission (handicap, sex, educational requirements), and information that will at least describe the major activities in each environment.

An initial classification of the surveyed retirement environments might be developed based on similarity of the activities. One way to approach this classification might be to group environments according to the saliency of people, data, or things to the major activities. Each of the saliency groups could then be arranged according to level of ability required.

Benchmark retirement environments could be selected for more intensive study by sampling a feasible number that will represent both levels (of ability required) and fields (patterns of people, data, and things) and at the same time allow for generalization from a benchmark to the environmental grouping it represents. These benchmark environments could then be studied more intensively to develop information on requirements for specific abilities (verbal, numerical, or spatial) and on specific-reinforcer characteristics (ability utilization, achievement, advancement, autonomy, and activity). The generalizability of the more detailed information for the benchmark environments should be confirmed by developing detailed descriptions of some of the other environments in the benchmark group. The researcher may be able to speed the development of the detailed description by using information (e.g., OAPs and ORPs) already available on work environments that are very similar to the retirement environments.

The classification of retirement environments is a necessary step in the prediction of retirement adjustment from the correspondence of retirement environment to retirement personality. If we are correct in our assertion that the best way to retire is to continue "working," research must be done to explore the similarity of retirement environments to work environments. Where the retirement environment is most similar to the work environment in which the individual was adjusted for significant periods of time, one would expect more transfer and a higher level of adjustment. This approach to improving the chances of transfer from work to retirement suggests that the classification of retirement environments should have as its goal the approximation of an available work-environment classification system (such as MOCS II).

The classification system for retirement environments would be especially useful when an appropriate single retirement environment was not available and a new one had to be designed. The system would aid in identifying parts of available environments that could be combined into a new retirement environment.

In the interim, we can create new retirement environments from existing classification systems of work environments. The process can be illustrated by using the MOCS II classification. If the individual had a work personality for which adjustment could be forecast to occupations in taxon 9D (which includes such occupations as programmer, accountant, and loan officer), one could combine elements of these occupations to create a new retirement job that would entail some programming, some accounting, and some fiscal knowledge. The new retirement job might be a small part-time business offering home budget planning or income tax preparation.

Because many people will not have professional retirement counseling available to them, it would be extremely useful if self-assessment methods were developed to describe the retirement personality in terms that are compatible with existing descriptive information on retirement and work environments. As an illustration, simple instruments for the self-ranking of abilities and needs (reinforcer preferences) can be developed for use in conjunction with a system like MOCS II. Research would be needed to show that self-rankings would produce results very similar to those obtained by using standard psychometric assessment instruments. For example, the simple ranking of reinforcer preferences based on the 20 needs of the MIQ could be compared with results obtained from taking the questionnaire.

If, as is likely, retirement environments provide less than an ideal correspondence for individuals, we should study how adjustment style variables might improve correspondence. Research would focus on ways in which counseling can enhance the use of adjustment style variables and on whether adjustment style variables can be modified. An individual may not realize that discorrespondence between the retirement personality and the retirement environment can be reduced by acting on the environment to change it (activeness) or by acting on self to bring about change (reactiveness). The counselor may facilitate the use of these adjustment style variables by helping to assess the likelihood that the individual will use them effectively. The assessment rests on a determination of the individual's levels of adjustment style variables and the flexibility of the environment (i.e., tolerance for discorrespondence, or the environment's requiring the individual to accommodate). In another case, the counselor might try to change the individual's levels of adjustment modes (activeness and reactiveness). Given a flexible environment and an individual who needs to present self as more active, the counselor might use assertiveness training to help the individual change to increase the typical level of activeness. Research is needed in these areas of counselor intervention.

Research is also needed to follow-up on the expected outcomes of retirement counseling and of self-planning for retirement. Measures of retirement satisfaction and retirement satisfactoriness might be adapted from existing work-adjustment instruments. Records of tenure in specific retirement environments will be important. Ideally, follow-up research should be continuous with periodic measurements of the indicators of adjustment (satisfaction and satisfactoriness). Follow-up information should be made available for use in refining both the model for retirement planning and the counseling techniques to be used.

Other research, of more relevance to personality theory, might address developmental questions: Does exposure to, and experience in, work environments change the personality structure and style (e.g., sharpening vs. leveling of profiles, raising or lowering of thresholds)? What changes in personality (structure, style) may be expected following the transition from work environments to retirement environments, given the likelihood that retirement will provide similar but not identical conditions?

REFERENCES

Gross, E. The worker and society. In H. Borow (Ed.), *Man in a world at work*. Boston: Houghton Mifflin, 1964.

Menninger, W. C. The meaning of work in Western society. In H. Borow (Ed.), *Man in a world at work*. Boston: Houghton Mifflin, 1964.

Palmore, E. Predicting longevity: A follow-up controlling for age. *The Gerontologist*, 1969, 9, 247-250.

Roe, A. *The psychology of occupations*. New York: Wiley, 1956.

Super, D. E. *The psychology of careers*. New York: Harper & Row, 1957.

10

Organizational and Societal Development

ORGANIZATIONAL USES FOR THE THEORY

With respect to organizations, the theory of work adjustment is most immediately relevant to business and industrial organizations. Specific areas where the theory applies include selection and placement of personnel, employee development and training, employee motivation and morale, job analysis, and job design. The relevance of the theory to business and industry is not surprising because it was first developed to organize available knowledge in vocational, personnel, industrial, and applied psychology that pertained to problems in work. This initial thrust was given shape and direction by incorporating fundamental concepts from other, more theoretical areas of psychology—the psychology of learning, motivation, experimental psychology, and differential psychology.

When selecting personnel for specific jobs, the central principle is the correspondence of the individual and the job environment, on the premise that correspondent individuals will be satisfactory workers who will stay in the job. Current selection procedures focus on selection equations that predict ability to perform and that describe the ability and task requirement aspects referred to in the theory of work adjustment. Although this focus is both desirable and useful, it is incomplete because it does not attend to the need satisfaction aspects of correspondence between individuals and environments. According to the theory, failure to attend to these need satisfaction aspects reduces the predictive power of selection equations. The theory, then, has two specific implications: first, ability selection equations should be developed on groups of satisfied workers; and, second, need satisfaction equations should also be developed and used. The use of need satisfaction equations, while not enhancing prediction of ability to do the job, does attend to the likelihood of selecting some workers who can satisfactorily perform on the job but will be dissatisfied. Such dissatisfaction can result in turnover, absences, and other undesirable behaviors. Need satisfaction equations make it possible to screen out applicants likely to be dissatisfied, to consider them for more appropriate environments, or to allow for modification of the reinforcer systems of the target environments to improve chances of satisfaction.

The most accurate predictions of performance capability in specific jobs are based on measures of job-specific skills. This approach, however, requires the development of many measures for the large number of component skills in each job. The task of developing measures for several jobs in a company becomes enormous and prohibitive in both cost and time, even when the measurement goals are limited to those skills judged to be most important. The model for operationalizing the theory uses the concept of reference dimensions, or principal ability components, to describe skills more parsimoniously on a smaller number of basic measures. The use of ability measurement rather than skill measurement allows a company to assess many applicants for many, varied jobs. It becomes possible to focus on a placement strategy of identifying the most suitable jobs for different applicants, thus making better use of the worker pool and more efficient use of the assessment procedures. In contrast, the approach based on job-specific skills focuses more narrowly on selecting for one job at a time, which leads to a continuing series of independent searches.

The assessment of reference abilities provides information on not only extant but also potential skills (aptitudes). This kind of information will be useful in programs for the training and development of employees. These programs are needed for the establishment of careers within the organization, wherein the company capitalizes on employee knowledge and experience gained in the service of the organization, on employee potential, and on the company's investment in training. The career concept provides a more rational basis for promotion than seniority alone. Reference dimensions also apply in the assessment of needs; the assessment of reference values provides information relevant for the prediction of satisfaction for the individual.

Employee training programs can be based on knowledge of trainee abilities and values and on the skill requirements and reinforcer system of the job. The goal of training, from the viewpoint of the theory of work adjustment, is to take an individual who is selected for appropriateness of reference dimensions (abilities, values) and to move that individual to skillfulness in job performance and to satisfaction in the work situation. This goal might be achieved in training by practicing a series of tasks that successively approximate the reinforcer system of the job.

Progression in training can proceed from simple to complex skills at a uniform rate in group training situations. The kinds and levels of skills to be included in the training would be best inferred from the group (average) profile of trainee abilities. Reinforcement during training in this group situation would require uniform schedules and uniform kinds and levels of reinforcers. The trainer might wish to base reinforcement of skill development on the group (average) profile of trainee needs and values. Given the existence of individual differences in beginning skill levels and in rates of learning, individualized training is desirable whenever feasible; it will also permit the trainer to individualize reinforcement for skill acquisition so that it will be most responsive to the unique reinforcer preferences of the trainee.

Ability and value information may also be used in the choice or design of modes of training to improve effectiveness. For example, training content presented in abstract verbal and numerical form would be more appropriate for trainees selected on the basis of high scores on verbal and numerical ability reference dimensions than for trainees scoring high on manual dexterity and eye-hand coordination. On the other hand, appropriateness would be reversed for training content involving concrete materials such as tools and machines. Similarly, group interaction techniques might be more appropriate and effective for trainees with strong preferences for social reinforcers (high scores on altruism and status value reference dimensions). Techniques that are premised on individual initiative might be more appropriate for trainees with strong preferences for self-reinforcers (high scores on autonomy and achievement).

Employee motivation, viewed in the context of the theory, derives from the individual employee seeking to achieve and maintain correspondence with the work environment. The two aspects of the desired correspondence are meeting task requirements for satisfactoriness and receiving preferred reinforcements for satisfaction. Workers who are seen as satisfactory and who are satisfied will maintain their typical work behavior over time. Because the maintenance of correspondence requires continuing interaction of the employees with their environments, employee motivation is a continuous phenomenon. When satisfactoriness, satisfaction, or both fall below acceptable tolerance levels but are perceived to be amenable to correction, the temporary state of discorrespondence motivates adjustment behavior. If, however, the state of discorrespondence is perceived to be uncorrectable (either before or after attempts at correction), motivation for adjustment to the situation will be lost and motivation to leave the job (either psychologically or physically) will be likely.

From the standpoint of the theory, satisfaction is a necessary component of employee morale. Good morale implies satisfaction with the conditions of work (both psychological and physical); poor morale results from low satisfaction coupled with the perception of inability to correct the situation. If poor morale is a problem, it may be partially addressed by attending to the source of low satisfaction, which is discorrespondence between needs/values and reinforcers. It may also be useful to explore the validity of the perception of powerlessness to correct the situation.

In institutional and organizational settings within both the private and public sectors, job analysis is a very important tool for effective personnel administration and management. It provides information basic for employee selection and placement, transfer and promotion, and for performance evaluation and compensation. Traditionally, job analysis has focused on the analysis and description of jobs in terms of task requirements, skills used, and conditions under which the employee will perform (including tools and equipment used, materials or subject matter involved, and physical and environmental demands). Job analysis approached from the viewpoint of the theory of work adjustment requires that attention be given to other aspects of the work environment as well. Specifically, the job analysis should include information important to the understanding and prediction of employee satisfaction and to the understanding of the continuing process of adjustment to work.

For understanding employee satisfaction, the analysis must include information about the reinforcer systems for the particular jobs being analyzed. Some of this information may be implicit in the description of the conditions under which the employee will perform. However, the information on reinforcer systems should not be limited to incidental inferences but should include a number of representative reinforcer dimensions. The descriptions of reinforcer systems should also use dimensions that are consonant, in both content and organization, with available systems for describing employee reinforcer preferences (needs and values). Such a rubric for describing reinforcer systems has been proposed in chapter 4, and it may be used in job analysis through an instrument like the Minnesota Job Description Questionnaire.

For understanding the continuing process of adjustment to work, the analysis must contain information about the personality and adjustment styles of employees and on the environment style of jobs. This information will be helpful in estimating the likelihood that individuals and environments will respond in particular ways as each attempts to adjust to the other in the interest of maintaining suitable correspondence. The job analysis should include information on the style characteristics of the environment. One set of environment-style dimensions has been presented earlier as a part of the theory in chapter 5.

Increasingly, organizations are finding it necessary or desirable to design new work environments or to redesign existing work environments. This emphasis on the design of work environments grows out of new product development and changing technologies in conjunction with the need or desire to maintain the existing work force insofar as that is feasible. One approach to the designing of new work environments might begin by constructing an inventory of task requirements in terms of skills required to meet production goals. These skill requirements can then be translated into the more manageable ability reference dimensions. With this information, workers can be selected from the existing work force. From this group of workers identified as potentially capable, one can assess the workers' preferred reinforcers (needs and values) and use that information to design the stimulus conditions for the new work environments. The goal of the design is the creation of reinforcer systems likely to satisfy the largest number of workers. By building on information about the abilities and values of the work force, the organization can create new work environments in ways that will maximize satisfactoriness and satisfaction of the workers.

In the redesign of work environments, as to accommodate technological change, organizations should obtain information on present ability requirements and reinforcer systems and examine these against the projected ability requirements and reinforcer systems of the redesigned environments. The examination will yield data on both new ability requirements and reinforcer changes. If we assume that the workers in the present work environments are satisfactory and satisfied and that this work force is to be maintained in the redesigned work environments, we seek to determine whether new ability requirements will be met or whether reinforcer changes will significantly affect the satisfaction of the worker. If it appears that new ability requirements will not be met, one might be required to modify the redesigned work environment or to select additional qualified workers to augment the work force. If reinforcer changes might affect satisfaction, the redesigned work environment might be modified to provide for the substitution or addition of appropriate reinforcers. Again, the approach suggested here builds on information about the worker abilities and values with the goal of maintaining worker satisfactoriness and satisfaction in the redesigned work environments.

SOCIAL USES FOR THE THEORY

The theory of work adjustment also provides a useful framework for conceptualizing some of the important social problems of our society. In previous chapters, we applied the theory to problems resulting from lack of career planning, unemployment, lack of planning for retirement, and disability. These problems, because they involve many individuals, may also be viewed in the larger context as social problems. Their solution requires information on which to base public policy and the implementation of policy. Public policy questions might include such issues as the opportunity to make an informed career choice, to engage in satisfying employment, to participate in work despite a disability, and to experience not only security and dignity but also satisfaction after retirement. Society must decide whether these opportunities are to be given to all of its members.

The theory of work adjustment, because it provides a way to conceptualize people and work and their interactions, specifies the kinds of information that would be useful in the discussion of such questions at the public policy formation stage. It also describes the adjustment process that is involved and, therefore, specifies the information needed to implement the policies that are adopted. For example, discussion of any of these policies would benefit from national statistics on the distribution of skills and abilities in the general population, the distribution of skill and ability requirements in present and future jobs, and projections of change in job availability in the labor market. Statistical information should also be developed on the distribution of needs and values in the general population and on the distribution of reinforcers available in present and future jobs.

Statistical information of this kind could be constructed from the sampling of segments of the population defined by other demographic variables. The state of the art in the sampling of populations makes the derivation of these useful statistics possible. If the statistical information were developed for skill/ability requirements and available reinforcers in jobs, and if any of the policies discussed above were adopted, the information could be used to develop the occupational ability patterns (OAPs) and occupational reinforcer patterns (ORPs) needed to implement the policy through the interactive-matching model of the theory. The OAP and ORP information could be used in a nationwide, computer-based system by such governmental units as state employment services and state vocational rehabilitation agencies in their work with individual clients. The information system could also be made available to educational institutions (public and private secondary schools and area vocational/technical schools, colleges, and universities) and to social agencies that provide counseling and vocational guidance services.

In education, the theory of work adjustment suggests some approaches that contribute to the original mission of education, that is, to bring out the latent potential of individuals and to develop it to the fullest possible extent. Our previous discussion of the inception and individuation of the personality stated that as individuals respond in social-educational environments and are reinforced in their responses, they develop repertoires of skills/abilities and needs/values. The implication for education is that, in addition to courses in basic skill areas (reading, math, language), schooling should include opportunities for behavior and skill learning in a wide range of activities designed to sample various combinations of abilities and to provide experience with various combinations of reinforcers. A large number of activities is not a goal in itself and may not enhance personality development; rather, we are advocating an enrichment of the basic curriculum by adding carefully selected experiences designed to bring out more complete personality development. This enrichment appears particularly important in the elementary and secondary years of education. To achieve a broad and still manageable sampling of activities that will provide appropriate experiences, educators could choose from a taxonomy that cross-classifies combinations of abilities and combinations of reinforcer-preference factors. Until such an activity taxonomy is developed, one could draw from existing taxonomies of work (based on ability requirements and reinforcers) and could simulate those activities in the educational environment. For example, a stock exchange exercise could be set up that would combine verbal, numerical, and social skills while it also combined reinforcers that included achievement, responsibility, and social status.

The theory also has implications for vocational/technical and professional education. It suggests that students be selected in relation to both the requisite abilities and the effective reinforcer systems of the occupations for which they are to be trained. Skill training can then make use of the most appropriate abilities and reinforcers. In the actual training of students, every effort should be made to approximate the known skill requirements and reinforcer systems of the target occupations. When successful, the training would result in not only appropriate levels of skill but also more realistic reinforcement expectations for the students.

Vocational/technical and professional training programs now focus almost exclusively on skill training. If the model presented in the theory of work adjustment is adopted in structuring training environments to be consonant with on-the-job environments, it also will be necessary to develop descriptions of reinforcer patterns for both the job environment and the training environment. The appropriate estimation methods were described earlier in chapter 4 in the discussion of the development of occupational reinforcer patterns using raters and an instrument like the Minnesota Job Description Questionnaire. For jobs, the raters might be first-line supervisors or experienced incumbents; for the training environment, the raters might be instructors or advanced students. If differences are found when the job and training reinforcer patterns are compared, one can restructure the reinforcer system of the training environment by increasing or decreasing the strength of particular reinforcers. If the goal is to increase safety reinforcers, for example, one might structure the training activities to produce a more predictable schedule. If the goal is to decrease safety reinforcers, one might introduce more unpredictability and variability into the schedule of training activities. Additional examples are given in table 10.1.

Table 10.1

EXAMPLES OF REINFORCER MODIFICATION IN TRAINING ENVIRONMENTS

ENVIRONMENTAL (COMFORT, SAFETY) REINFORCERS	
ADD OR INCREASE REINFORCERS	DELETE OR DECREASE REINFORCERS
Structure training and work activities to yield a steady, continuing, paced and predictable schedule	Introduce nonpredictable and variably applied periods of inactivity
Arrange work stations to maximize students' working alone	Arrange work stations to maximize physical proximity of students
Require that projects be completed by each student independently	Assign projects for completion by groups of students
Increase number and variety of projects and schedule to avoid continuous work on the same problem	Standardize training projects so that they remain essentially the same from day to day
Grade all projects on an objective, automatic basis that is clearly understood beforehand by all students	Allow more individualized bases for grading that are keyed more to individuals' progress than to an objective normative standard
Regularly provide current information on employment opportunities and earnings for the target occupation	Focus only on immediate training objectives and not on employment
Provide for the best maintenance of equipment and the work environment	Use funds and time allocated for maintenance to increase practice opportunity in skill training

Table 10.1 – *Continued*

SOCIAL (ALTRUISM, STATUS) REINFORCERS	
ADD OR INCREASE REINFORCERS	DELETE OR DECREASE REINFORCERS
Assign students to work groups and stations on the basis of sociograms	Make random assignments to work groups and stations
Emphasize the right-versus-wrong aspects of procedures, services, and dealings with others following high standards of behavior	Focus more on getting results than on standards of behavior
Call attention frequently to the ways in which the training will result in helping other people	Focus primarily on self accomplishment and the achievement of skillfulness
Establish a hierarchical system of progression through well-defined levels of accomplishment that is recognized by use of appropriate titles and insignia	Avoid recognizing differential accomplishment and foster a more egalitarian climate
Provide for student experience in overseeing the carrying out of projects by other students	Delegate very little authority to students
Increase the number of student awards given out	Eliminate any existing student awards systems

SELF (ACHIEVEMENT, AUTONOMY) REINFORCERS	
ADD OR INCREASE REINFORCERS	DELETE OR DECREASE REINFORCERS
Seek to match difficulty levels of tasks/ projects to individual student ability levels	Standardize task-difficulty levels and task progression for all students
Teach students to recognize their levels of accomplishment by comparisons with objective standards/models of competency	Rely solely on global or overall instructor evaluation of students' progress
Build in procedures that encourage student experimentation with techniques, approaches, design, and choice of objectives	Use highly prescribed standard approaches to problem solving and project completion
Allow for a wide latitude of student choice in selecting, scheduling, and completing projects	Operate on a fixed schedule of projects to be completed at prescribed times

Note: Reprinted from *Job satisfaction and work adjustment: Implications for vocational education* by R. V. Dawis and L. H. Lofquist, (Columbus, Ohio: National Center for Research in Vocational Education, The Ohio State University, 1981), pp. 19-20.

Little information is now available on the reinforcer systems that exist in vocational/technical and professional training environments. It would be desirable to begin a systematic program for developing educational reinforcer patterns (ERPs). The availability of ERPs would help the transfer of training and enhance the likelihood of subsequent job satisfaction and career tenure.

Similarly, the model in the theory suggests new approaches to the design of retirement environments and communities. The major thrust would be to provide opportunities to use abilities and to experience reinforcers in enough breadth to accommodate the requirements of different retirees. Taxonomies of abilities and reinforcers such as those described in the discussion of adjustment to retirement (chap. 9) will be useful in achieving this goal. Retirement environments would be regarded as places where one continues to engage in the activities and to enjoy the benefits of "working," rather than as comfortable retreats that are removed from the real (working) world.

The model can also help to monitor the changes brought about by automation and the rapid development of new technologies, and it can deal with the effects of these changes on workers. The changes will probably affect specific skills and skill patterns, but they will not alter the basic abilities and ability patterns. Similarly, they will alter specific reinforcers and reinforcer patterns but not basic reinforcer factors. Even when skills become obsolete and reinforcers change, the assessment of abilities and of reinforcer factors provides information that is essential for the development of new skills and the structuring of new reinforcer systems. It follows that a nationwide program designed to facilitate the rapid assessment of ability requirements and reinforcer factors in new or emerging jobs is necessary for the most effective societal adaptation to technological change. We believe that technological advancement will not necessarily mean the wholesale elimination of jobs and lack of employment opportunities for workers; it will, however, require planning of better strategies to ensure worker readjustment.

11

Implications for the Study of Behavior

Our goal in writing this book was to elaborate on the theory of work adjustment, to report on research done on the theory, and to relate the theory to the broader research literature on work behavior. In doing so, we have concluded that the concepts in the theory of work adjustment might be generalizable to other areas of human behavior. In other words, it might serve as a more general theory of behavior and, in particular, as a theory of personality because it is rooted in basic psychological concepts as they might relate to a major part of human behavior—work.

We began by defining psychology simply as the study of behavior. Other disciplines, such as sociology, anthropology, and economics, also study behavior, but their preferred concepts do not focus on individual behavior itself. Their primary conceptual focus is on such derivations of individual behavior as the behavior of groups, institutions, cultures, classes, markets, and economies. It is psychology that has chosen individual behavior as the primary focus of study. It is psychology that includes in its technical terminology such terms related to individual behavior as response, stimulus, reinforcement, response latency, and response generalization.

Even in psychology, much of the study of individual behavior has been relatively isolated from the natural life settings in which behavior occurs. This isolation was the understandable result of the transition in psychology from a philosophic approach to a scientific one and of the consequent change in emphasis from subjective analysis to objective experimentation.

As psychology developed as an experimental science, much

attention was given to the laboratory study of specific behaviors under highly controlled conditions. This work led to the development of basic principles of behavior, such as respondent and operant conditioning. Much of the work has been done with animals, but the principles have been shown to generalize to human behavior. Ideally, behavior principles developed in the laboratory should be applicable to behavior in real life settings; however not enough work has been done to make these applications.

Some psychologists have studied behavior in naturalistic settings. Their study has been largely directed at the treatment of human problems. This strong focus on problem solving has led to the development of decision rules for practice that have little connection to the basic principles that have been developed in the laboratory. If applied psychology is to be most effective, it should be premised more completely on basic principles of behavior. What is needed are more studies of behavior in naturalistic settings, using approaches that adopt the basic behavior principles developed in the laboratory. The following paragraphs describe some considerations for understanding behavior that should be taken into account by this approach.

To understand behavior, we must pay attention to both response and stimulus. The study of response alone is not psychologically meaningful; only by linking it to stimulus can we understand what is happening.

Discrete behaviors, even when studied in stimulus-response terms, yield limited understanding of behavior unless they are studied in the context of the larger pattern of individual behavior. Similarly, stimuli should be studied in the context of the larger stimulus pattern, or the environment.

The study of individual behavior in stimulus-response terms will bring limited understanding if it includes only the simple addition of discrete behavioral units or the combination of selected discrete units. More understanding will arise from the study of individual-environment interaction in the context of the larger stimulus-response patterns, which is S-R studied at a molar level.

The study of human behavior should take individual differences into account. It has been well documented that individual differences are not simply random error, but instead they are lawful phenomena in their own right. "Laws" of human behavior are difficult to state in terms that apply to all individuals. Behavioral laws are best thought of as probabilistic statements. Rather than limiting our understanding of behavior, the consideration of individual differences should enlarge our comprehension (through the discovery of new laws) and sharpen our focus (through the increased precision resulting from delimiting the subset of individuals for whom a given behavioral law would apply). In other words, behavior studied from the perspective of individual differences should obviate the stating of laws that are too broad and become trivial in the effort to encompass all individuals. At the same time, this perspective would produce behavioral laws that are valid for the greatest number of individuals.

Because all behavior takes place in an environment, the study of behavior must also recognize that environments differ in ways that have significance for the formulation of behavioral laws. In the same way that it is extremely difficult to state a behavioral law that applies to all individuals, it is extremely difficult to state a behavioral law that will hold for all environments. Behavioral laws must attend selectively to differences in individuals and in environments. Perhaps we could think of behavioral laws as occurring in four classes: those that are valid for most individuals in most environments, most individuals in some environments, some individuals in most environments, and some individuals in some environments.

Behavior can be understood by studying contemporaneously observed stimuli and responses in an individual-environment interaction. This understanding, when stated in terms of behavioral laws, will be more valid and reliable if information is available on previous individual-environment interactions and if continuing observations are obtained over time. Confidence in the utility of behavioral laws increases with evidence of the repeatability of the individual-environment interaction being studied.

In developing the theory of work adjustment (see chap. 5), we sought to construct a conceptual framework to provide direction for the study of a specific class of behaviors (work adjustment) occurring in a naturalistic setting (the work environment). The basic concepts in the theory build upon the foundation of stimulus and response formulations that have utility in the laboratory study of behavior. For example, the concepts of skills and abilities are derived from response dimensions that have been studied in laboratory research on topics such as sensation and perception, perceptual and motor skills, and cognitive psychology (information processing). The concepts of needs and values are derived from stimulus dimensions studied in the laboratory in such areas as reinforcement and conditioning. The theory requires the operationalization of these concepts in ways that incorporate both individual differences and environment differences. The theory also provides for the study of behavior from both a historical (retrospective) and a predictive (prospective) viewpoint.

The theory of work adjustment, arising from a stimulus-response paradigm, conceptualizes behavior at a molar level. It uses response and stimulus dimensions chosen to be optimally descriptive, manageable in number, and combined so as to reflect both the individual and the environment functioning as integrated systems in an interactive adjustment process. The dimensions specified in the theory (abilities, values, and personality style) are viewed not as separate or discrete dimensions but as combinations and patterns. The particular combination or pattern for each set of dimensions has greater significance than each dimension in the set considered by itself. The patterns provide a better representation of reality because they reflect the underlying interconnectedness of single dimensions and better represent the integration of the individual and the overall organization of the environment in real life.

THE THEORY OF WORK ADJUSTMENT AS A THEORY OF PERSONALITY

If the propositions, corollaries, and operationalized model of the theory of work adjustment are a useful way for viewing adjustment problems in work, career selection, career change, marriage, family, educational settings, and rehabilitation, we may ask whether this psychological theory can be considered a theory of personality. If we adapt the theory by removing the modifer *work* from its constructs, definitions, propositions, corollaries, and measures, and if we substitute the appropriate modifier for a particular class of adjustment problems (e.g., marital or disability), the result may well be productive from the standpoint of both the generation of research and the implications for practice. The content and structure of the theory appear to apply to several adjustment problems. Although our central concern is adjustment to work, we believe that the theory, with some modification, has contributions to make as a less circumscribed personality theory. The appropriateness of these assertions may be judged by testing the theory against criteria that have typically been used in discussions of whether or not a psychological theory should be considered a theory of personality.

Hall and Lindzey (1970) in their *Theories of Personality* explored the nature of personality and of personality theory. They extracted several characteristics and criteria from the literature that serve to clarify both the definition of the term *personality* and the nature of a theory. In the following paragraphs, we will discuss how the theory of work adjustment might be evaluated against these characteristics and criteria; page references to the Hall and Lindzey work are given in parentheses.

"Personality theories are functional in their orientation. They are concerned with questions that make a difference in the adjustment of the organism. They center about issues of crucial importance for the survival of the individual" (page 4). The theory of work adjustment is functional in orientation in that it directly addresses adjustment problems in work (the activity in which most individuals exhibit most of their behavior in their lifetimes). In our society, adjustment to work is required for economic, social, and psychological survival. The concepts and the model of the theory are also useful in dealing with adjustment and survival in other interactions between person and environment, as in marriage and family.

"Personality theorists have customarily assigned a crucial role to the motivational process" (page 5). Correspondence, and its dynamic expression in corresponsiveness, are the central concepts in the theory of work adjustment that provide the basis for a motivational process in adjustment. The achievement and maintenance of the correspondence needed for satisfaction constitute the motivational forces in this process.

"The personality theorist's conviction [is] that an adequate understanding of human behavior will evolve only from the study of the whole person. . . . [T]he subject should be viewed from the vantage of the entire functioning person in his natural habitat" (page 6). In the theory of work adjustment, the work personality, which encompasses both structure and style, reflects the major behavioral dimensions of the whole person. Analogous constructs are used to describe the central features of the target environment in which the individual seeks to adjust. Interaction between individual and environment takes place in a naturalistic setting.

"One of the most distinctive features of personality theory is its function as an integrative theory. . . . [The theory assists in] bringing together and organizing the diverse findings of specialists" (page 6). The theory of work adjustment is developed from learning theory and differential psychology and draws upon research in such areas as vocational psychology, industrial-organizational psychology, and counseling psychology. It has been used to integrate and organize knowledge across these diverse fields of applied psychology.

We must also ask whether the theory of work adjustment is indeed a theory. Hall and Lindzey (1970) specified some criteria typically used to answer this question: "A theory is a set of conventions created by the theorist" (page 10). "Not only must the assumptions be stated clearly but also the assumptions and the elements within the theory must be explicitly combined and related to one another. . . . [The theory must have syntax, i.e.,] rules for the systematic interaction between the assumptions and their embedded concepts" (page 11). "The assumptions must be relevant in that they bear upon the empirical events with which the theory is concerned" (page 11).

Further, they wrote that empirical definitions should permit "precise interaction of certain terms or concepts within the theory with empirical data. . . . [Operational definitions] attempt to specify operations by means of which the relevant variables or concepts can be measured" (page 12). "A theory is . . . useful or not useful . . . primarily in terms of how efficiently the theory can generate predictions or propositions concerning relevant events which turn out to be verified (true)" (pages 10-11).

The utility of a theory has two components: "Verifiability . . . the capacity of the theory to generate predictions which are confirmed when the relevant empirical data are collected" and "comprehensiveness . . . the scope or completeness of these derivations" (page 12). A theory should have heuristic influence, or the capacity to "generate research by suggesting ideas or even by arousing disbelief and resistance. . . ." (page 13). A theory "leads to the collection or observation of relevant empirical relations not yet observed" (page 12). It should permit the "incorporation of known empirical findings within a logically consistent and reasonably simple framework" (page 13).

We believe that the theory of work adjustment meets this list of criteria and can, as a consequence, be thought of as a theory of personality. Using Hall and Lindzey's set of substantive attributes by which personality theories can be compared, the theory of work adjustment can be further described as being:

Strong on *uniqueness* and *individuality*;

Toward the *molar* end of a molecular-molar dimension, with respect to the breadth of the unit of behavior used to analyze personality:

Holistic in the sense of field emphasis;

Purposive (goal striving, purpose seeking) rather than mechanistic;

Conscious (rational, aware) rather than unconscious (unaware) with respect to determinants of behavior;

Hedonistic in the sense of reward and effect, with reinforcement central in retention and learning of responses and preferences for conditions for responding;

Focused more on the effect than on association (contiguity);

Focused more on the *acquisitions (outcomes) of learning* (the developed, relatively stable response and preference repertoire) than on the learning process (modification of behavior);

Focused more on *continuity of behavior* rather than on independent and separated stages, in the development of personality;

Focused more on *homeostasis* (maintaining a balanced psychological state) than on change through learning; and

Focused more on *objective reality* than on perceived (subjective) reality (does not require introduction of a self-concept).

The theory of work adjustment also deals more with the content of behavior than with general principles or laws. It assigns substantial importance to both heredity and environment in the development of the individual personality, and it views early developmental experiences as central to establishing the adult personality. Its emphasis, however, is on the adjustment of the product of the developmental years (stable personality) to contemporaneous factors.

IMPLICATIONS FOR OTHER AREAS OF PSYCHOLOGY

If the theory of work adjustment can be viewed more broadly as a theory of personality, it has implications for the study of behavior in areas other than vocational psychology. Its constructs should be useful in the study of such topics as motivation, learning, human development, social behavior, and even abnormal behavior.

In understanding motivation, the general principle that individuals behave in ways designed to achieve and maintain correspondence with their environments seems to underlie much of voluntary or self-directed behavior. The correspondence to be achieved and maintained cannot be described in terms limited to either the individual or the environment without regard for the other. It must be described in terms of the fit between the two. The theory of work adjustment specifies the significant descriptors of individuals and of environments in stimulus-response terms that help to determine the goodness of fit.

The focus is placed on response and reinforcement, or rather on response dimensions and reinforcer dimensions. Response dimensions are observed as response capabilities (skills/abilities) for individuals and as response demands (skill/ability requirements) for environments. Reinforcer dimensions are observed as reinforcer preferences (needs/values) for individuals and as reinforcer conditions (reinforcer patterns and clusters) for environments. The response dimensions set the limits of the behavior manifested in the pursuit of correspondence, whereas the reinforcer dimensions determine the likelihood of behavior within these limits. This line of reasoning leads us to the conclusion that the central constructs in motivation within this theoretical framework are correspondence and reinforcement. Because the satisfaction of individuals is predictable from reinforcement correspondence, measured satisfaction can be viewed as both an outcome and an index of motivation.

The study of individual differences in motivation is enhanced by the inclusion of personality style dimensions. Differences in flexibility (tolerance for discorrespondence), for example, will determine the likelihood of adjustment behavior. Across individuals, the lower the flexibility thresholds, the higher the likelihood of adjustment behavior. For a given individual, position on the flexibility dimension in relation to the threshold provides another index of motivation. Similar implications with respect to motivation could be derived from other personality style dimensions such as pace and perseverance.

In a typical individual-environment interaction, the constructs central to motivation are correspondence and reinforcement, with personality style dimensions playing an important role in the achievement and maintenance of correspondence. Typically, both individual and environment change, and a continuous adjustment interaction between the two serves to maintain correspondence. When the changes involved are relatively small, the changes in level of motivation are minimal and the observed motivation can be described as continuing "maintenance motivation." When changes are larger, one would expect significant changes in the level of motivation.

Large changes in the environment may result from such events as management changes, introduction of new technology, changes in the work force, promotion and transfer. These changes may bring a very different reinforcer system and changed ability requirements. The changes will also upset the correspondence balance and require that the individual redress the balance by making an adjustment. Very drastic changes might result in little or no observable motivation, from which one might infer that the individual sees no possibility for successful adjustment.

Large changes in the individual may also bring significant changes in level of motivation. Examples of such changes include the sudden experience of physical disability or illness that results in serious impairment of abilities; unexpected emotional trauma, such as loss of a closely related person or loss of employment; and dramatic ideological conversion (religious, political). In the case of physical disability, the goodness of fit of the correspondence is disturbed by behavioral limitations that not only make it impossible to meet task requirements but also limit the ability of the individual to experience preferred reinforcers associated with response to task demands. We believe that, in the study of significant changes in motivation resulting from large changes in the environment or the individual, physical disability may be one of the most promising areas for research.

If one accepts the view that motivation is a condition for learning, the factors affecting motivation that are described above may be expected to have their effects on learning. Working from a model in which correspondence is central, the initial level of motivation in a learning experiment might be established from knowledge of the fit between individual needs and environment reinforcers or by manipulation of the environmental reinforcer system to produce different target levels of correspondence and, therefore, different initial levels of motivation. Procedures of this sort might be used to control the motivational factor in a learning experiment or to study the contribution of motivation in the learning situation.

In the development of personality, an individual's pattern and level of abilities and values result from the person's response and reinforcement history. They are, therefore, the result of previous learning, and, if assessed, can be used as operational indicators of the initial state of subjects in a learning experiment. Individual differences in learning are more readily accounted for if one has knowledge of the initial state of subjects, of their patterns and levels of abilities and values. Knowledge of abilities and values can also be used in the design of training programs and methods.

The theory of work adjustment used as a theory of personality in the study of human development provides a structure for the identification of significant dimensions on which development takes place. It also provides a stimulus-response orientation for the study of the different effects of response and reinforcement history on the developing individual. The approach appears to provide a more precise specification of the origins, individuation, and stabilization of personality. For example, given initial levels and rates of development, it should be possible to forecast the stabilized levels and patterns of abilities. With information about environments as specified in the theory, one may then operationally define human potential in terms of predicted correspondence for future environments. Having identified the most correspondent future environments, the development of human potential would involve training to acquire appropriate skills to meet task requirements while providing reinforcers appropriate to the individual's needs and consonant with the targeted future environments.

In the study of the development of an individual's personality, the correspondence principle is central to understanding the shaping of the personality. The object of achieving correspondence with one's environment is present from the beginnings of personality development and continues throughout life. In the early stages, the individual is acting on environment and experiencing the response requirements and reinforcer systems of the environment. In a sense, the individual is testing out a variety of available environments. When the response and reinforcement conditions are experienced by the individual as correspondent, the individual will appear to an observer as satisfied (happy) and as capable, responding at specifiable levels of ability. As an individual experiences both a variety of environments and recurrence of similar environments, the personality structure may be observed to exhibit increasing differences in levels and patterns of the significant personality dimensions. In the periods of inception and individuation of the personality, rate of development and differentiation may be viewed as a function in part of the range of available environments and the frequency of experience with these environments.

Stabilization of the personality occurs with stabilization of biological growth and of experiences in environments. Stabilization of the personality may be objectively observed when repeated measurements of the significant personality dimensions show little or no change in levels and patterns. Stabilization of the personality may occur early, late, or not at all for particular individuals. Although it may be convenient to describe development in terms of stages (inception, individuation, and stabilization), the more significant phenomenon is the fact of individual differences in rate and type of personality development.

The stabilization of the personality as indicated by the stability of repeated measurements of personality dimensions establishes one major premise for a trait approach to the description of human behavior. The relative independence of the personality dimensions identified in the theory of work adjustment—the low intercorrelations among ability, value, and style dimensions—validates the other major premise of trait theory. This trait approach, which has been known as the theory of relatively unique traits, has provided the foundation for much of applied psychology, such as in prediction and selection problems in industrial/organizational psychology, educational psychology, and military psychology.

One can also study social behavior using the conceptual framework of the theory of work adjustment. If one substitutes the modifier *social* for the modifier *work* in the model, it is possible to describe social behavior as the interaction between the social personality and the social environment and to view the outcome of the interaction in terms of social satisfactoriness, social satisfaction, and the maintenance of the social interaction (social tenure). The social environment can be defined as another individual, a group of some size, an organization, or a culture. These social environments have social task requirements and social reinforcer systems. The social personality, in turn, can be defined as having social skills, abilities, needs, and values. The social task requirements can be described in terms of social-ability requirements, and the social needs and values can be described in terms of social-reinforcer preferences. The basic principle governing the social interaction is correspondence, the mutual establishment and maintenance of a satisfying and satisfactory social relationship.

The study of social behavior in this framework requires the mapping of the domains of social abilities and reinforcers. Social abilities, for example, might be categorized as afferent (social-task/reinforcer perception), mediational (social memory/reasoning), and efferent (social response and reinforcer use directed toward such goals as persuasion, domination, and manipulation). Social ability patterns might be utilized in describing both individuals and environments. Similarly, patterns of preferences for social reinforcers might be identified for individuals and patterns of social reinforcers for environments. The study of social behavior using this interactive model would probably be enhanced by the use of personality style constructs as likely moderators of the social interaction between individual and environment.

From this theoretical perspective, abnormal behavior might be defined as remaining in a discorrespondent environment or as leaving a correspondent environment, when in either case the opposite behavior is predicted within normative limits. In other words, the acceptance of dissatisfaction or the rejection of satisfaction is not justifiable by normative expectations and is translated into inappropriate behavior. The task, then, becomes one of attempting to redress the abnormal state by establishing correspondence or by improving the perception of correspondence/discorrespondence. In either case, the objective is to motivate appropriate behavior. The prognosis and the choice of specific procedures to accomplish this should be based on thorough assessment of both the individual and the environment against the individual's prior history as normative background.

We want to emphasize that we have not empirically tested these implications for the study of behavior that flow from viewing the theory of work adjustment as a more general theory of personality. We do, however, believe that they are eminently reasonable and that they provide alternative and feasible approaches to the study of behavior.

REFERENCE

Hall, C. S., & Lindzey, G. *Theories of personality*. New York: Wiley, 1970.

APPENDIXES

Appendix A
Research Instruments

Instruments developed by the Work Adjustment Project for use in research on and application of the Theory of Work Adjustment:

Minnesota Importance Questionnaire, Paired Form
Minnesota Importance Questionnaire, Ranked Form
Minnesota Job Description Questionnaire
Minnesota Satisfaction Questionnaire
Minnesota Satisfactoriness Scales
Biographical Information Form
Personality Style Rating Form, Experimental
Adjustment Style Rating Form, Experimental

Do not write on this booklet

minnesota importance questionnaire

1975 Edition

paired form

Vocational Psychology Research

UNIVERSITY OF MINNESOTA

Directions

The purpose of this questionnaire is to find out what you consider **important** in your **ideal job,** the kind of job you would most like to have.

On the following pages you will find **pairs** of statements about work.

    —Read each **pair** of statements carefully.

    —Decide which statement of the **pair** is **more** important to you in your **ideal** job.

    —For each pair mark your choice on the answer sheet. **Do not mark this booklet.** (Directions on how to mark the answer sheet are given below.)

Do this for **all** pairs of statements. Work as rapidly as you can. Read each pair of statements, mark your choice, then move on to the next pair. Be sure to make a choice for **every** pair. **Do not** go back to change your answer to any pair.

Remember: You are to decide which statement of the pair is **more important** to **you** in your **ideal** job. Mark your choice on the answer sheet, **not** on this booklet.

How to Mark the Answer Sheet

First of all

    Print your name in the space provided, and fill in the other information requested.

To fill in the answer sheet

    Start where it is marked "Page 1."

    There is a box for each pair of statements. The number in the middle of the box is the number of that pair. "a" and "b" in the box stand for the two statements of the pair.

    If you think statement "a" is more important to you than statement "b", mark an "X" over the "a" on the answer sheet, as shown in the example below:

    However, if you think statement "b" is more important to you than statement "a", mark an "X" over the "b" on the answer sheet, as shown in the example below:

Mark Only One Answer for Each Pair of Statements.

    Mark **either** "a" **or** "b" for each pair. **Do this for all pairs of statements.** Remember, **do not** mark your answer on this booklet. Use the answer sheet.

Ask yourself: Which is **more important** to me in my **ideal** job?

1.
   a. I could be busy all the time.
      OR
   b. The job would provide an opportunity for advancement.

2.
   a. I could try out some of my own ideas.
      OR
   b. My co-workers would be easy to make friends with.

3.
   a. The job could give me a feeling of accomplishment.
      OR
   b. I could do something that makes use of my abilities.

4.
   a. The company would administer its policies fairly.
      OR
   b. I could be busy all the time.

5.
   a. I could try out some of my own ideas.
      OR
   b. I could be "somebody" in the community.

6.
   a. The job would provide an opportunity for advancement.
      OR
   b. My co-workers would be easy to make friends with.

7.
   a. I could tell people what to do.
      OR
   b. I could work alone on the job.

8.
   a. I could get recognition for the work I do.
      OR
   b. The company would administer its policies fairly.

9.
   a. My co-workers would be easy to make friends with.
      OR
   b. The job would provide for steady employment.

10.
   a. The job could give me a feeling of accomplishment.
      OR
   b. The job would provide an opportunity for advancement.

11.
   a. My boss would train the workers well.
      OR
   b. I could work alone on the job.

12.
   a. I could do the work without feeling that it is morally wrong.
      OR
   b. The job would have good working conditions.

Ask yourself: Which is **more important** to me in my **ideal** job?

a. I could be busy all the time.
13.   OR
b. The job could give me a feeling of accomplishment.

a. I could do something that makes use of my abilities.
14.   OR
b. The job would provide an opportunity for advancement.

a. I could tell people what to do.
15.   OR
b. The company would administer its policies fairly.

a. My co-workers would be easy to make friends with.
16.   OR
b. My pay would compare well with that of other workers.

a. I could try out some of my own ideas.
17.   OR
b. I could work alone on the job.

a. I could get recognition for the work I do.
18.   OR
b. I could do the work without feeling that it is morally wrong.

a. The job would provide for steady employment.
19.   OR
b. I could make decisions on my own.

a. I could do things for other people.
20.   OR
b. I could be "somebody" in the community.

a. My boss would back up the workers (with top management).
21.   OR
b. My boss would train the workers well.

a. The job would have good working conditions.
22.   OR
b. I could do something different every day.

a. I could do something that makes use of my abilities.
23.   OR
b. I could be busy all the time.

a. The job could give me a feeling of accomplishment.
24.   OR
b. I could tell people what to do.

Ask yourself: Which is **more important** to me in my **ideal** job?

25.
a. The company would administer its policies fairly.
OR
b. The job would provide an opportunity for advancement.

26.
a. I could do something that makes use of my abilities.
OR
b. My co-workers would be easy to make friends with.

27.
a. I could try out some of my own ideas.
OR
b. The job could give me a feeling of accomplishment.

28.
a. I could be busy all the time.
OR
b. I could work alone on the job.

29.
a. The job would provide an opportunity for advancement.
OR
b. I could do the work without feeling that it is morally wrong.

30.
a. I could tell people what to do.
OR
b. I could get recognition for the work I do.

31.
a. The company would administer its policies fairly.
OR
b. I could make decisions on my own.

32.
a. The job would provide for steady employment.
OR
b. My pay would compare well with that of other workers.

33.
a. I could do things for other people.
OR
b. My co-workers would be easy to make friends with.

34.
a. My boss would back up the workers (with top management).
OR
b. I could work alone on the job.

35.
a. I could do the work without feeling that it is morally wrong.
OR
b. My boss would train the workers well.

36.
a. I could do something different every day.
OR
b. I could get recognition for the work I do.

Ask yourself: Which is **more important** to me in my **ideal** job?

37.
a. I could make decisions on my own.
OR
b. The job would have good working conditions.

38.
a. I could do something that makes use of my abilities.
OR
b. I could tell people what to do.

39.
a. The company would administer its policies fairly.
OR
b. The job could give me a feeling of accomplishment.

40.
a. I could be busy all the time.
OR
b. My pay would compare well with that of other workers.

41.
a. I could try out some of my own ideas.
OR
b. I could tell people what to do.

42.
a. I could get recognition for the work I do.
OR
b. My co-workers would be easy to make friends with.

43.
a. The company would administer its policies fairly.
OR
b. I could work alone on the job.

44.
a. I could do the work without feeling that it is morally wrong.
OR
b. My pay would compare well with that of other workers.

45.
a. I could make decisions on my own.
OR
b. I could try out some of my own ideas.

46.
a. The job would provide for steady employment.
OR
b. I could work alone on the job.

47.
a. I could do things for other people.
OR
b. I could do the work without feeling that it is morally wrong.

48.
a. I could get recognition for the work I do.
OR
b. I could be "somebody" in the community.

Ask yourself: Which is **more important** to me in my **ideal** job?

49.
a. I could make decisions on my own.
    OR
b. My boss would back up the workers (with top management).

50.
a. The job would provide for steady employment.
    OR
b. My boss would train the workers well.

51.
a. I could do something different every day.
    OR
b. I could do things for other people.

52.
a. The job would have good working conditions.
    OR
b. I could be "somebody" in the community.

53.
a. I could tell people what to do.
    OR
b. I could be busy all the time.

54.
a. The job would provide an opportunity for advancement.
    OR
b. My pay would compare well with that of other workers.

55.
a. I could do something that makes use of my abilities.
    OR
b. The company would administer its policies fairly.

56.
a. I could be busy all the time.
    OR
b. My co-workers would be easy to make friends with.

57.
a. The job could give me a feeling of accomplishment.
    OR
b. My pay would compare well with that of other workers.

58.
a. I could try out some of my own ideas.
    OR
b. The job would provide an opportunity for advancement.

59.
a. The company would administer its policies fairly.
    OR
b. I could do the work without feeling that it is morally wrong.

60.
a. I could get recognition for the work I do.
    OR
b. My pay would compare well with that of other workers.

Ask yourself: Which is **more important** to me in my **ideal** job?

61.
    a. My co-workers would be easy to make friends with.
        OR
    b. I could make decisions on my own.

62.
    a. The job would provide for steady employment.
        OR
    b. I could try out some of my own ideas.

63.
    a. I could work alone on the job.
        OR
    b. I could do things for other people.

64.
    a. I could be "somebody" in the community.
        OR
    b. I could do the work without feeling that it is morally wrong.

65.
    a. The job would provide an opportunity for advancement.
        OR
    b. I could tell people what to do.

66.
    a. My boss would train the workers well.
        OR
    b. I could make decisions on my own.

67.
    a. The job would provide for steady employment.
        OR
    b. I could do something different every day.

68.
    a. I could do things for other people.
        OR
    b. The job would have good working conditions.

69.
    a. My boss would back up the workers (with top management).
        OR
    b. I could get recognition for the work I do.

70.
    a. My co-workers would be easy to make friends with.
        OR
    b. I could tell people what to do.

71.
    a. The company would administer its policies fairly.
        OR
    b. I could try out some of my own ideas.

72.
    a. My pay would compare well with that of other workers.
        OR
    b. I could work alone on the job.

Ask yourself: Which is **more important** to me in my **ideal** job?

73.
    a. I could do the work without feeling that it is morally wrong.
       OR
    b. My co-workers would be easy to make friends with.

74.
    a. My boss would back up the workers (with top management).
       OR
    b. The job would have good working conditions.

75.
    a. I could work alone on the job.
       OR
    b. I could make decisions on my own.

76.
    a. The job would provide for steady employment.
       OR
    b. I could do the work without feeling that it is morally wrong.

77.
    a. I could get recognition for the work I do.
       OR
    b. I could do things for other people.

78.
    a. I could be "somebody" in the community.
       OR
    b. I could make decisions on my own.

79.
    a. My boss would back up the workers (with top management).
       OR
    b. The job would provide for steady employment.

80.
    a. My boss would train the workers well.
       OR
    b. I could do things for other people.

81.
    a. I could do something different every day.
       OR
    b. I could be "somebody" in the community.

82.
    a. I could get recognition for the work I do.
       OR
    b. I could try out some of my own ideas.

83.
    a. My pay would compare well with that of other workers.
       OR
    b. I could tell people what to do.

84.
    a. I could do something that makes use of my abilities.
       OR
    b. The job would have good working conditions.

Ask yourself: Which is **more important** to me in my **ideal** job?

85.
a. I could do something different every day.
        OR
b. The job could give me a feeling of accomplishment.

86.
a. My boss would train the workers well.
        OR
b. I could be busy all the time.

87.
a. My co-workers would be easy to make friends with.
        OR
b. The company would administer its policies fairly.

88.
a. My pay would compare well with that of other workers.
        OR
b. I could try out some of my own ideas.

89.
a. I could do something that makes use of my abilities.
        OR
b. I could do something different every day.

90.
a. The job could give me a feeling of accomplishment.
        OR
b. The job would have good working conditions.

91.
a. I could work alone on the job.
        OR
b. My co-workers would be easy to make friends with.

92.
a. I could do the work without feeling that it is morally wrong.
        OR
b. I could try out some of my own ideas.

93.
a. I could get recognition for the work I do.
        OR
b. The job would provide for steady employment.

94.
a. My boss would train the workers well.
        OR
b. I could do something that makes use of my abilities.

95.
a. I could be busy all the time.
        OR
b. The job would have good working conditions.

96.
a. I could do things for other people.
        OR
b. I could make decisions on my own.

Ask yourself: Which is **more important** to me in my **ideal** job?

97.
a. The job would provide for steady employment.
    OR
b. I could be "somebody" in the community.

98.
a. I could work alone on the job.
    OR
b. I could get recognition for the work I do.

99.
a. I could do things for other people.
    OR
b. My boss would back up the workers (with top management).

100.
a. I could make decisions on my own.
    OR
b. I could do the work without feeling that it is morally wrong.

101.
a. My boss would train the workers well.
    OR
b. I could be "somebody" in the community.

102.
a. My boss would back up the workers (with top management).
    OR
b. I could do something different every day.

103.
a. I could get recognition for the work I do.
    OR
b. I could make decisions on my own.

104.
a. I could be busy all the time.
    OR
b. I could do something different every day.

105.
a. My boss would train the workers well.
    OR
b. The job could give me a feeling of accomplishment.

106.
a. The job would have good working conditions.
    OR
b. The job would provide an opportunity for advancement.

107.
a. My pay would compare well with that of other workers.
    OR
b. The company would administer its policies fairly.

108.
a. I could do the work without feeling that it is morally wrong.
    OR
b. I could work alone on the job.

Ask yourself: Which is **more important** to me in my **ideal** job?

109.
a. My boss would train the workers well.
   OR
b. The job would have good working conditions.

110.
a. My boss would back up the workers (with top management).
   OR
b. I could do something that makes use of my abilities.

111.
a. The job would provide for steady employment.
   OR
b. I could do things for other people.

112.
a. The job could give me a feeling of accomplishment.
   OR
b. My co-workers would be easy to make friends with.

113.
a. I could do something different every day.
   OR
b. My boss would train the workers well.

114.
a. I could do things for other people.
   OR
b. I could try out some of my own ideas.

115.
a. I could do something that makes use of my abilities.
   OR
b. I could be "somebody" in the community.

116.
a. My boss would back up the workers (with top management).
   OR
b. The job could give me a feeling of accomplishment.

117.
a. The job would provide an opportunity for advancement.
   OR
b. I could do something different every day.

118.
a. I could tell people what to do.
   OR
b. The job would have good working conditions.

119.
a. I could do the work without feeling that it is morally wrong.
   OR
b. My boss would back up the workers (with top management).

120.
a. My pay would compare well with that of other workers.
   OR
b. I could make decisions on my own.

Ask yourself: Which is **more important** to me in my **ideal** job?

121.
    a. I could be "somebody" in the community.
        OR
    b. I could work alone on the job.

122.
    a. My boss would train the workers well.
        OR
    b. I could get recognition for the work I do.

123.
    a. I could make decisions on my own.
        OR
    b. I could do something different every day.

124.
    a. The job would have good working conditions.
        OR
    b. The job would provide for steady employment.

125.
    a. My pay would compare well with that of other workers.
        OR
    b. I could do something that makes use of my abilities.

126.
    a. I could do something different every day.
        OR
    b. I could tell people what to do.

127.
    a. My boss would back up the workers (with top management).
        OR
    b. I could be "somebody" in the community.

128.
    a. I could try out some of my own ideas.
        OR
    b. I could be busy all the time.

129.
    a. I could work alone on the job.
        OR
    b. The job would provide an opportunity for advancement.

130.
    a. I could tell people what to do.
        OR
    b. I could do the work without feeling that it is morally wrong.

131.
    a. The job would have good working conditions.
        OR
    b. The company would administer its policies fairly.

132.
    a. My boss would train the workers well.
        OR
    b. The job would provide an opportunity for advancement.

Ask yourself: Which is **more important** to me in my **ideal** job?

133.
a. My boss would back up the workers (with top management).
   OR
b. I could be busy all the time.

134.
a. The job could give me a feeling of accomplishment.
   OR
b. I could be "somebody" in the community.

135.
a. I could do something that makes use of my abilities.
   OR
b. I could do things for other people.

136.
a. I could do the work without feeling that it is morally wrong.
   OR
b. I could do something different every day.

137.
a. The job would have good working conditions.
   OR
b. I could get recognition for the work I do.

138.
a. My pay would compare well with that of other workers.
   OR
b. I could do things for other people.

139.
a. I could be "somebody" in the community.
   OR
b. My co-workers would be easy to make friends with.

140.
a. I could try out some of my own ideas.
   OR
b. My boss would back up the workers (with top management).

141.
a. The job could give me a feeling of accomplishment.
   OR
b. I could work alone on the job.

142.
a. I could do the work without feeling that it is morally wrong.
   OR
b. I could be busy all the time.

143.
a. The job would provide an opportunity for advancement.
   OR
b. I could get recognition for the work I do.

144.
a. I could tell people what to do.
   OR
b. I could make decisions on my own.

Ask yourself: Which is **more important** to me in my **ideal** job?

145.
a. The company would administer its policies fairly.
    OR
b. The job would provide for steady employment.

146.
a. I could try out some of my own ideas.
    OR
b. I could do something that makes use of my abilities.

147.
a. My pay would compare well with that of other workers.
    OR
b. The job would have good working conditions.

148.
a. I could do something different every day.
    OR
b. The company would administer its policies fairly.

149.
a. My boss would train the workers well.
    OR
b. I could tell people what to do.

150.
a. My boss would back up the workers (with top management).
    OR
b. The job would provide an opportunity for advancement.

151.
a. I could be busy all the time.
    OR
b. I could be "somebody" in the community.

152.
a. I could do things for other people.
    OR
b. The job could give me a feeling of accomplishment.

153.
a. I could do something that makes use of my abilities.
    OR
b. The job would provide for steady employment.

154.
a. I could do something different every day.
    OR
b. I could work alone on the job.

155.
a. I could try out some of my own ideas.
    OR
b. My boss would train the workers well.

156.
a. My co-workers would be easy to make friends with.
    OR
b. My boss would back up the workers (with top management).

Ask yourself: Which is **more important** to me in my **ideal** job?

a. I could be "somebody" in the community.
157.   OR
b. My pay would compare well with that of other workers.

a. I could do things for other people.
158.   OR
b. The company would administer its policies fairly.

a. The job would provide for steady employment.
159.   OR
b. I could tell people what to do.

a. The job would provide an opportunity for advancement.
160.   OR
b. I could make decisions on my own.

a. I could be busy all the time.
161.   OR
b. I could get recognition for the work I do.

a. I could do the work without feeling that it is morally wrong.
162.   OR
b. The job could give me a feeling of accomplishment.

a. I could work alone on the job.
163.   OR
b. I could do something that makes use of my abilities.

a. The job would have good working conditions.
164.   OR
b. My co-workers would be easy to make friends with.

a. I could do something different every day.
165.   OR
b. My pay would compare well with that of other workers.

a. My boss would train the workers well.
166.   OR
b. The company would administer its policies fairly.

a. I could tell people what to do.
167.   OR
b. My boss would back up the workers (with top management).

a. The job would provide an opportunity for advancement.
168.   OR
b. I could be "somebody" in the community.

Ask yourself: Which is **more important** to me in my **ideal** job?

169.
- a. I could do things for other people.
  OR
- b. I could be busy all the time.

170.
- a. The job could give me a feeling of accomplishment.
  OR
- b. The job would provide for steady employment.

171.
- a. I could make decisions on my own.
  OR
- b. I could do something that makes use of my abilities.

172.
- a. I could work alone on the job.
  OR
- b. The job would have good working conditions.

173.
- a. I could do something different every day.
  OR
- b. I could try out some of my own ideas.

174.
- a. My co-workers would be easy to make friends with.
  OR
- b. My boss would train the workers well.

175.
- a. My boss would back up the workers (with top management).
  OR
- b. My pay would compare well with that of other workers.

176.
- a. I could be "somebody" in the community.
  OR
- b. The company would administer its policies fairly.

177.
- a. I could tell people what to do.
  OR
- b. I could do things for other people.

178.
- a. The job would provide an opportunity for advancement.
  OR
- b. The job would provide for steady employment.

179.
- a. I could be busy all the time.
  OR
- b. I could make decisions on my own.

180.
- a. I could get recognition for the work I do.
  OR
- b. The job could give me a feeling of accomplishment.

Ask yourself: Which is **more important** to me in my **ideal** job?

181.
a. I could do something that makes use of my abilities.
OR
b. I could do the work without feeling that it is morally wrong.

182.
a. The job would have good working conditions.
OR
b. I could try out some of my own ideas.

183.
a. My co-workers would be easy to make friends with.
OR
b. I could do something different every day.

184.
a. My boss would train the workers well.
OR
b. My pay would compare well with that of other workers.

185.
a. The company would administer its policies fairly.
OR
b. My boss would back up the workers (with top management).

186.
a. I could tell people what to do.
OR
b. I could be "somebody" in the community.

187.
a. The job would provide an opportunity for advancement.
OR
b. I could do things for other people.

188.
a. I could be busy all the time.
OR
b. The job would provide for steady employment.

189.
a. I could make decisions on my own.
OR
b. The job could give me a feeling of accomplishment.

190.
a. I could get recognition for the work I do.
OR
b. I could do something that makes use of my abilities.

Please continue on the next page.

On this page consider each statement and decide whether or not it is **important** to have in your **ideal job.**

—If you think that the statement is **important** for your **ideal job,** mark an X in the **"Yes"** box on your answer sheet.

—If you think that the statement is **not important** for your **ideal job,** mark an X in the **"No"** box on your answer sheet.

On my **ideal job** it is important that . . .

191. I could do something that makes use of my abilities.
192. the job could give me a feeling of accomplishment.
193. I could be busy all the time.
194. the job would provide an opportunity for advancement.
195. I could tell people what to do.
196. the company would administer its policies fairly.
197. my pay would compare well with that of other workers.
198. my co-workers would be easy to make friends with.
199. I could try out some of my own ideas.
200. I could work alone on the job.
201. I could do the work without feeling that it is morally wrong.
202. I could get recognition for the work I do.
203. I could make decisions on my own.
204. the job would provide for steady employment.
205. I could do things for other people.
206. I could be "somebody" in the community.
207. my boss would back up the workers (with top management).
208. my boss would train the workers well.
209. I could do something different every day.
210. the job would have good working conditions.

> **Please check your answer sheet to see that you have marked only one choice in each of the 210 boxes.**

MINNESOTA
IMPORTANCE QUESTIONNAIRE

1975 Revision

RANKED FORM

Vocational Psychology Research

UNIVERSITY OF MINNESOTA

Ⓒ Copyright, 1975

DIRECTIONS

The purpose of this questionnaire is to find out what you consider **important** in your **ideal job,** the kind of job you would most like to have.

On the following pages are **groups** of five statements about work.

— Read each group of statements carefully.

— Rank the five statements in each group in terms of their **importance** to you in your **ideal** job.

— Use the number "1" for the statement which is **most important** to you in your **ideal** job, the number "2" for the statement which is **next most important** to you, and so on.

— Use the number "5" for the statement **least important** to you in your **ideal** job.

— Write down your rankings in the correct spaces on the answer sheet.

Please turn to the next page for instructions on how to mark your answer sheet.

HOW TO MARK THE ANSWER SHEET

First of all

Print your name in the space provided and fill in the other information requested.

To fill in the answer sheet

— Start where it says "Page 1".

— There is a box for each of the statements in each group. The letters at the left side of the boxes stand for the statements in your booklet.

— For example, your ranking of a group of statements might look like this:

(booklet)   (answer sheet)

group 1	On my ideal job . . .		
	a.	I could be busy all the time.	
	b.	the job would provide for steady employment.	
	c.	I could do things for other people.	
	d.	I could try out some of my own ideas.	
	e.	my boss would train the workers well.	

		group 1
begin page 1	a	*1*
	b	*3*
	c	*5*
	d	*2*
	e	*4*

This means that, of the five statements, you consider statement "a" (I could be busy all the time) the **most important** (ranked "1") to you in your **ideal** job; statement "d" (I could try out some of my own ideas) the **next most important** (ranked "2"); statement "b" (ranked "3") the **next most important**; statement "e" (ranked "4") the **next most important**; and statement "c" (ranked "5") the **least important** to you in your **ideal** job.

You will find some of the rankings more difficult to make than others, but it is **important** that you rank **every statement** in each group.

Be Sure Your Answers are Numbers, Not Letters.

On your answer sheet enter your rankings of statements for each group.

Remember: "1" = **most important** to you in your **ideal** job; "2" = **next most important**, and so on, to "5" for **least important** to you in your **ideal** job.

---

group
1

On my ideal job . . .

    a.   I could be busy all the time.

    b.   I could do things for other people.

    c.   I could try out some of my own ideas.

    d.   my pay would compare well with that of other workers.

    e.   the job would provide an opportunity for advancement.

---

group
2

On my ideal job . . .

    a.   I could do things for other people.

    b.   I could do something different every day.

    c.   the job could give me a feeling of accomplishment.

    d.   my boss would train the workers well.

    e.   the company would administer its policies fairly.

---

group
3

On my ideal job . . .

    a.   I could do the work without feeling that it is morally wrong.

    b.   my boss would back up the workers (with top management).

    c.   I could do something different every day.

    d.   I could do something that makes use of my abilities.

    e.   I could be busy all the time.

---

group
4

On my ideal job . . .

    a.   the company would administer its policies fairly.

    b.   I could try out some of my own ideas.

    c.   I could do something that makes use of my abilities.

    d.   my co-workers would be easy to make friends with.

    e.   I could be "somebody" in the community.

On your answer sheet enter your rankings of statements for each group.

Remember: "1" = **most important** to you in your **ideal** job; "2" = **next most important,** and so on, to "5" for **least important** to you in your **ideal** job.

---

group
5

On my ideal job . . .

a.   my boss would train the workers well.

b.   I could plan my work with little supervision.

c.   my boss would back up the workers (with top management).

d.   I could try out some of my own ideas.

e.   the job would have good working conditions.

---

group
6

On my ideal job . . .

a.   I could get recognition for the work I do.

b.   I could do the work without feeling that it is morally wrong.

c.   I could plan my work with little supervision.

d.   I could do things for other people.

e.   my co-workers would be easy to make friends with.

---

group
7

On my ideal job . . .

a.   my boss would back up the workers (with top management).

b.   the company would administer its policies fairly.

c.   my pay would compare well with that of other workers.

d.   I could get recognition for the work I do.

e.   I could tell people what to do.

---

group
8

On my ideal job. . .

a.   I could do something different every day.

b.   my co-workers would be easy to make friends with.

c.   I could make decisions on my own.

d.   the job would have good working conditions.

e.   my pay would compare well with that of other workers.

On your answer sheet enter your rankings of statements for each group.

Remember: "1" = **most important** to you in your **ideal** job: "2" = **next most important,** and so on, to "5" for **least important** to you in your **ideal** job.

---

group
9

On my ideal job . . .

a.   I could do something that makes use of my abilities.

b.   I could tell people what to do.

c.   the job would have good working conditions.

d.   the job would provide for steady employment.

e.   I could do things for other people.

---

group
10

On my ideal job . . .

a.   I could make decisions on my own.

b.   I could be busy all the time.

c.   the job would provide for steady employment.

d.   the company would administer its policies fairly.

e.   I could plan my work with little supervision.

---

group
11

On my ideal job . . .

a.   the job could give me a feeling of accomplishment.

b.   I could make decisions on my own.

c.   I could tell people what to do.

d.   I could do the work without feeling that it is morally wrong.

e.   I could try out some of my own ideas.

---

group
12

On my ideal job . . .

a.   my co-workers would be easy to make friends with.

b.   the job would provide for steady employment.

c.   the job would provide an opportunity for advancement.

d.   my boss would back up the workers (with top management).

e.   the job could give me a feeling of accomplishment.

On your answer sheet enter your rankings of statements for each group.

Remember: "1" = **most important** to you in your **ideal** job: "2" = **next most important,** and so on, to "5" for **least important** to you in your **ideal** job.

---

group
13

On my ideal job . . .

    a.   I could plan my work with little supervision.

    b.   the job would provide an opportunity for advancement.

    c.   I could be "somebody" in the community.

    d.   I could tell people what to do.

    e.   I could do something different every day.

---

group
14

On my ideal job . . .

    a.   my pay would compare well with that of other workers.

    b.   the job could give me a feeling of accomplishment.

    c.   I could work alone on the job.

    d.   I could plan my work with little supervision.

    e.   I could do something that makes use of my abilities.

---

group
15

On my ideal job . . .

    a.   I could tell people what to do.

    b.   my boss would train the workers well.

    c.   my co-workers would be easy to make friends with.

    d.   I could be busy all the time.

    e.   I could work alone on the job.

---

group
16

On my ideal job . . .

    a.   the job would provide for steady employment.

    b.   my pay would compare well with that of other workers.

    c.   my boss would train the workers well.

    d.   I could be "somebody" in the community.

    e.   I could do the work without feeling that it is morally wrong.

On your answer sheet enter your rankings of statements for each group.

Remember: "1" = **most important** to you in your **ideal** job; "2" = **next most important**, and so on, to "5" for **least important** to you in your **ideal** job.

---

group
17

On my ideal job . . .

   a.   I could work alone on the job.

   b.   I could be "somebody" in the community.

   c.   I could do things for other people.

   d.   my boss would back up the workers (with top management).

   e.   I could make decisions on my own.

---

group
18

On my ideal job . . .

   a.   I could try out some of my own ideas.

   b.   I could get recognition for the work I do.

   c.   I could do something different every day.

   d.   I could work alone on the job.

   e.   the job would provide for steady employment.

---

group
19

On my ideal job . . .

   a.   the job would provide an opportunity for advancement.

   b.   I could do something that makes use of my abilities.

   c.   I could get recognition for the work I do.

   d.   I could make decisions on my own.

   e.   my boss would train the workers well.

---

group
20

On my ideal job . . .

   a.   the job would have good working conditions.

   b.   I could work alone on the job.

   c.   the company would administer its policies fairly.

   d.   the job would provide an opportunity for advancement.

   e.   I could do the work without feeling that it is morally wrong.

On your answer sheet enter your rankings of statements for each group.

Remember: "1" = **most important** to you in your **ideal** job; "2" = **next most important**, and so on, to "5" for **least important** to you in your **ideal** job.

group
21

On my ideal job . . .

a. I could be "somebody" in the community.

b. the job would have good working conditions.

c. I could be busy all the time.

d. the job could give me a feeling of accomplishment.

e. I could get recognition for the work I do.

Check your answer sheet to see that you have used the **numbers 1 to 5** to rank **every statement** in each group.

Then, continue on the next page.

On this page consider each statement and decide whether or not it is **important** to have in your **ideal** job.

- If you think that the statement is **important** for your **ideal** job, mark an X in the "**Yes**" box on your answer sheet.
- If you think that the statement is **not important** for your **ideal** job, mark an X in the "**No**" box on your answer sheet.

On my **ideal** job it is important that . . .

1. I could do something that makes use of my abilities.
2. The job could give me a feeling of accomplishment.
3. I could be busy all the time.
4. The job would provide an opportunity for advancement.
5. I could tell people what to do.
6. The company would administer its policies fairly.
7. My pay would compare well with that of other workers.
8. My co-workers would be easy to make friends with.
9. I could try out some of my own ideas.
10. I could work alone on the job.
11. I could do the work without feeling that it is morally wrong.
12. I could get recognition for the work I do.
13. I could make decisions on my own.
14. The job would provide for steady employment.
15. I could do things for other people.
16. I could be "somebody" in the community.
17. My boss would back up the workers (with top management).
18. My boss would train the workers well.
19. I could do something different every day.
20. The job would have good working conditions.
21. I could plan my work with little supervision.

Check your answer sheet to see that you have marked only one choice for each of the 21 statements.

minnesota
job description questionnaire

Form S

Confidential   **For Research Purposes Only**

On the following pages you are asked to rank statements
on the basis of how well they describe the job of:

_____

Statements about this job are in groups of five. You are asked to consider *each group* of five *individually* and rank the five statements in terms
of *how well they describe the job,* using the numbers "1" to "5." Then go
to the next group of five statements and make the same kind of ranking.

For example, your answers on a group of statements might look like
this:

Workers on this job . . .

   __4__   get full credit for the work they do.

   __3__   are of service to other people.

   __1__   have freedom to use their own judgment.

   __5__   do new and original things on their own.

   __2__   have the chance to get ahead.

This means that, of the five statements, you consider "have freedom to
use their own judgment" as most descriptive of the job; "have the
chance to get ahead" as the next most descriptive statement; and so on.

You will find some of these comparisons more difficult to make than
others, but it is *important* that you rank *every statement* in each group.

All information will be held in strictest confidence.

vocational psychology research
university of minnesota

Code Number

Please rank the five statements in each group on the basis of how well *they* describe *the job mentioned on the front page. Write a "1" by the statement which* best *describes the job; write a "2" by the statement which provides the* next best *description; continue ranking all five statements, using a "5" for the statement which describes the job* least well.

Workers on this job . . .

_____are busy all the time.

_____have work where they do things for other people.

_____try out their own ideas.

_____are paid well in comparison with other workers.

_____have opportunities for advancement.

Workers on this job . . .

_____have work where they do things for other people.

_____have something different to do every day.

_____get a feeling of accomplishment.

_____have bosses who train their workers well.

_____have a company which administers its policies fairly.

Workers on this job . . .

_____do work without feeling that it is morally wrong.

_____have bosses who back up their workers (with top management).

_____have something different to do every day.

_____make use of their individual abilities.

_____are busy all the time.

Workers on this job . . .

_____have a company which administers its policies fairly.

_____try out their own ideas.

_____make use of their individual abilities.

_____have co-workers who are easy to make friends with.

_____have the position of "somebody" in the community.

Please rank the five statements in each group on the basis of how well they describe the job written on the third page. Write a "1" by the statement which best describes the job; write a "2" by the statement which provides the next best description; continue ranking all five statements, using a "5" for the statement which describes the job least well.

Workers on this job . . .

_____have bosses who train their workers well.

_____plan their work with little supervision.

_____have bosses who back up their workers (with top management).

_____try out their own ideas.

_____have good working conditions.

Workers on this job . . .

_____receive recognition for the work they do.

_____do work without feeling that it is morally wrong.

_____plan their work with little supervision.

_____have work where they do things for other people.

_____have co-workers who are easy to make friends with.

Workers on this job . . .

_____have bosses who back up their workers (with top management).

_____have a company which administers its policies fairly.

_____are paid well in comparison with other workers.

_____receive recognition for the work they do.

_____tell other workers what to do.

Workers on this job . . .

_____have something different to do every day.

_____have co-workers who are easy to make friends with.

_____make decisions on their own.

_____have good working conditions.

_____are paid well in comparison with other workers.

---

please continue on the next page

Please rank the five statements in each group on the basis of how well they describe the job written on the third page. Write a "1" by the statement which best describes the job; write a "2" by the statement which provides the next best description; continue ranking all five statements, using a "5" for the statement which describes the job least well.

Workers on this job . . .

_____make use of their individual abilities.

_____tell other workers what to do.

_____have good working conditions.

_____have steady employment.

_____have work where they do things for other people.

Workers on this job . . .

_____make decisions on their own.

_____are busy all the time.

_____have steady employment.

_____have a company which administers its policies fairly.

_____plan their work with little supervision.

Workers on this job . . .

_____get a feeling of accomplishment.

_____make decisions on their own.

_____tell other workers what to do.

_____do work without feeling that it is morally wrong.

_____try out their own ideas.

Workers on this job . . .

_____have co-workers who are easy to make friends with.

_____have steady employment.

_____have opportunities for advancement.

_____have bosses who back up their workers (with top management).

_____get a feeling of accomplishment.

Please rank the five statements in each group on the basis of how well they describe the job written on the third page. Write a "1" by the statement which best describes the job; write a "2" by the statement which provides the next best description; continue ranking all five statements, using a "5" for the statement which describes the job least well.

Workers on this job . . .

_____plan their work with little supervision.

_____have opportunities for advancement.

_____have the position of "somebody" in the community.

_____tell other workers what to do.

_____have something different to do every day.

Workers on this job . . .

_____are paid well in comparison with other workers.

_____get a feeling of accomplishment.

_____do their work alone.

_____plan their work with little supervision.

_____make use of their individual abilities.

Workers on this job . . .

_____tell other workers what to do.

_____have bosses who train their workers well.

_____have co-workers who are easy to make friends with.

_____are busy all the time.

_____do their work alone.

Workers on this job . . .

_____have steady employment.

_____are paid well in comparison with other workers.

_____have bosses who train their workers well.

_____have the position of "somebody" in the community.

_____do work without feeling that it is morally wrong.

---

please continue on the next page

Please rank the five statements in each group on the basis of how well they describe the job written on the third page. Write a "1" by the statement which best describes the job; write a "2" by the statement which provides the next best description; continue ranking all five statements, using a "5" for the statement which describes the job least well.

Workers on this job . . .

_____do their work alone.

_____have the position of "somebody" in the community.

_____have work where they do things for other people.

_____have bosses who back up their workers (with top management).

_____make decisions on their own.

Workers on this job . . .

_____try out their own ideas.

_____receive recognition for the work they do.

_____have something different to do every day.

_____do their work alone.

_____have steady employment.

Workers on this job . . .

_____have opportunities for advancement.

_____make use of their individual abilities.

_____receive recognition for the work they do.

_____make decisions on their own.

_____have bosses who train their workers well.

Workers on this job . . .

_____have good working conditions.

_____do their work alone.

_____have a company which administers its policies fairly.

_____have opportunities for advancement.

_____do work without feeling that it is morally wrong.

Please rank these five statements.

Workers on this job . . .

_____have the position of "somebody" in the community.

_____have good working conditions.

_____are busy all the time.

_____get a feeling of accomplishment.

_____receive recognition for the work they do.

===

On the rest of this page we are asking you to do something different. *This time, consider each statement* individually *and decide* whether or not *it describes the job.*

—*If you think that the statement describes the job, circle "Yes."*

—*If you think that the statement does not describe the job, circle "No."*

Workers on this job . . .	Circle your answer for each statement	
1. make use of their individual abilities	Yes	No
2. get a feeling of accomplishment	Yes	No
3. are busy all the time	Yes	No
4. have opportunities for advancement	Yes	No
5. tell other workers what to do	Yes	No
6. have a company which administers its policies fairly	Yes	No
7. are paid well in comparison with other workers	Yes	No
8. have co-workers who are easy to make friends with	Yes	No
9. try out their own ideas	Yes	No
10. do their work alone	Yes	No
11. do work without feeling that it is morally wrong	Yes	No
12. receive recognition for the work they do	Yes	No
13. make decisions on their own	Yes	No
14. have steady employment	Yes	No
15. have work where they do things for other people	Yes	No
16. have the position of "somebody" in the community	Yes	No
17. have bosses who back up their workers (with top management)	Yes	No
18. have bosses who train their workers well	Yes	No
19. have something different to do every day	Yes	No
20. have good working conditions	Yes	No
21. plan their work with little supervision	Yes	No

please continue on the next page

Please answer these questions as a supervisor of people working on the job of_____.

1. How long have you been a supervisor of people working on this job?
   _____years   _____months

2. How many workers do you usually supervise on this job? (not including yourself)?_____
   How many are men?_____   How many are women?_____

3. Have you ever been a worker on this job? (check one)
   ☐ No
   ☐ Yes—how long did you work on this job?
   _____years   _____months

   Are you now a worker on this job, in addition to being a supervisor? (check one)
   ☐ Yes   ☐ No

4. Compared with other supervisors of people working on this job, how well would you say you are acquainted with this job? (check one)
   ☐ *Not as well acquainted* as most supervisors on this job
   ☐ *About as well acquainted* as most supervisors on this job
   ☐ *Better acquainted* than most supervisors on this job

5. Please answer the following questions about yourself.
   Sex: ☐ Male ☐ Female   Age_____
   Circle the number of years of schooling completed in *each* category.

Grade and High School	Business or Trade School	College (including graduate and professional school)
7 8 9 10 11 12	0 1 2 3 4 5	0 1 2 3 4 5 6 7

   Your job title_____

On the preceding pages you answered questions about the characteristics of the occupation written at the top of this page. Please list below **any other characteristics** which you think make people **satisfied** or **not satisfied** in that occupation.

_____

_____

_____

Thank you very much for your assistance.

minnesota satisfaction questionnaire

Vocational Psychology Research

UNIVERSITY OF MINNESOTA

Confidential

Your answers to the questions and all other information you give us will be held in strictest confidence.

Name_____Today's Date_____ 19____
       Please Print

1. Check one: ☐ Male   ☐ Female

2. When were you born?_____ 19____

3. Circle the number of years of schooling you completed:

4 5 6 7 8	9 10 11 12	13 14 15 16	17 18 19 20
Grade School	High School	College	Graduate or Professional School

4. What is your present job called?_____

_____

5. What do you do on your present job?_____

_____

_____

6. How long have you been on your present job?_____years _____months

7. What would you call your **occupation,** your usual line of work?_____

_____

8. How long have you been in this line of work?_____years _____months

minnesota satisfaction questionnaire

The purpose of this questionnaire is to give you a chance to tell **how you feel about your present job,** what things you are **satisfied** with and what things you are **not satisfied** with.

On the basis of your answers and those of people like you, we hope to get a better understanding of the things people **like and dislike about their jobs.**

On the following pages you will find statements about your **present** job.

- Read each statement carefully.

- Decide **how satisfied you feel about the aspect of your job** described by the statement.

  Keeping the statement in mind:

  — if you feel that your job gives you **more than you expected,** check the box under **"Very Sat."** (Very Satisfied);

  — if you feel that your job gives you **what you expected,** check the box under **"Sat."** (Satisfied);

  — if you **cannot make up your mind** whether or not the job gives you what you expected, check the box under **"N"** (Neither Satisfied nor Dissatisfied);

  — If you feel that your job gives you **less than you expected,** check the box under **"Dissat."** (Dissatisfied);

  — if you feel that your job gives you **much less than you expected,** check the box under **"Very Dissat."** (Very Dissatisfied).

- Remember: Keep the statement in mind when deciding **how satisfied you feel about that aspect of your job.**

- Do this for **all** statements. Please answer **every** item.

Be frank and honest. Give a true picture of your feelings about your **present job.**

Ask yourself: How **satisfied** *am I with this aspect of my job?*

> **Very Sat.** *means I am very satisfied with this aspect of my job.*
>
> **Sat.** *means I am satisfied with this aspect of my job.*
>
> **N** *means I can't decide whether I am satisfied or not with this aspect of my job.*
>
> **Dissat.** *means I am dissatisfied with this aspect of my job.*
>
> **Very Dissat.** *means I am very dissatisfied with this aspect of my job.*

On my present job, this is how I feel about . . .	Very Dissat.	Dissat.	N	Sat.	Very Sat.
1. The chance to be of service to others.	☐	☐	☐	☐	☐
2. The chance to try out some of my own ideas.	☐	☐	☐	☐	☐
3. Being able to do the job without feeling it is morally wrong.	☐	☐	☐	☐	☐
4. The chance to work by myself.	☐	☐	☐	☐	☐
5. The variety in my work.	☐	☐	☐	☐	☐
6. The chance to have other workers look to me for direction.	☐	☐	☐	☐	☐
7. The chance to do the kind of work that I do best.	☐	☐	☐	☐	☐
8. The social position in the community that goes with the job.	☐	☐	☐	☐	☐
9. The policies and practices toward employees of this company.	☐	☐	☐	☐	☐
10. The way my supervisor and I understand each other.	☐	☐	☐	☐	☐
11. My job security.	☐	☐	☐	☐	☐
12. The amount of pay for the work I do.	☐	☐	☐	☐	☐
13. The working conditions (heating, lighting, ventilation, etc.) on this job.	☐	☐	☐	☐	☐
14. The opportunities for advancement on this job.	☐	☐	☐	☐	☐
15. The technical "know-how" of my supervisor.	☐	☐	☐	☐	☐
16. The spirit of cooperation among my co-workers.	☐	☐	☐	☐	☐
17. The chance to be responsible for planning my work.	☐	☐	☐	☐	☐
18. The way I am noticed when I do a good job.	☐	☐	☐	☐	☐
19. Being able to see the results of the work I do.	☐	☐	☐	☐	☐
20. The chance to be active much of the time.	☐	☐	☐	☐	☐
21. The chance to be of service to people.	☐	☐	☐	☐	☐
22. The chance to do new and original things on my own.	☐	☐	☐	☐	☐
23. Being able to do things that don't go against my religious beliefs.	☐	☐	☐	☐	☐
24. The chance to work alone on the job.	☐	☐	☐	☐	☐
25. The chance to do different things from time to time.	☐	☐	☐	☐	☐
	Very Dissat.	Dissat.	N	Sat.	Very Sat.

Ask yourself: How **satisfied** am I with this aspect of my job?

    Very Sat. means I am very satisfied with this aspect of my job.

    Sat. means I am satisfied with this aspect of my job.

    N means I can't decide whether I am satisfied or not with this aspect of my job.

    Dissat. means I am dissatisfied with this aspect of my job.

    Very Dissat. means I am very dissatisfied with this aspect of my job.

On my present job, this is how I feel about . . .	Very Dissat.	Dissat.	N	Sat.	Very Sat.
26. The chance to tell other workers how to do things.	☐	☐	☐	☐	☐
27. The chance to do work that is well suited to my abilities.	☐	☐	☐	☐	☐
28. The chance to be "somebody" in the community.	☐	☐	☐	☐	☐
29. Company policies and the way in which they are administered.	☐	☐	☐	☐	☐
30. The way my boss handles his/her employees.	☐	☐	☐	☐	☐
31. The way my job provides for a secure future.	☐	☐	☐	☐	☐
32. The chance to make as much money as my friends.	☐	☐	☐	☐	☐
33. The physical surroundings where I work.	☐	☐	☐	☐	☐
34. The chances of getting ahead on this job.	☐	☐	☐	☐	☐
35. The competence of my supervisor in making decisions.	☐	☐	☐	☐	☐
36. The chance to develop close friendships with my co-workers.	☐	☐	☐	☐	☐
37. The chance to make decisions on my own.	☐	☐	☐	☐	☐
38. The way I get full credit for the work I do.	☐	☐	☐	☐	☐
39. Being able to take pride in a job well done.	☐	☐	☐	☐	☐
40. Being able to do something much of the time.	☐	☐	☐	☐	☐
41. The chance to help people.	☐	☐	☐	☐	☐
42. The chance to try something different.	☐	☐	☐	☐	☐
43. Being able to do things that don't go against my conscience.	☐	☐	☐	☐	☐
44. The chance to be alone on the job.	☐	☐	☐	☐	☐
45. The routine in my work.	☐	☐	☐	☐	☐
46. The chance to supervise other people.	☐	☐	☐	☐	☐
47. The chance to make use of my best abilities.	☐	☐	☐	☐	☐
48. The chance to "rub elbows" with important people.	☐	☐	☐	☐	☐
49. The way employees are informed about company policies.	☐	☐	☐	☐	☐
50. The way my boss backs up his/her employees (with top management).	☐	☐	☐	☐	☐
	Very Dissat.	Dissat.	N	Sat.	Very Sat.

Ask yourself: How **satisfied** *am I with this aspect of my job?*

Very Sat. *means I am very satisfied with this aspect of my job.*

Sat. *means I am satisfied with this aspect of my job.*

N *means I can't decide whether I am satisfied or not with this aspect of my job.*

Dissat. *means I am dissatisfied with this aspect of my job.*

Very Dissat. *means I am very dissatisfied with this aspect of my job.*

On my present job, this is how I feel about . . .	Very Dissat.	Dissat.	N	Sat.	Very Sat.
51. The way my job provides for steady employment.	☐	☐	☐	☐	☐
52. How my pay compares with that for similar jobs in other companies.	☐	☐	☐	☐	☐
53. The pleasantness of the working conditions.	☐	☐	☐	☐	☐
54. The way promotions are given out on this job.	☐	☐	☐	☐	☐
55. The way my boss delegates work to others.	☐	☐	☐	☐	☐
56. The friendliness of my co-workers.	☐	☐	☐	☐	☐
57. The chance to be responsible for the work of others.	☐	☐	☐	☐	☐
58. The recognition I get for the work I do.	☐	☐	☐	☐	☐
59. Being able to do something worthwhile.	☐	☐	☐	☐	☐
60. Being able to stay busy.	☐	☐	☐	☐	☐
61. The chance to do things for other people.	☐	☐	☐	☐	☐
62. The chance to develop new and better ways to do the job.	☐	☐	☐	☐	☐
63. The chance to do things that don't harm other people.	☐	☐	☐	☐	☐
64. The chance to work independently of others.	☐	☐	☐	☐	☐
65. The chance to do something different every day.	☐	☐	☐	☐	☐
66. The chance to tell people what to do.	☐	☐	☐	☐	☐
67. The chance to do something that makes use of my abilities.	☐	☐	☐	☐	☐
68. The chance to be important in the eyes of others.	☐	☐	☐	☐	☐
69. The way company policies are put into practice.	☐	☐	☐	☐	☐
70. The way my boss takes care of the complaints of his/her employees.	☐	☐	☐	☐	☐
71. How steady my job is.	☐	☐	☐	☐	☐
72. My pay and the amount of work I do.	☐	☐	☐	☐	☐
73. The physical working conditions of the job.	☐	☐	☐	☐	☐
74. The chances for advancement on this job.	☐	☐	☐	☐	☐
75. The way my boss provides help on hard problems.	☐	☐	☐	☐	☐
	Very Dissat.	Dissat.	N	Sat.	Very Sat.

Ask yourself: How **satisfied** *am I with this aspect of my job?*

     Very Sat. *means I am very satisfied with this aspect of my job.*

     Sat. *means I am satisfied with this aspect of my job.*

     N *means I can't decide whether I am satisfied or not with this aspect of my job.*

     Dissat. *means I am dissatisfied with this aspect of my job.*

     Very Dissat. *means I am very dissatisfied with this aspect of my job.*

On my present job, this is how I feel about . . .	Very Dissat.	Dissat.	N	Sat.	Very Sat.
76. The way my co-workers are easy to make friends with.	☐	☐	☐	☐	☐
77. The freedom to use my own judgment.	☐	☐	☐	☐	☐
78. The way they usually tell me when I do my job well.	☐	☐	☐	☐	☐
79. The chance to do my best at all times.	☐	☐	☐	☐	☐
80. The chance to be "on the go" all the time.	☐	☐	☐	☐	☐
81. The chance to be of some small service to other people.	☐	☐	☐	☐	☐
82. The chance to try my own methods of doing the job.	☐	☐	☐	☐	☐
83. The chance to do the job without feeling I am cheating anyone.	☐	☐	☐	☐	☐
84. The chance to work away from others.	☐	☐	☐	☐	☐
85. The chance to do many different things on the job.	☐	☐	☐	☐	☐
86. The chance to tell others what to do.	☐	☐	☐	☐	☐
87. The chance to make use of my abilities and skills.	☐	☐	☐	☐	☐
88. The chance to have a definite place in the community.	☐	☐	☐	☐	☐
89. The way the company treats its employees.	☐	☐	☐	☐	☐
90. The personal relationship between my boss and his/her employees.	☐	☐	☐	☐	☐
91. The way layoffs and transfers are avoided in my job.	☐	☐	☐	☐	☐
92. How my pay compares with that of other workers.	☐	☐	☐	☐	☐
93. The working conditions.	☐	☐	☐	☐	☐
94. My chances for advancement.	☐	☐	☐	☐	☐
95. The way my boss trains his/her employees.	☐	☐	☐	☐	☐
96. The way my co-workers get along with each other.	☐	☐	☐	☐	☐
97. The responsibility of my job.	☐	☐	☐	☐	☐
98. The praise I get for doing a good job.	☐	☐	☐	☐	☐
99. The feeling of accomplishment I get from the job.	☐	☐	☐	☐	☐
100. Being able to keep busy all the time.	☐	☐	☐	☐	☐
	Very Dissat.	Dissat.	N	Sat.	Very Sat.

minnesota
satisfactoriness
scales

Vocational Psychology Research

UNIVERSITY OF MINNESOTA

Employee Name _____ Job _____

Rated by _____ Date _____

> Please check the best answer for each question
>
> Be sure to answer all questions

	not as well	*about the same*	*better*
Compared to others in his/her work group, how well does the employee . . .			
1. Follow company policies and practices?	☐	☐	☐
2. Accept the direction of his/her supervisor?	☐	☐	☐
3. Follow standard work rules and procedures?	☐	☐	☐
4. Accept the responsibility of his/her job?	☐	☐	☐
5. Adapt to changes in procedures or methods?	☐	☐	☐
6. Respect the authority of his/her supervisor?	☐	☐	☐
7. Work as a member of a team?	☐	☐	☐
8. Get along with his/her supervisors?	☐	☐	☐
9. Perform repetitive tasks?	☐	☐	☐
10. Get along with his/her co-workers?	☐	☐	☐
11. Perform tasks requiring variety and change in methods?	☐	☐	☐

	not as good	*about the same*	*better*
Compared to others in his/her work group . . .			
12. How good is the quality of his/her work?	☐	☐	☐
13. How good is the quantity of his/her work?	☐	☐	☐

	yes	*not sure*	*no*
If you could make the decision, would you . . .			
14. Give him/her a pay raise?	☐	☐	☐
15. Transfer him/her to a job at a higher level?	☐	☐	☐
16. Promote him/her to a position of more responsibility?	☐	☐	☐

> Please check the best answer for each question
>
> Be sure to answer all questions

Compared to others in his/her work group, how often does the employee . . .

	less	about the same	more
17. Come late for work?	☐	☐	☐
18. Become overexcited?	☐	☐	☐
19. Become upset and unhappy?	☐	☐	☐
20. Need disciplinary action?	☐	☐	☐
21. Stay absent from work?	☐	☐	☐
22. Seem bothered by something?	☐	☐	☐
23. Complain about physical ailments?	☐	☐	☐
24. Say 'odd' things?	☐	☐	☐
25. Seem to tire easily?	☐	☐	☐
26. Act as if he/she is not listening when spoken to?	☐	☐	☐
27. Wander from subject to subject when talking?	☐	☐	☐

28. Now will you please consider this worker with respect to overall competence, the effectiveness of job performance, proficiency, and general overall value. Take into account all the elements of successful job performance, such as knowledge of the job and functions performed, quantity and quality of output, relations with other people (subordinates, equals, superiors), ability to get the work done, intelligence, interest, response to training, and the like. In other words, how closely does he/she approximate the ideal, the kind of worker you want more of? With all these factors in mind, where would you rank this worker as compared with the other people whom you now have doing the same work? (or, if he/she is the only one, how does he/she compare with those who have done the same work in the past?)

In the top ¼ .... ☐

In the top half but not among the top ¼ .... ☐

In the bottom half but not among the lowest ¼ .... ☐

In the lowest ¼ .... ☐

Biographical Information
Vocational Assessment Clinic

This form is designed to obtain information about your personal history that will be useful in vocational assessment. It consists of three parts: Part I asks about your educational history, work history, and vocationally related activities; Part II asks for information about your childhood and adolescent years; and Part III asks about your present situation. (Use the back of the page for additional information that does not fit in the space given.)

Part I

Section A: Educational History

1. How many years of school have you finished?
   _____ less than high school graduate
   _____ high school graduate
   _____ voc/tech school graduate
   _____ some college
   _____ college graduate
   _____ some graduate work or professional school
   _____ graduate or professional degree

2. Rank the following types of courses putting first (Rank 1) that area in which you had the most courses in junior high school and/or high school, and putting last (Rank 5) that area in which you had the fewest courses.
   Business   1. _____
   Math   2. _____
   Science   3. _____
   Shop/Technical 4. _____
   Social Studies 5. _____

3. List and describe below job-related training and/or education you have had beyond high school training. (This would include any trade school, college or university, vocational-technical or business school, correspondence, extension or special courses or programs, apprenticeship or service school.)

Where Taken	Dates	Course Program or Major Area of Study	Degree or Certification
_____	___ to ___	_____	_____
_____	___ to ___	_____	_____
_____	___ to ___	_____	_____
_____	___ to ___	_____	_____
_____	___ to ___	_____	_____
_____	___ to ___	_____	_____

4. Have you taken any independent study/reading courses? ☐ yes ☐ no
   If yes, how many? _____

5. List any self-improvement courses you have taken (e.g., human relations, assertiveness training, Dale Carnegie, speed reading, how-to-study).
   _____
   _____

Section B: Work History

1. At what age did you start working regularly for pay? _____
   ☐ part-time   or   ☐ full-time?

2. How many different jobs have you had in the last five years? _____

3. List and describe below and on the following page your *last five* jobs *beginning with your current or most recent job.* (Do not include military service.)
   Job Title _____
   Employer/Address _____
   Dates: _____ to _____   Pay per month $_____   Hours per week_____
   Describe what you do (did) on this job _____
   _____

   How do (did) you like this job? (Check one)
         ☐ I hate(d) it   ☐ I like(d) it
         ☐ I dislike(d) it   ☐ I am (was) enthusiastic about it
         ☐ I don't (didn't) like it   ☐ I love(d) it
         ☐ I am (was) indifferent to it
   Job Title _____
   Employer/Address _____
   Dates: _____ to _____   Pay per month $_____   Hours per week_____
   Describe what you do (did) on this job _____
   _____

   Did you like this job? (Check one)
         ☐ I liked it
         ☐ It was okay
         ☐ I mostly didn't like it
   Job Title _____
   Employer/Address _____
   Dates: _____ to _____   Pay per month $_____   Hours per week_____
   Describe what you do (did) on this job _____
   _____

   Did you like this job? (Check one)
         ☐ I liked it
         ☐ It was okay
         ☐ I mostly didn't like it
   Job Title _____
   Employer/Address _____
   Dates: _____ to _____   Pay per month $_____   Hours per week_____
   Describe what you do (did) on this job _____
   _____

   Did you like this job? (Check one)
         ☐ I liked it
         ☐ It was okay
         ☐ I mostly didn't like it
   Job Title _____
   Employer/Address _____
   Dates: _____ to _____   Pay per month $_____   Hours per week_____
   Describe what you do (did) on this job _____
   _____

   Did you like this job? (Check one)
         ☐ I liked it

☐ It was okay
☐ I mostly didn't like it

4. Which one of the jobs on the preceding pages did you hold for the *longest* period of time? _____

5. Which one of the jobs did you *like best*? _____

6. If these jobs (longest and liked best) are the same, only check the boxes under *longest*. If these jobs are *not* the same, check the boxes on the left for the job you held the *longest* and the boxes on the right for the job you *liked best*.

	Longest	*Liked best*
Did you see the finished product of your work?	☐ yes ☐ sometimes ☐ no	☐ yes ☐ sometimes ☐ no
Did you supervise others?	☐ yes ☐ no	☐ yes ☐ no
Did you develop projects that others completed?	☐ yes ☐ no	☐ yes ☐ no
Did you receive praise from your supervisor well done?	☐ yes ☐ no	☐ yes ☐ no
How much time did you spend outdoors?	☐ most or all ☐ about half ☐ little or none	☐ most or all ☐ about half ☐ little or none
Did you have much free time on the job?	☐ yes ☐ sometimes ☐ no	☐ yes ☐ sometimes ☐ no
How did you work most of the time?	☐ alone ☐ with a few people ☐ with many people	☐ alone ☐ with a few people ☐ with many people
How were you supervised?	☐ supervised most of the time ☐ not supervised most of the time	☐ supervised most of the time ☐ not supervised most of the time
Who set your work routine?	☐ followed a set routine, paced for you ☐ operated within a loose routine, paced yourself ☐ established your own routine and pacing	☐ followed a set routine, paced for you ☐ operated within a loose routine, paced yourself ☐ established your own routine and pacing

7. Have you ever:

created or redesigned your own job?	☐ yes ☐ no
suggested changes in company policy or practice?	☐ yes ☐ no
asked for a raise in pay?	☐ yes ☐ no
refused to do a task required by your job?	☐ yes ☐ no
put off doing tasks required by your job until you didn't have to do them?	☐ yes ☐ no
changed work methods in your job?	☐ yes ☐ no

8. For *each* of the following work tasks, check *one* of the boxes (seldom, sometimes, or frequently) for the job you held the *longest*; then check *one* of the boxes for the job you *liked best*. If these jobs are the same, check only the boxes under *longest*.

	Longest			Liked Best		
	Seldom	Some-times	Fre-quently	Seldom	Some-times	Fre-quently
Working with numbers	☐	☐	☐	☐	☐	☐
Working with words, ideas	☐	☐	☐	☐	☐	☐
Working with forms patterns, graphs	☐	☐	☐	☐	☐	☐
Advising or counseling others	☐	☐	☐	☐	☐	☐
Waiting on people	☐	☐	☐	☐	☐	☐
Teaching or supervising	☐	☐	☐	☐	☐	☐
Speaking to or com-municating with others	☐	☐	☐	☐	☐	☐
Selling or entertaining	☐	☐	☐	☐	☐	☐
Placing or moving large objects	☐	☐	☐	☐	☐	☐
Driving or steering equipment	☐	☐	☐	☐	☐	☐
Handling small objects, use of fingers (like typing)	☐	☐	☐	☐	☐	☐
Observing or tending things or machines	☐	☐	☐	☐	☐	☐

9. How many jobs have you obtained:

        through friends or family? _____

        through a placement or employment agency? _____

        through being contacted by the company? _____

        through want ads or applying in person? _____

10. Were you ever in the military service? ☐ yes ☐ no

        If yes: What branch? _____

        How long? _____ years

        Rank at entry? _____

        Rank at discharge? _____

        Awards? (List) _____

        Did you receive any occupational training? ☐ yes ☐ no

        If yes, for what occupation(s)? _____

        Type of discharge _____

        How did you feel about the military service?

            ☐ I liked it   ☐ It was okay   ☐ I mostly didn't like it

Section C: Related Activities

1. For each of the following general kinds of activities check *one* of the boxes (seldom, sometimes, or frequently) that best describes how much you were involved in that kind of activity in the *last five years*.

	Seldom or not at all	Some-times	Fre-quently
Team sports like basketball or hockey	☐	☐	☐
Fixing things, working on cars	☐	☐	☐
Eating out	☐	☐	☐
Activities like model building or watch repair	☐	☐	☐

	Seldom or not at all	Some-times	Fre-quently
Individual sports like skiing, bowling	☐	☐	☐
Walking or jogging	☐	☐	☐
Self-improvement activities like physical fitness, yoga	☐	☐	☐
Driving around	☐	☐	☐
Outdoor activities (other than sports)	☐	☐	☐
Attending art galleries, concerts, plays	☐	☐	☐
Home carpentry, repairs or painting	☐	☐	☐
Watching television, weekly serials or sports	☐	☐	☐
Watching plays, documentaries, educational TV	☐	☐	☐
Playing musical instruments or singing	☐	☐	☐
Composing music, writing stories, designing	☐	☐	☐
Craft activities like knitting, leatherwork	☐	☐	☐
Games like pool, pinball or cards	☐	☐	☐
Listening to music	☐	☐	☐
Going to the movies	☐	☐	☐
Housework or household activities	☐	☐	☐
Activities like carving or composing photographs	☐	☐	☐
Attending sports events, drag races	☐	☐	☐
Going to taverns or bars	☐	☐	☐
Reading best sellers	☐	☐	☐
Playing bingo, games of chance	☐	☐	☐
Reading classical literature or history	☐	☐	☐
Stamp collecting or working crossword puzzles	☐	☐	☐
Reading community newspapers, magazines like *McCall's*	☐	☐	☐
Reading books, reports, manuals that relate to your job	☐	☐	☐
Reading newspapers and magazines like *Time, Newsweek*	☐	☐	☐
Writing letters to newspapers, city hall, Congressmen	☐	☐	☐

2. List the awards or prizes you have received for things you have done. _____

3. What kinds of organizations or clubs have you been a member of in the *past five years*?
    What offices or active committee memberships have you held?
    Community organizations: (name/office held) _____
    _____
    Church or religious organizations: (name/office held) _____
    _____
    Hobby, interest, or study groups: (name/office held) _____
    _____
    Political organizations: (name/office held) _____
    _____
    Social organizations: (name/office held) _____
    _____
    Business, trade, labor union, or professional organizations: (name/office held) _____
    _____

4. Do you have any health problems that limit your activities?   ☐ yes ☐ no

5. How many times in the last five years have you been hospitalized for longer than a
    week? (Do not count hospitalizations for check-ups.) _____

6. How many houses or apartments have you lived in in the last five years? _____

Part II

The questions in this part of the form are about *the time period before you were 18 years old*. Answer the questions with that time period in mind.

1. How many adults did you typically live with? _____

2. How many people younger than you did you typically live with? _____

3. How many years did you live on a farm? _____   in a small town or city (less than 100,000)? _____   in a large city? _____

4. Number of different communities or cities you lived in _____

5. Number of different residences you lived in (count each address, including apartment houses) _____

6. Did you leave home before age 18?   ☐ yes   ☐ no

7. What work did you do for pay during this period? (Check all that apply)
   _____ babysitting   _____ store clerk
   _____ paper route   _____ farm work, laborer
   _____ busboy, waitress   _____ other (name them) _____

8. How did you spend your free time outside work or school?
   ☐ mostly alone
   ☐ mostly with one or two friends
   ☐ mostly in groups of three or more

9. Did you have any health problems that restricted your activities?
   ☐ yes   ☐ no   If yes, what were these? _____
   _____

10. How many times were you hospitalized for longer than a week? (Do not count hospitalizations for check-ups.) _____

11. Did you attend public school?   ☐ yes   ☐ no   If yes, how many years? _____

12. Did you attend private or parochial schools?   ☐ yes   ☐ no
    If yes, for how many years? _____

13. In school did you break the rules? (Check one)
    ☐ never   ☐ sometimes
    ☐ almost never   ☐ frequently

14. In school were you punished for breaking the rules? (Check one)
    ☐ never   ☐ sometimes
    ☐ almost never   ☐ frequently

15. For *each* of the following activities check *one* of the boxes (seldom, sometimes, or frequently) that best describes how much you were into that kind of activity.

	Seldom or not at all	Some-times	Fre-quently
Art work or craft activities	☐	☐	☐
Building or fixing things	☐	☐	☐
Community activities, organizations	☐	☐	☐
Dancing	☐	☐	☐
Extra-curricular school activities	☐	☐	☐
Going to concerts	☐	☐	☐
Going to the movies	☐	☐	☐
Hanging around	☐	☐	☐
Housework or household tasks	☐	☐	☐
Listening to music	☐	☐	☐
Outdoor activities other than sports	☐	☐	☐
Playing musical instruments or singing	☐	☐	☐
Reading	☐	☐	☐
Sports	☐	☐	☐
Television	☐	☐	☐
Time with friends	☐	☐	☐
Working	☐	☐	☐

16. Were you happy with your life during this period of time? (Check one)

☐ yes   ☐ somewhat   ☐ no

Part III

The following questions are about your present situation.

1. How many people do you live with *now*? _____

2. How many are over the age of 16? _____

3. How many times have you been married? _____

4. If you are currently married, how long have you been married? _____ years

5. Spouse's age _____, years of education _____, occupation _____

6. Father's age _____, years of education _____, occupation _____

7. Mother's age _____, years of education _____, occupation _____

8. List your brothers' and sisters' ages, years of education, and occupation.

	Age	*Yrs. of Ed.*	*Occupation*
Brothers	____	_____	_____
	____	_____	_____
	____	_____	_____
Sisters	____	_____	_____
	____	_____	_____
	____	_____	_____

9. List your children's ages, sex, years of education, and occupation (if any).

Age	*Sex*	*Yrs. of Ed.*	*Occupation*
___	___	___	_____
___	___	___	_____
___	___	___	_____
___	___	___	_____

10. How many people do you see *socially* outside work on a weekly basis? _____

11. How many of them are from a high income level? _____

12. How many are from a lower income level? _____

13. Of the people you see weekly, how many do you know through work? _____

14. In your home who makes the decisions about paying bills? (Check one only)
    ☐ yourself   ☐ other person
    ☐ you and other person   ☐ not relevant to you

15. Who makes decisions about caring for or disciplining the children? (Check one only)
    ☐ yourself   ☐ other person
    ☐ you and other person   ☐ not relevant to you

16. Who makes the decisions about what you do for fun or entertainment? (Check one only)
    ☐ yourself   ☐ other person
    ☐ you and other person   ☐ not relevant to you

17. Do you keep a budget and account of your spending? (Check one)
    ☐ keep exact records and follow a budget
    ☐ keep records and manage according to a general plan
    ☐ never budget or keep records

18. Do you know how much retirement income you will have? (Check one)
    ☐ yes, exactly
    ☐ yes, generally
    ☐ no

19. How much life insurance do you have? (Check one)
    ☐ none
    ☐ less than three times my yearly earnings
    ☐ three times my yearly earnings or more
    ☐ don't really know

20. How many dependents other than yourself do you support? _____

21. In a *typical week*, how much time do you spend:

	none or a few hours	5 to 10 hours	10 to 20 hours	over 20 hours
Working (including work in the home, also transportation to and from work)	☐	☐	☐	☐
Personal activities like dressing, grooming, eating	☐	☐	☐	☐
Television	☐	☐	☐	☐
Organization activities	☐	☐	☐	☐

	none or a few hours	5 to 10 hours	10 to 20 hours	over 20 hours
Time with people in your home	☐	☐	☐	☐
Time with people from outside your home	☐	☐	☐	☐
Physical exercise	☐	☐	☐	☐
Hobbies or interest activities	☐	☐	☐	☐
Attending classes and doing class homework	☐	☐	☐	☐
Reading (other than for school)	☐	☐	☐	☐
Other (please describe):				
_____	☐	☐	☐	☐
_____	☐	☐	☐	☐

Release of Information Request
Vocational Assessment Clinic

In order to improve our services to you and to people who seek vocational counseling in the future, we are developing a clinic service which will continuously require information and feedback about approaches to vocational choice and decision-making. In this work we would like your assistance and suggestions and would appreciate comments you could make to your counselor. We would also like to obtain your permission to use testing and other information for vocational research and are therefore asking you to read the following paragraph and sign, if you are willing to assist us.

_____

I understand that the information obtained in this questionnaire and other test sources will be used for counseling purposes, including consultations by the Clinic staff. I also agree that the information developed by the staff may be used for research purposes, with the understanding that any and all information will be confidential. If information is used subsequently for research, I have been informed that I will not be identified by name, nor in any manner which would make my identity known.

Signed: _____

Counselor: _____

Date: _____

Personality Style Rating Form, Experimental

Celerity — quickness of response in interacting with the environment.

Low _____ High
     1   2   3   4   5

Pace — level of effort typically expended in interaction with the environment.

Low _____ High
     1   2   3   4   5

Rhythm — typical pattern of pace.

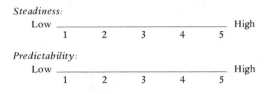

    Steadiness:
    Low _____ High
         1   2   3   4   5

    Predictability:
    Low _____ High
         1   2   3   4   5

Endurance — likelihood of maintaining interaction with the environment.

Low _____ High
     1   2   3   4   5

Adjustment Style Rating Form, Experimental

Flexibility — tolerance for discorrespondence with the environment before acting to reduce the discorrespondence.

Low _____ High
     1   2   3   4   5

Activeness — likelihood of acting to change the environment to reduce discorrespondence.

Low _____ High
     1   2   3   4   5

Reactiveness — likelihood of acting on self to change the expression of personality structure to reduce discorrespondence.

Low _____ High
     1   2   3   4   5

Perseverance — likelihood of maintaining adjustment behavior under conditions of continuing discorrespondence.

Low _____ High
     1   2   3   4   5

Appendix B
The Minnesota Importance
Questionnaire (MIQ) Report

MIQ answer sheets are computer scored by Vocational Psychology Research, Department of Psychology, University of Minnesota, 75 East River Road, Minneapolis, MN, 55455. Hand-scoring the MIQ is very time-consuming. A computer-generated printout provides a profile of need and value scores on the first page and a listing of occupations for which satisfaction is predicted or not predicted on the second page. Figure 1 shows a standard MIQ computer report.

The report in Figure 1 presents the following information: In the upper left-hand corner of the first page, following the date of administration, an LCT (Logically Consistent Triad) score is shown. This score represents the degree of logical consistency of response of the individual.

The MIQ need scales, with their abbreviated scale statements, are listed in the left-hand column in six groups according to their membership in a value cluster. The value clusters are ordered to reflect diametrically opposed values. The Achievement Value is followed by the contrasting Comfort Value. In similar fashion, the Status Value is followed by the Altruism Value and the Safety Value by the Autonomy Value.

Need scores are given for each need scale under the column heading "Score." While need scores can range from −4.0 to +4.0, in practice almost all scores will fall within the range from −1.0 to +3.0, the scale that is used in the report. The score for each need scale is plotted as an "X" and is usually accompanied by dashes on either side of the "X" to indicate the range within which this score might have varied had the individual been more consistent in responding.

Similarly, the score for each value is plotted as a "V," and the score itself is identified by an asterisk. (Any obtained scores that are lower than −1.0 or higher than +3.0 are plotted at −1.0 or +3.0 respectively, using XX.)

The profile scale, shown on the top and bottom of the MIQ report, may be regarded as a scale of importance of each need to the individual. The scale range is divided into regions of Importance and Unimportance by a 0.0 point. These regions are indicated by "Important" and "Unimp."

The second page of the MIQ report lists ninety representative, or benchmark, occupations grouped into six clusters. These clusters designate groups of occupations with similar Occupational Reinforcer Patterns. An Occupational Reinforcer Pattern (ORP) describes the reinforcers for the 20 MIQ needs present in an occupation. A separate ORP has been developed for each of these occupations.

Each cluster is characterized by a predominant reinforcer pattern expressed in value terms. For example, Cluster A (ACH-AUT-Alt) lists occupations for which the reinforcers for the Achievement (ACH) and Autonomy (AUT) values are high and the reinforcers for Altruism (Alt) value are moderate. Within each cluster, the 15 representative occupations are listed in alphabetical order.

Next to this listing, the column labeled the "C Index" gives the correspondence index. This index indicates the degree to which the individual's MIQ profile corresponds to the ORP of each occupation that is listed. The C Index is a correlation coefficient and may, therefore, range from −1.00 to +1.00. The closer the C Index is to +1.00, the higher is the correspondence of the MIQ profile to the ORP. Conversely, the closer the C Index is to the −1.00 end of the possible range, the higher is the discorrespondence between MIQ profile and ORP.

The column labeled "Pred. Sat." (predicted satisfaction) lists a symbol S, L, or N for each occupation. S (satisfied) indicates a high probability of satisfaction with the occupation; L (likely satisfied) indicates a moderate probability; and N (not satisfied) indicates little or no probability of satisfaction. The ranges of correlation coefficients (C Index) are from +0.50 to +1.00 for S, +0.10 to +0.49 for L, and −1.00 to +0.09 for N.

In addition to the standard MIQ report, an extended MIQ report may be requested. The extended report differs from the standard report in that it provides correspondence information for all occupations for which ORP information is available. The advantage of the extended report is that, in addition to the 90 benchmark occupations, other occupations are shown in their appropriate clusters. Within each cluster, occupations are listed alphabetically.

With either the standard or extended MIQ reports, additional copies of the report, and/or sets of punched data cards containing MIQ scale scores, may be requested.

In the event that an individual's LCT (Logically Consistent Triad) score drops below *33%* for the paired form or *50%* for the ranked form, the MIQ profile is considered to be questionable because of the extraordinarily high level of inconsistent response. In such cases, the MIQ report is accompanied by an additional report containing an analysis of the distribution, by scale, of the response inconsistency. An example of such a report is shown in Figure 2.

In Figure 2, the LCT score is given along with the score designating the point at which responses become questionable from a logical consistency standpoint. The report also indicates whether or not the inconsistency of response shows a pattern of random or nonrandom responding (in Figure 2 this pattern is shown to be nonrandom). The report then lists the 20 MIQ scales in increasing order of consistency and provides a Scale Logically-Consistent-Triad score (Scale LCT %) for each scale. A logically consistent triad is defined as a pattern of response in which A is chosen over B, B over C, and A over C. (By contrast, a logically inconsistent triad is one where A is chosen over B, B over C, and C over A, which does not follow logically from the first two choices.) The higher Scale LCT % scores indicate higher degrees of logical consistency.

Figure 1

A Sample MIQ Report

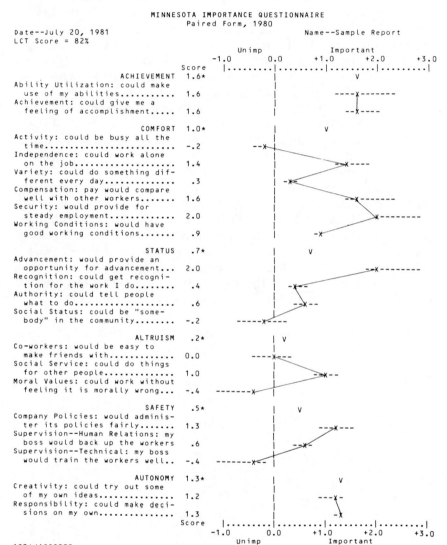

MINNESOTA IMPORTANCE QUESTIONNAIRE
Paired Form, 1980

Date--July 20, 1981   Name--Sample Report
LCT Score = 82%

Figure 1, continued

MINNESOTA IMPORTANCE QUESTIONNAIRE

Correspondence Report for Sample Report   Date: July 20, 1981
MIQ profile is compared with Occupational Reinforcer Patterns (ORP'S)
for 90 representative occupations. Correspondence is indicated by
the C-Index. A prediction of Satisfied (S) results from C values
greater than .50, Likely Satisfied (L) for C values between .10 and
.49, and Not Satisfied (N) for C values less than .10. Occupations
are clustered by similarity of Occupational Reinforcer Pattern.

	C Index	Pred. Sat.		C Index	Pred. Sat.
Cluster A (ACH-AUT-Alt)	.30	L	Cluster B (ACH-Com)	.15	L
Architect	.25	L	Bricklayer	-.07	N
Dentist	.21	L	Carpenter	.24	L
Family Practitioner (M.D.)	.21	L	Cement Mason	-.16	N
Interior Designer-Decorator	.43	L	Elevator Repairer	.48	L
Lawyer	.35	L	Heavy Equipment Operator	.30	L
Minister	.13	L	Landscape Gardener	-.11	N
Nurse, Occupational Health	.12	L	Lather	-.05	N
Occupational Therapist	.33	L	Millwright	.10	L
Optometrist	.39	L	Painter/Paperhanger	.11	L
Psychologist, Counseling	.21	L	Patternmaker, Metal	.28	L
Recreation Leader	.15	L	Pipefitter	.34	L
Speech Pathologist	.28	L	Plasterer	-.13	N
Teacher, Elementary School	.23	L	Plumber	.37	L
Teacher, Secondary School	.28	L	Roofer	-.04	N
Vocational Evaluator	.36	L	Salesperson, Automobile	.43	L
Cluster C (ACH-Aut-Com)	.44	L	Cluster D (ACH-STA-Com)	.57	S
Alteration Tailor	.27	L	Accountant, Certified Public	.43	L
Automobile Mechanic	.25	L	Airplane Co-Pilot, Commercial	.25	L
Barber	.46	L	Cook (Hotel-Restaurant)	.48	L
Beauty Operator	.44	L	Department Head, Supermarket	.38	L
Caseworker	.28	L	Drafter, Architectural	.41	L
Claim Adjuster	.51	S	Electrician	.44	L
Commercial Artist, Illustrat.	.56	S	Engineer, Civil	.45	L
Electronics Mechanic	.39	L	Engineer, Time Study	.59	S
Locksmith	.28	L	Farm-Equipment Mechanic I	.52	S
Maintenance Repairer, Factory	.41	L	Line-Installer-Repairer (Tel)	.13	L
Mechanical-Engineering Tech.	.40	L	Machinist	.54	S
Office-Machine Servicer	.53	S	Programmer (Bus., Eng., Sci.)	.65	S
Photoengraver (Stripper)	.54	S	Sheet Metal Worker	.50	S
Sales Agent, Real Estate	.32	L	Statistical-Machine Servicer	.56	S
Salesperson, General Hardware	.15	L	Writer, Technical Publication	.61	S
Cluster E (COM)	.19	L	Cluster F (Alt-Com)	.21	L
Assembler, Production	.05	N	Airplane-Flight Attendant	.02	N
Baker	.16	L	Clerk, Gen. Ofc., Civil Svc.	.03	N
Bookbinder	.28	L	Dietitian	.56	S
Bookkeeper I	.31	L	Fire Fighter	.16	L
Bus Driver	.17	L	Librarian	.28	L
Key-Punch Operator	.10	L	Medical Technologist	.21	L
Meat Cutter	.16	L	Nurse, Professional	.15	L
Post-Office Clerk	.13	L	Orderly	-.08	N
Production Helper (Food)	.24	L	Physical Therapist	.34	L
Punch-Press Operator	.11	L	Police Officer	.13	L
Sales, General (Dept. Store)	.20	L	Receptionist, Civil Service	.29	L
Sewing-Machine Operator, Auto	.03	N	Secretary (General Office)	.26	L
Solderer (Production Line)	.16	L	Taxi Driver	.12	L
Telephone Operator	.17	L	Telephone Installer	.42	L
Teller (Banking)	.18	L	Waiter-Waitress	.18	L

Vocational Psychology Research . . . Department of Psychology
University of Minnesota . . . Minneapolis, MN 55455

Figure 2

Logical Consistency of the MIQ (1980 Edition)

Paired Form

Date--June 9, 1981   Name--A Sample Report

Logically Consistent Triad Score = 29%

Questionable LCT Range Begins at 33%

MIQ Scores are Questionable

Analysis of the data indicates a non-random pattern.
Listed below are the 20 MIQ vocational need scales in decreasing
order of their Logically Consistent Triad scores (Scale LCT %).
The scales at the top of the list represent those needs for which
the respondent's judgments were least consistent, and those at
the bottom represent those needs which the respondent judged most
consistently.

MIQ Scale	Scale LCT %	MIQ Scale	Scale LCT %
Independence	7	Social Status	33
Coworkers	21	Supervision--Technical	33
Authority	25	Achievement	33
Responsibility	28	Ability Utilization	35
Security	28	Social Service	40
Recognition	28	Creativity	42
Supervision--Human Relations	32	Variety	53
Advancement	32	Moral Values	65
Working Conditions	32	Activity	69
Company Policies & Practices	33	Compensation	83

REFERENCES

References

Allport, G. W., Vernon, P. E., & Lindzey, G. *Manual: Study of Values.* Boston: Houghton Mifflin, 1970.

Anastasi, A. *Differential psychology.* (3rd ed.). New York: Macmillan, 1958.

Anderson, L. M. *Longitudinal changes in level of work adjustment.* Unpublished doctoral dissertation, University of Minnesota, 1969.

Baehr, M. E. A simplified procedure for the measurement of employee attitudes. *Journal of Applied Psychology,* 1953, *37,* 163-167.

Bakke, E. W. *The unemployed man.* New York: Dutton, 1934.

Bakke, E. W. *The unemployed worker.* New Haven: Yale University Press, 1940.

Bentz, V. J. A test-retest experiment on the relationship between age and mental ability. *American Psychologist,* 1953, *8,* 319-320.

Betz, E. L. Need reinforcer correspondence as a predictor of job satisfaction. *Personnel and Guidance Journal,* 1969, *47,* 878-883.

Betz, E. L. *Occupational reinforcer patterns and need-reinforcer correspondence in the prediction of job satisfaction.* Unpublished doctoral dissertation, University of Minnesota, 1971.

Borgen, F. H., Weiss, D. J., Tinsley, H. E. A., Dawis, R. V., & Lofquist, L. H. The measurement of occupational reinforcer patterns. *Minnesota Studies in Vocational Rehabilitation,* XXV, 1968.

Brayfield, A. H., & Crockett, W. H. Employee attitudes and employee performance. *Psychological Bulletin,* 1955, *52,* 396-424.

Brayfield, A. H., & Rothe, H. F. An index of job satisfaction. *Journal of Applied Psychology,* 1951, *35,* 307-311.

Campbell, J. P., Dunnette, M. D., Lawler, E. E., III, & Weick, K. E., Jr. *Managerial behavior, performance, and effectiveness.* New York: McGraw-Hill, 1970.

Campbell, J. P., & Pritchard, R. D. Motivation theory in industrial and organizational psychology. In M. D. Dunnette (Ed.), *Handbook of industrial and organizational psychology.* Chicago: Rand McNally, 1976.

Carlson, R. E., Dawis, R. V., England, G. W., & Lofquist, L. H. The measurement of employment satisfactoriness. *Minnesota Studies in Vocational Rehabilitation,* XIV, 1963.

Cherry, N. Do career officers give good advice? *British Journal of Guidance and Counseling,* 1974, *2,* 27-40.

Cheung, F. M. *A threshold model of flexibility as a personality style dimension in work adjustment.* Unpublished doctoral dissertation, University of Minnesota, 1975.

Dawis, R. V., England, G. W., & Lofquist, L. H. A theory of work adjustment. *Minnesota Studies in Vocational Rehabilitation,* XV, 1964.

Dawis, R. V., & Lofquist, L. H. *Minnesota Occupational Classification System.* Work Adjustment Project, Department of Psychology, University of Minnesota, Minneapolis, 1974.

Dawis, R. V., & Lofquist, L. H. Personality style and the process of work adjustment. *Journal of Counseling Psychology,* 1976, *23,* 55-59.

Dawis, R. V., & Lofquist, L. H. A note on the dynamics of work adjustment. *Journal of Vocational Behavior,* 1978, *12,* 76-79.

Dawis, R. V., Lofquist, L. H., Henly, G. A., & Rounds, J. B., Jr. *Minnesota Occupational Classification System II.* Vocational Psychology Research, Department of Psychology, University of Minnesota, Minneapolis, 1979/1982.

Dawis, R. V., Lofquist, L. H., & Weiss, D. J. A theory of work adjustment (a revision). *Minnesota Studies in Vocational Rehabilitation,* XXIII, 1968.

Desmond, R. E., & Weiss, D. J. Measurement of ability requirements of occupations. *Proceedings of the 78th Annual Convention of the American Psychological Association,* 1970, 149-150.

Eberly, R. E. *Biographical determinants of vocational values.* Unpublished doctoral dissertation, University of Minnesota, 1980.

Eberly, R. E., Rounds, J. B., Jr., Dawis, R. V., & Williams, R. *Vocational needs of three adult male groups: Neuropsychiatric patients, rehabilitation clients, and college students.* Unpublished research paper, Work Adjustment Project, Department of Psychology, University of Minnesota, 1976.

Elizur, D., & Tziner, A. Vocational needs, job rewards, and satisfaction: A canonical analysis. *Journal of Vocational Behavior,* 1977, *10,* 205-211.

Engdahl, B. E. *The structure of biographical data and its relationship to vocational needs and values.* Unpublished doctoral dissertation, University of Minnesota, 1980.

England, G. W. Personal value systems of American managers. *Academy of Management Journal,* 1967, *10,* 53-68.

England, G. W., & Lee, R. The relationship between managerial values and managerial success in the United States, Japan, India, and Australia. *Journal of Applied Psychology,* 1974, *59,* 411-419.

Farris, G. F. A predictive study of turnover. *Personnel Psychology,* 1971, *24,* 311-328.

Fine, S. A. A structure of worker function. *Personnel and Guidance Journal,* 1955, *34,* 66-73.

Fleishman, E. A. Dimensional analysis of psychomotor abilities. *Journal of Experimental Psychology,* 1954, *48,* 437-454.

Flint, P. L. *Sex differences in perceptions of occupational reinforcers.* Unpublished doctoral dissertation, University of Minnesota, 1980.

French, J. W. *Manual for kit of selected tests for reference aptitude and achievement factors.* Princeton: Educational Testing Service, 1954.

Friedmann, E. A., & Havighurst, R. *The meaning of work and retirement.* Chicago: University of Chicago Press, 1954.

Fruehling, R. T. *Vocational needs and their life history correlates for high school students.* Unpublished doctoral dissertation, University of Minnesota, 1980.

Gay, E. G., Weiss, D. J., Hendel, D. D., Dawis, R. V., & Lofquist, L. H. Manual for the Minnesota Importance Questionnaire. *Minnesota Studies in Vocational Rehabilitation,* XXVIII, 1971.

Ghiselli, E. E. *The validity of occupational aptitude tests.* New York: Wiley, 1966.

Gibson, D. L., Weiss, D. J., Dawis, R. V., & Lofquist, L. H. Manual for the Minnesota Satisfactoriness Scales. *Minnesota Studies in Vocational Rehabilitation,* XVII, 1970.

Gray, B. L. *A longitudinal study of extracurricular activities, vocational needs, and individual need stability during adolescence*. Unpublished doctoral dissertation, University of Minnesota, 1974.

Gross, E. The worker and society. In H. Borow (Ed.), *Man in a world at work*. Boston: Houghton Mifflin, 1964.

Hall, C. S., & Lindzey, G. *Theories of personality*. New York: Wiley, 1970.

Hardin, E. *Measurement of physical output at the job level*. Research and Technical Report 10. Industrial Relations Center, University of Minnesota, 1951.

Harman, H. H. *Modern factor analysis*. Chicago: University of Chicago Press, 1970.

Harrower, G. F., & Cox, K. J. The results obtained from a number of occupational groupings on the professional level with the Rorschach group method. *Bulletin of the Canadian Psychological Association*, 1942, *2*, 31-33.

Hathaway, S. R., & McKinley, J. C. *Minnesota Multiphasic Personality Inventory: Manual for administration and scoring*. New York: Psychological Corporation, 1967.

Heron, A. The establishment for research purposes of two criteria of occupational adjustment. *Occupational Psychology*, 1952, *26*, 78-85. (a)

Heron, A. A psychological study of occupational adjustment. *Journal of Applied Psychology*, 1952, *36*, 385-387. (b)

Herzberg, F., Mausner, B., & Snyderman, B. B. *The motivation to work*. New York: Wiley, 1959.

Holland, J. L. *Making vocational choices: A theory of careers*. Englewood Cliffs, N.J.: Prentice-Hall, 1973.

Hoppock, R. *Job satisfaction*. New York: Harper, 1935.

Humphrey, C. C. *A multi trait-multi method assessment of personality styles in work adjustment*. Unpublished doctoral dissertation, University of Minnesota, 1980.

Hunt, E. P., and Smith, P. Vocational psychology and choice of employment. *Occupational Psychology*, 1945, *19*, 109-116.

Ivancevich, J. M. Predicting job performance by use of ability tests and studying job satisfaction as a moderating variable. *Journal of Vocational Behavior*, 1976, *9*, 87-97.

Johnson, G. H. An instrument for the measurement of job satisfaction. *Personnel Psychology*, 1955, *8*, 27-37.

Katzell, R. A. Personal values, job satisfaction, and job behavior. In H. Borow (Ed.), *Man in a world at work*. Boston: Houghton Mifflin, 1964.

Kerr, W. A. On the validity and reliability of the Job Satisfaction tear ballot. *Journal of Applied Psychology*, 1948, *32*, 275-281.

Lichter, D. J. *The prediction of job satisfaction as an outcome of career counseling*. Unpublished doctoral dissertation, University of Minnesota, 1980.

Locke, E. A. The nature and causes of job satisfaction. In M. D. Dunnette (Ed.), *Handbook of industrial and organizational psychology*. Chicago: Rand McNally, 1976.

Locke, E. A., Mento, A. J., & Katcher, B. L. The interactions of ability and motivation in performance. An exploration of the meaning of moderators. *Personnel Psychology*, 1978, *31*, 269-280.

Lofquist, L. H., & Dawis, R. V. *Adjustment to work*. New York: Appleton-Century-Crofts, 1969.

Maslow, A. H. *Motivation and personality*. New York: Harper, 1954.

Menninger, W. C. The meaning of work in Western society. In H. Borow (Ed.), *Man in a world at work*. Boston: Houghton Mifflin, 1964.

Meresman, J. F. *Biographical correlates of vocational needs*. Unpublished doctoral dissertation, University of Minnesota, 1975.

Morse, N. C. *Satisfactions in the white-collar job*. Ann Arbor: University of Michigan, 1953.

Muchinsky, P. M., & Tuttle, M. L. Employee turnover: An empirical and methodological assessment. *Journal of Vocational Behavior*, 1979, *14*, 43-77.

Palmore, E. Predicting longevity: A follow-up controlling for age. *The Gerontologist*, 1969, *9*, 247-250.

Paterson, D. G., Gerken, C. d'A., & Hahn, M. E. *The Minnesota Occupational Rating Scales and Counseling Profile*. Chicago: Science Research Associates, 1941.

Paterson, D. G., Gerken, C. d'A., & Hahn, M. E. *Revised Minnesota Occupational Rating Scales*. Minneapolis: University of Minnesota Press, 1953.

Pervin, L. A. Performance and satisfaction as a function of individual environment fit. *Psychological Bulletin*, 1968, *69*, 56-68.

Pieper, J. *Leisure, the basis of culture*. New York: Pantheon Books, 1952.

Porter, L. W., & Steers, R. M. Organizational, work, and personal factors in employee turnover and absenteeism. *Psychological Bulletin*, 1973, *80*, 151-176.

Rabinowitz, S., & Hall, D. T. Organizational research on job involvement. *Psychological Bulletin*, 1977, *84*, 265-288.

Robinson, J. P., Athanasiou, R., & Head, K. B. *Measures of occupational attitudes and occupational characteristics*. Survey Research Center, University of Michigan, Ann Arbor, 1969.

Roe, A. A Rorschach study of a group of scientists and technicians. *Journal of Consulting Psychology*, 1946, *10*, 317-327.

Roe, A. Analysis of group Rorschachs of biologists. *Rorschach Research Exchange*, 1949, *13*, 25-43.

Roe, A. Analysis of group Rorschachs of physical scientists. *Journal of Projective Techniques*, 1950, *14*, 385-398.

Roe, A. Analysis of group Rorschachs of psychologists and anthropologists. *Journal of Projective Techniques*, 1952, *16*, 212-224.

Roe, A. *The psychology of occupations*. New York: Wiley, 1956.

Rokeach, M. *The nature of human values*. New York: Free Press, 1973.

Rothe, H. F. Output rates among butter wrappers: I. Work curves and their stability. *Journal of Applied Psychology*, 1946, *30*, 199-211. (a)

Rothe, H. F. Output rates among butter wrappers: II. Frequency distributions and an hypothesis regarding the "restriction of output." *Journal of Applied Psychology*, 1946, *30*, 320-327. (b)

Rothe, H. F. Output rates among machine operators: I. Distributions and their reliability. *Journal of Applied Psychology*, 1947, *31*, 484-489.

Rothe, H. F. Output rates among chocolate dippers. *Journal of Applied Psychology*, 1951, *35*, 94-97.

Rounds, J. B., Jr. *The comparative and combined utility of need and interest data in the prediction of job satisfaction*. Unpublished doctoral dissertation, University of Minnesota, 1981.

Rounds, J. B., Jr., Dawis, R. V., & Lofquist, L. H. Life history correlates of vocational needs for a female adult sample. *Journal of Counseling Psychology*, 1979, *26*, 487-496.

Rounds, J. B., Jr., Henly, G. A., Dawis, R. V., Lofquist, L. H., & Weiss, D. J. *Manual for the Minnesota Importance Questionnaire: A measure of vocational needs and values*. Department of Psychology, University of Minnesota, Minneapolis, 1981.

Salazar, R. C. *The prediction of satisfaction and satisfactoriness for counselor training graduates*. Unpublished doctoral dissertation, University of Minnesota, 1981.

Schaffer, R. H. Job satisfaction as related to need satisfaction in work. *Psychological Monographs*, 1953, *67*, (Whole No. 364).

Scott, T. B., Dawis, R. V., England, G. W., & Lofquist, L. H. A definition of work adjustment. *Minnesota Studies in Vocational Rehabilitation*, X, 1960.

Seaburg, D. J., Rounds, J. B., Jr., Dawis, R. V., & Lofquist, L. H. *Values as second order needs*. Paper presented at the 84th annual meeting of the American Psychological Association, Washington, D.C., September 1976.

Sheehy, G. *Passages*. New York: E. P. Dutton, 1974.

Shubsachs, A. P. W., Rounds, J. B., Jr., Dawis, R. V., & Lofquist, L. H. Perception of work reinforcer systems: Factor structure. *Journal of Vocational Behavior*, 1978, *13*, 54-62.

Sloan, E. B. *An investigation of relationships between vocational needs and personality.* Unpublished doctoral dissertation, University of Minnesota, 1979.

Smith, P. C., Kendall, L. N., & Hulin, C. L. *The measurement of satisfaction in work and retirement.* Chicago: Rand McNally, 1969.

Special Task Force to the Secretary of Health, Education, and Welfare. *Work in America.* Cambridge, Mass.: The MIT Press, 1973.

Steiner, M. E. The use of projective techniques in industry. *Rorschach Research Exchange,* 1948, *12,* 171-174.

Strong, E. K., Jr. *Vocational interests of men and women.* Stanford, Calif.: Stanford University Press, 1943.

Strong, E. K., Jr. *Vocational interests 18 years after college.* Minneapolis: University of Minnesota Press, 1955.

Stulman, D. A. *Experimental validation of the independence and creativity scales of the Minnesota Importance Questionnaire.* Unpublished doctoral dissertation, University of Minnesota, 1974.

Super, D. E. *The psychology of careers.* New York: Harper & Row, 1957.

Super, D. E. (Ed.). *The use of multifactor tests in guidance.* Washington, D.C.: American Personnel and Guidance Association, 1958.

Super, D. E. The structure of work values in relation to status, achievement, interests, and adjustment. *Journal of Applied Psychology,* 1962, *42,* 231-239.

Super, D. E. *Work Values Inventory Manual.* Boston: Houghton Mifflin, 1970.

Super, D. E. The Work Values Inventory. In D. G. Zytowski (Ed.), *Contemporary approaches to interest measurement.* Minneapolis: University of Minnesota Press, 1973.

Taylor, K. D., & Weiss, D. J. Prediction of individual job termination from measured job satisfaction and biographical data. *Journal of Vocational Behavior,* 1972, *2,* 123-132.

Terkel, S. *Working.* New York: Pantheon Books, 1972.

Thorndike, R. L., & Hagen, E. *10,000 careers.* New York: Wiley, 1959.

Thorndike, R. M., Weiss, D. J., & Dawis, R. V. The canonical correlation of vocational interests and vocational needs. *Journal of Counseling Psychology,* 1968, *15,* 101-106.

Tilgher, A. *Work: What it has meant to men through the ages.* New York: Harcourt, 1930.

Twery, R., Schmid, J., & Wrigley, C. Some factors in job satisfaction: A comparison of three methods of analysis. *Educational and Psychological Measurement,* 1958, *18,* 189-202.

Tyler, L. E. *The psychology of individual differences.* (3rd ed.). New York: Appleton-Century-Crofts, 1965.

U.S. Department of Labor. *Worker trait requirements for 4000 jobs.* Washington, D.C.: U.S. Government Printing Office, 1956.

U.S. Department of Labor. *Manual for the USES General Aptitude Test Battery.* Washington, D.C.: U.S. Government Printing Office, 1970.

U.S. Department of Labor. *Survey of job satisfaction.* Washington, D.C.: U.S. Government Printing Office, 1973.

U.S. Department of Labor. *Dictionary of occupational titles.* (4th ed.). Washington, D.C.: U.S. Government Printing Office, 1977.

U.S. Department of Labor. *Manual for the USES General Aptitude Test Battery, Section II: Occupational aptitude pattern structure.* Washington, D.C.: U.S. Government Printing Office, 1979.

U.S. Department of Labor. *Occupational outlook handbook, 1982-83.* Washington, D.C.: U.S. Government Printing Office, 1982.

Vander Noot, T., Kunde, T., & Heneman, H. G., Jr. Comparability of absence rates. *Personnel Journal,* 1958, *36,* 380-382.

Viteles, M. S. *Industrial psychology.* New York: Norton, 1932.

Vroom, V. H. *Work and motivation.* New York: Wiley, 1964.

Weber, M. *The Protestant ethic and the spirit of capitalism.* New York: Scribner, 1930.

Weiss, D. J., Dawis, R. V., England, G. W., & Lofquist, L. H. Construct validation studies of the Minnesota Importance Questionnaire. *Minnesota Studies in Vocational Rehabilitation,* XVIII, 1964.

Weiss, D. J., Dawis, R. V., England, G. W., & Lofquist, L. H. An inferential approach to occupational reinforcement. *Minnesota Studies in Vocational Rehabilitation,* XIX, 1965.

Weiss, D. J., Dawis, R. V., England, G. W., & Lofquist, L. H. Manual for the Minnesota Satisfaction Questionnaire. *Minnesota Studies in Vocational Rehabilitation,* XXII, 1967.

Weiss, D. J., Dawis, R. V., Lofquist, L. H., & England, G. W. Instrumentation for the theory of work adjustment. *Minnesota Studies in Vocational Rehabilitation,* XXI, 1966.

Wiener, Y., & Klein, K. L. The relationship between vocational interests and job satisfaction: Reconciliation of divergent results. *Journal of Vocational Behavior,* 1978, *13,* 298-304.

GLOSSARY

Glossary

Abilities. Reference dimensions for skills.

Abilities, mature. Abilities that show stability on repeated measurement.

Ability dimensions. More basic dimensions that represent common elements of skill dimensions. Reference dimensions for the description of skills.

Ability pattern. Description of an individual in terms of relative levels of different abilities.

Ability requirement pattern. Description of an environment in terms of the relative levels of different abilities required of an individual for adjustment.

Ability tests. Measures of ability dimensions.

Activeness. Reducing discorrespondence by acting to change the environment. Acting on the environment to increase correspondence.

Adjustment. Continuous and dynamic process by which an individual seeks to achieve and maintain correspondence with an environment.

Adjustment mode. Approach used by the individual to reduce discorrespondence or increase correspondence. Description of individual adjustment in terms of activeness or reactiveness.

Adjustment style. Description of an individual on personality dimensions of flexibility activeness, reactiveness, and perseverance.

Behavior development, decline stage. Period in which some response capabilities are affected by physiological changes associated with aging.

Behavior development, differentiation stage. Period in which the individual is observed to try out, develop, and expand response capabilities in terms of their variety, range, and complexity.

Behavior development, stability stage. Period characterized by the crystallization and maintenance of a response repertoire.

Career. Tenure in an occupation. Sequence of positions held in the span of occupational tenure.

Celerity. Quickness of response in interacting with the environment.

Correspondence. Degree to which the requirements of either the worker or the work environment are met by each other. Harmonious relationship between the individual and the environment. Suitability of the individual to the environment and of the environment for the individual. Consonance or agreement between the individual and the environment. Reciprocal and complementary relationship between the individual and the environment. Relationship in which the individual and the environment are corresponsive, i.e., mutually responsive.

Disability. Ability loss. Significant decrease in the level of one ability or more in the ability set.

Disabling conditions. Changes or limitations in physical and bodily functions that can, but do not necessarily, have a significant effect on an individual's ability levels.

Endurance. Likelihood of maintaining interaction with the environment.

Factor analysis. Mathematical method of identifying a smaller number of more basic dimensions (factors) that underlie several observed dimensions.

Flexibility. Tolerance for discorrespondence with the environment before acting to reduce the discorrespondence. Range on an axis of discorrespondence from 0 to T_L (lower threshold).

Incentives. Rewards that are contingent upon performance and known to an individual in advance.

Individual differences. Differences among people on any given behavioral dimension. Differences in an individual's standing in a group from one behavioral dimension to another. Differences in an individual's standing in a group on a given behavioral dimension from one time to another. Combinations of the above.

Interests. Preferences (liking or disliking) for various kinds of activities.

Interests, exhibited. Preferences for activities inferred from observations of an individual's participation in activities or from records of such participation.

Interests, expressed or stated. Preferences for activities as stated by an individual.

Interests, latent. Interests that appear much later than usual, i.e., well after physical maturity.

Interests, measured. Preferences for activities as expressed by the individual on a structured, standardized psychometric instrument designed to sample a broad domain of activities.

Interests, validated. Preferences for activities established from the agreement between expressed or stated, measured, and exhibited interests.

Interests, vicarious. Interests that are based on someone else's experience.

Job. Group of similar positions in the employing organization.

Memory. Unique reference system against which present experience can be compared and evaluated.

Need reinforcers. Classes of stimulus conditions the presence or absence of which is associated with satisfaction of needs.

Needs. An individual's requirements for reinforcers at given levels of reinforcement strength. An individual's preferences for stimulus conditions experienced to have been reinforcing.

Occupation. Group of similar jobs found in several employing organizations.

Occupational aptitude pattern. Description of the minimum levels of abilities required by a given occupation.

Occupational reinforcer pattern. Description of the relative presence or absence of need reinforcers in a given occupation.

Pace. Level of effort typically expended in interaction with the work environment.

Perseverance. Persisting in adjustment activity. Tolerance of discorrespondence with the environment, as indicated by length of stay, before leaving it. Length of time an individual seeks to reduce intolerable discorrespondence.

Personality description, exhibited. Description of an individual's personality based on records compiled by observers.

Personality description, expressed or stated. Self-reported description of an individual's personality in terms of the likelihood of behaving in particular ways.

Personality description, measured. Description of an individual's personality made within the framework of a psychometric instrument constructed to sample and scale a broad range of human behaviors in systematic fashion.

Personality description, validated. Description of personality based on the agreement of exhibited and measured personality descriptions.

Personality structure. Status characteristics of the work personality. Skills and needs. Abilities and values as reference dimensions for skills and needs. The individual's set of abilities, set of values, and the relationships among and between these abilities and values.

Personality structure, crystallization of. Retention of a particular set of abilities and values in the personality structure.

Personality structure, inception of. Initial development of abilities and values.

Personality structure, individuation of. Process of crystallization and stabilization of abilities and values.

Personality structure, stabilization of. Maintenance of abilities and values at relatively constant levels of strength and hierarchical ordering.

Personality style. Process characteristics of the work personality. The individual's typical ways of interacting with the environment. Description of the individual on dimensions of celerity, pace, rhythm, and endurance. Description of how an individual utilizes abilities in the context of values in terms of quickness or slowness of responding, level of activity, pattern of activity, and length of responding.

Position. Set of tasks performed by one worker.

Psychological needs. Requirements for reinforcers at particular strengths regardless of their derivation. Measured as self-reported requirements or as observed requirements.

Reactiveness. Reducing discorrespondence by acting on self to change expression of personality structure. Changing the expression or manifestation of personality structure to increase correspondence.

Reinforcement. Process of providing reinforcers that maintain or increase response rate.

Reinforcement strength. Frequency level of responding associated with a given reinforcer. Frequency level of responding that is experienced (*actual*), reported by an individual (*stated*), or reported by an observer (*observed*).

Reinforcer factors. Reference dimensions for the description of reinforcers.

Reinforcer pattern. Description of an environment in terms of the relative presence or absence of different kinds of reinforcers.

Reinforcers. Stimulus conditions observed to be consistently associated with an increased rate of response over the base rate. Stimulus conditions that are associated with the maintenance of response and the likelihood of future response.

Response cues. Stimulus conditions that signal what response is appropriate and when to respond.

Responses. Reactions to the environment or actions on the environment.

Rewards. Stimulus conditions intended to serve as effective reinforcers.

Rhythm. Typical pattern of pace.

Satisfaction. Refers to an individual's satisfaction with the work environment. Result of an individual's requirements being fulfilled by the work environment. Internal indicator of correspondence. The individual worker's appraisal of the extent to which his or her requirements are fulfilled by the work environment.

Satisfactoriness. Satisfaction of the work environment with the individual. Result of an individual fulfilling the requirements of the work environment. External indicator of correspondence. Work environment's appraisal of the extent to which its requirements are fulfilled by the individual worker.

Skill dimension. Common skill identified for several individuals, defined in terms of level of difficulty, economy of effort, and efficiency.

Skills. Recurring response sequences that become more refined with repetition. Behaviors requiring the exercise or use of several different abilities in combination.

Social norms. Standards of behavior that have developed from the society's collective experience. Prescriptions for socially acceptable behavior in a variety of environmental settings.

Stable psychological needs. Needs showing little change over successive measurements.

Tenure. Remaining on and being retained on the job. Length of stay in an environment.

Tenure, occupational. Length of time spent in a specific occupation irrespective of organizational membership or positions held.

Tenure, organizational. Length of time spent in an organization irrespective of the positions held.

Tenure, position or job. Length of time spent in a particular position or job.

Threshold, lower (T_L). Point on the axis of discorrespondence that separates the range of tolerable discorrespondence from the range of intolerable discorrespondence.

Threshold, upper (T_U). Point on the axis of discorrespondence at which discorrespondence becomes so intolerable that the individual leaves the environment.

Value dimensions. Basic dimensions that represent common elements in need dimensions. Reference dimensions for the description of needs.

Values. Reference dimensions for needs.

Work. Interaction between an individual and a work environment in which each has requirements of the other.

Work adjustment. Continuous and dynamic process by which a worker seeks to achieve and maintain correspondence with a work environment.

Work adjustment indicators. Individual satisfaction, individual's satisfactoriness, and tenure.

Work environment celerity. Speed of responding required of the worker.

Work environment endurance. Duration of responding required of the worker.

Work environment pace. Level of effort required of the worker.

Work environment rhythm. Typical patterns of work environment pace.

Work environment structure. Skill requirements and need reinforcers. Ability requirement patterns and reinforcer clusters as reference dimensions for skill requirements and need reinforcers.

Work environment style. Description of the work environment in terms of its celerity, pace, rhythm, and endurance.

Work personality. Principal characteristics of the individual in relation to work adjustment. Work personality structure and work personality style. Abilities, values, and style dimensions that are most relevant to the understanding of work behavior.

INDEXES

Author Index

241

Subject Index

René V. Dawis and **Lloyd H. Lofquist** both earned their masters and doctoral degrees in psychology at the University of Minnesota. Dawis has served, successively, as director of the Work Adjustment Project, professor in the industrial relations department and, since 1968, professor in the department of psychology at Minnesota, where he is also director of the counseling psychology graduate program. Lofquist worked as a counseling psychologist at the Veterans Administration Hospital in Minneapolis and has been professor of psychology at the University of Minnesota since 1956; he is now chair of the department of psychology at Minnesota. Dawis and Lofquist are co-authors of *Adjustment to Work* (1969); Lofquist has also written *Vocational Counseling with the Physically Handicapped* and is co-author of *Problems in Counseling.*